Claire Moore   Catrin Elen Morris

Ready for
PLANET ENGLISH

Elementary

The pleasure of learning

PUBLISHING

Ready for PLANET ENGLISH

Presentations & Grammar

Welcome Unit

- Introduction to English as a global language
- Activation of known vocabulary and structures

- Revision of vocabulary: countries, nationalities, languages, continents, cardinal and ordinal numbers
- Practice introducing yourself

- Countries fact files: a quick glance at facts and numbers of the main English-speaking countries all over the world

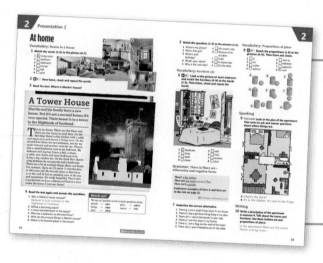

Presentation 1

- Lexical approach
- Reading Comprehension activating vocabulary and grammar structures in real contexts
- Grammar boxes with links to the **Grammar Reference & Practice**, followed by simple practice exercises
- Speaking tasks to activate **key competences**

Presentation 2

- Second text in the form of an interview or newspaper article
- Activation of the second grammar point
- Oral production which aims to develop **Critical Thinking** skills

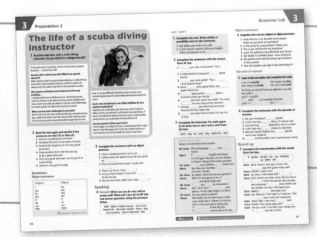

Grammar Lab

- A page dedicated to grammar practice with links to **Grammar Reference & Practice**

Vocabulary & Communication

Vocabulary & Listening

- Supplementary vocabulary page with activities to facilitate learning and comprehension
- Links to the illustrated **Words Plus** pages
- Links to the **Pronunciation Bank** in the **Digital Book**
- Oral comprehension tasks with vocabulary in context

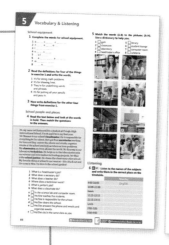

Video & Life Skills

- The Darsha & Harry sitcom videos to learn the main communicative functions as well as 4 stand-alone videos about different lifestyles.

Skills & Strategies

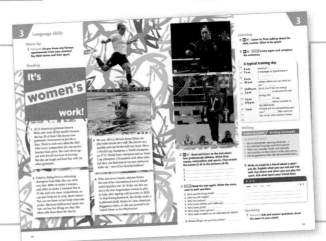

Language Skills

- A double page spread of skills practice: Reading, Listening, Speaking and Writing
- The symbol **CERT** indicates that it is an exam practice activity for external certification

Learn to Learn

- Strategies to improve presentation and production, and to increase fluency and self-confidence in English

Quick Check

- Multiple-choice tests to assess unit's key vocabulary, grammar structures and language functions
- End of unit test in class or a self-assessment tool
- Quick-mark system gives instant assessment

Words Plus

- Visual presentation of key lexical sets to contextualize learning
- Extension, personalization and organization tasks for vocabulary assimilation
- Guided, contextualized and freer practice of target vocabulary
- **Remember!** boxes highlighting false friends and exceptions

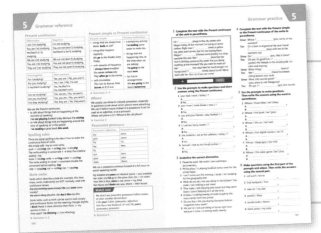

Grammar Reference & Practice

- Concise, clearly presented and labelled grammar tables
- **Watch out!** boxes highlighting exceptions and common grammar errors
- Links to specific practice exercises for target structures

3

Irregular Verbs

- Tables with the past simple and past participle forms of the main regular and irregular verbs
- Phonetic transcription for pronunciation

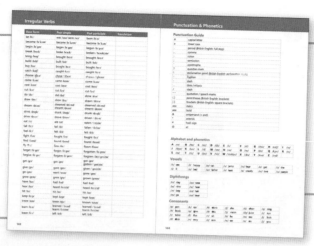

Punctuation and Phonetics

- Key to Punctuation Guide
- Alphabet and Phonetics
- Vowels, Diphthongs and Consonants with international phonetic symbol

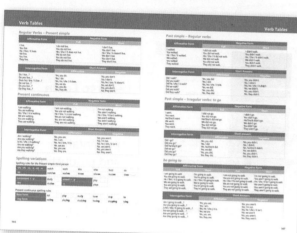

Verb Tables

- Tables with main regular and irregular verbs
- Full and short forms
- Past, Present and Future verb forms
- Affirmative, Negative, Interrogative forms and Short answers
- Spelling variations for third person singular and *-ing* form

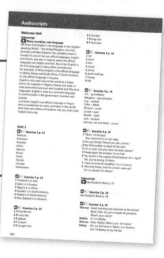

Audio and video scripts

- Complete audio and video scripts from course

Map

- Detailed maps of the UK and the USA

🔊 **15** Audio tracks you can listen to on the **DIGITAL BOOK** or downloadable with the ELI LINK app

▶ Video on the **DIGITAL BOOK** or downloadable with the ELI LINK app

CERT Preparation for external certification

▶ **Words Plus** Extra vocabulary practice

✓ **DIGITAL BOOK** ▶ **Pronunciation Bank: /h/** Links to the pronunciation worksheets with speaking tasks in the DIGITAL BOOK

ELIDigiBook

The DIGITAL BOOK is an interactive and digital version of the text book, to be used in class on an interactive whiteboard (IWB), or at home for independent study.

The **DIGITAL BOOK** presents the whole book in browsable multimedia form and brings all the course resources together in one place: interactive exercises and self-correction, audio and video All the videos have subtitles.

You will be able to add notes, documents, pictures, links and voice memos to your digital book from the toolbar. It will also be possible to create mind maps to help learn and revise key concepts.

Accessible intuitive tasks.

There is a karaoke function with every audio track.

The DIGITAL BOOK provides extra resources:

- direct access to the dedicated website where you will find further resources related to the course topics
- **Culture videos** with worksheets
- An **interactive table** with audio English phonetic symbol pronunciation

Contents

Different countries, one global language

1 ▶ Watch the video. Name at least six countries where English is the first official language.

2 ▶ First or second language? Watch the video again and fill in the gaps.

Alaska

Canada

USA

Bermuda

Puerto Rico

Hawaii

Belize **Jamaica**

Trinidad and Tobago

Guyana

Pitcain

Countries where English is used as first and official language

Countries where English is used as a Lingua Franca or official language

Falkland Islands

Hi, I'm Aisha and I'm from Lagos, in Nigeria. English is my _____ language.

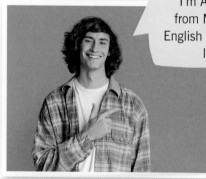

Hi, guys, I'm Brad and I'm Australian. I'm from Melbourne and English is my _____ language.

Hey guys, I'm Theo and I'm American, from Chicago. English is my _____ language.

Hello, everyone, I'm Naira and I'm from New Delhi in India. English is my _____ language.

Cardinal and ordinal numbers

1 → one	1st → the first
2 → two	2nd → the second
3 → three	3rd → the third
4 → four	4th → the fourth
10 → ten	10th → the tenth
11 → eleven	11th → the eleventh
21 → twenty-one	21st → the twenty-first
32 → thirty-two	32nd → the thirty-second
43 → forty-three	43rd → the forty-third

Introducing yourself

Hi, I'm Brad.
My name's Lily.
I'm from Chicago in the USA.

Hi, my name's Lily. I'm from Hong Kong and English is my _____ language.

Hi, I'm Kevin and I'm from Liverpool in Great Britain. English is my _____ language.

3 **Which continent? Complete the table with the names of the six continents and countries from the box.**

South America ● Oceania ● Europe ● Canada ● India ● Nigeria ● New Zealand ● Zimbabwe ● The USA

Continents		North America		Asia			Africa
Countries	The UK		Guyana			Australia	South Africa

Countries fact files

The UK
Country: The United Kingdom
(England, Scotland, Wales, Northern Ireland)
Capital city: London
Population: 67,886,000
Official language: English
Currency: Pound sterling (GBP)

Ireland
Country: Republic of Ireland
Capital city: Dublin
Population: 4,977,400
Official languages: Irish, English
Currency: Euro (EUR)

Malta
Country: Republic of Malta
Capital city: Valletta
Population: 514,564
Official languages: Maltese, English
Currency: Euro (EUR)

The USA
Country: The United States of America
Capital city: Washington, D.C.
Population: 328,239,523
Official language: English
Currency: United States dollar (USD)

Canada
Country: Canada
Capital city: Ottawa
Population: 38,005,238
Official languages: English, French
Currency: Canadian dollar (CAD)

Guyana
Country: Co-operative Republic of Guyana
Capital city: Georgetown
Population: 786,390
Official language: English
Currency: Guyanese dollar (GYD)
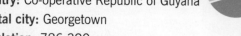

South Africa
Country: The Republic of South Africa
Capital city: Pretoria
Population: 59,622,350
Official languages: English and 10 others
Currency: South African rand (ZAR)

Nigeria
Country: Federal Republic of Nigeria
Capital city: Abuja
Population: 206,630,269
Official languages: English and others
Currency: Naira (NGN)

Liberia
Country: Republic of Liberia
Capital city: Monrovia
Population: 5,073,290
Official language: English
Currency: Liberian dollar (LRD)

Zimbabwe
Country: Republic of Zimbabwe
Capital city: Harare
Population: 14,215,809
Official languages: English and others
Currency: Zimbabwean dollar

Hong Kong
Country: Hong Kong Special Administrative
Region of the People's Republic of China (HKSAR)
Population: 7,500,700
Official languages: Chinese, English
Currency: Hong Kong dollar (HKD)

Australia
Country: Commonwealth of Australia
Capital city: Canberra
Population: 25,694,500
Official language: English
Currency: Australian dollar (AUD)

New Zealand
Country: New Zealand
Capital city: Wellington
Population: 5,095,020
Official languages: English, Maori
Currency: New Zealand dollar (NZD)

1

Two teenagers having fun on a longboard in a street in Bogotá, Colombia

My World

Fact

According to science, friends can make you happy, healthy and even beautiful and attractive.

The Big Question

How many friends do you have? Do you have a best friend? Why is he or she your best friend?

Unit Objectives

Vocabulary & Listening	Grammar	Language Skills	Video & Life Skills
• Countries and nationalities • Continents • Appearance • The family	• Subject pronouns • *to be* • Demonstratives • Possessive adjectives • Possessive 's • Plural of nouns	Reading: Ed Sheeran's favorites Listening: A young book lover Speaking: Talking about a school club Writing: Writing about your favorite things	▶ Nadiya's family Respect others: • Value other cultures

Nice to meet you!

Vocabulary: Countries and nationalities

1 🔊 1 **Write the nationalities in the table. Then listen and check.**

> Polish • Chinese • ~~Mexican~~ • British • American
> Spanish • Vietnamese • Turkish • Italian • Brazilian

Country	Nationality
Mexico	Mexican
America	
Brazil	
Italy	
Spain	
Britain	
Poland	
Turkey	
China	
Vietnam	

Vocabulary: Continents

2 **Complete the sentences with the names of the continents.**

> Europe • Asia • Africa • North America • Oceania
> South America

1 Thailand is in _____.
2 Spain is in _____.
3 Nigeria is in _____.
4 Ecuador is in _____.
5 Alaska is in _____.
6 New Zealand is in _____.

3 🔊 2 **Now listen and check.**

4 **Count the objects and write the numbers.**

A fourteen   B _____   C _____

D _____   E _____   F _____

5 **Read the conversation. Where is Duc from?**

Alejandro Hi, Agata. I'm Alejandro.
          We're in the same class!
Agata   Hi, Alejandro! Are you Spanish?
Alejandro No, I'm not Spanish. I'm from
          Ecatepec.
Agata   Ecatepec? Oh, you're Mexican!
Alejandro Yes, that's right. Are you Italian?
Agata   No, I'm not from Italy,
          I'm from Warsaw. I'm Polish.
Alejandro Cool. This is my friend, Duc.
          He's from Saigon.
Agata   Hi, Duc. Nice to meet you.
          Is Saigon in China?
Duc   Hi, Agata. No, it isn't in China,
          it's in the south of Vietnam!
Agata   Oh, you're Vietnamese! Are you
          in our class too, Duc?
Duc   I'm not sure...
Alejandro How old are you?
Duc   I'm sixteen.
Alejandro No, you aren't in our class.
          We're seventeen in class 2A.
Agata   You're with Amalia and Osman.
          They aren't in our class. They're in
          class 1B.
Duc   Are they sixteen too?
Agata   Yes.
Duc   Oh OK, cool.
Alejandro See you in class, Agata!
Agata   OK, bye, Alejandro! Bye Duc.
Duc   See you.

6 **Write the names of the students.**

1 He's from Mexico.   Alejandro
2 They're in the same class. _____
                            and _____
3 She isn't Italian.   _____
4 She's Polish.   _____
5 He's from Saigon.   _____
6 He isn't seventeen.   _____
7 They are sixteen.   _____
                            and _____
8 They aren't in class 2A. _____,
                            _____
                            and _____

7 Complete the students' identity cards.

SUMMERHILL LANGUAGE SCHOOL
STUDENT IDENTITY CARD

Name	Alejandro Martínez
Age	(1) _17_
City	Ecatepec
Nationality	(2)_____

SUMMERHILL LANGUAGE SCHOOL
STUDENT IDENTITY CARD

Name	Agata Cwalinski
Age	(3)_____
City	(4)_____
Nationality	Polish

SUMMERHILL LANGUAGE SCHOOL
STUDENT IDENTITY CARD

Name	(5)_____ Pham
Age	(6)_____
City	Saigon
Nationality	(7)_____

Grammar: Verb *to be*

> *I'm Alejandro.*
> *Is Saigon in China?*
> *I'm not Spanish.*
> *You aren't in our class.*
> *How old are you?*

Find more examples of the verb *to be* in the conversation and underline them.

➡ Grammar reference p. 112

8 Underline the correct alternative.

1 I'*m* / '*s* from Mexico.
2 My friends *is* / *are* eighteen.
3 *Are you* / *You are* Polish?
4 Paula *isn't* / *aren't* Brazilian.
5 How old *is* / *are* your mother?
6 Kate and her friends *are* / *aren't* American, they're Australian.

Grammar: *this, these, that, those*

> ***This** is my friend, Duc.* →●
> *Who are **these** students?* →●●
> ***That** room is our classroom.* ——→●
> ***Those** students aren't American.* ——→●●

➡ Grammar reference p. 112

9 Write plural and singular sentences.

1 That student is in my class.
   Those students are in my class.
2 These T-shirts are new.
   _____
3 Those teachers aren't French.
   _____
4 This girl in the photo isn't my friend.
   _____

Functions
Greetings and introductions

Hi/Hello, I'm Alejandro.
This is my friend, Duc.
Nice to meet you.
See you. / Bye.

Speaking

10 In pairs, practice the conversation. Use the model. Change the words in red.

A Hi, Francisco. I'm Juan and this is my friend Lisa.
B Hi, Juan! Hi, Lisa. Nice to meet you.
A Nice to meet you too.
B Are you Brazilian?
A No, I'm not Brazilian. I'm from Madrid and she's from Barcelona.
B You're Spanish!
A Yes, that's right.
B How old are you?
A I'm sixteen.
B Me too! OK, see you Juan.
A Bye!

Possessive adjectives

*He's in **my** Spanish class.*
***His** name's James.*
***Her** name's Sylvia.*
*Is **your** sister pretty?*

Is she tall?

1 **Joe and Lucy are talking about Lucy's family. Read the conversation. Does Lucy have brothers and sisters?**

Joe   Do you have brothers and sisters, Lucy?

Lucy   Yes, I do. I have one brother. His name's James. And one sister. Her name's Sylvia. And you?

Joe   I don't have brothers or sisters. I'm an only child. Is your sister pretty?

Lucy   Yes, she's very pretty! She's slim with long, curly, brown hair.

Joe   Does she have brown eyes?

Lucy   No, she doesn't. Sylvia's eyes are green and she has freckles.

Joe   And your brother?

Lucy   He has very curly hair like my dad. But James's eyes are blue and Dad doesn't have blue eyes. His eyes are brown.

Joe   Is James tall?

Lucy   Yes, he is. He's quite tall.

Joe   What color hair does he have?

Lucy   He has blond hair and he has glasses.

Joe   Is he on the soccer team?

Lucy   Yes, he is. Why?

Joe   You're kidding! I think we are on the same team!

Lucy   No way!

Watch out!

Where there are two or more types of adjectives, the order is always: size → quality → color.

*She's slim with **long, curly, brown** hair.*

2 **Complete the descriptions of the people.**

1   Sylvia _*is*_ slim with _____, _____, brown hair. Her eyes are _____ and she _____ freckles.

2   James _____ tall with _____, blond hair. He has _____ eyes and _____.

3   Lucy's father has _____ hair. His eyes _____ brown.

Grammar: Possessive *'s*

Sylvia's eyes are green.

Find one more example of possessive *'s* in the conversation. Underline it.

➡ Grammar reference p. 112

3 **Complete the sentences with the possessive adjectives from the box.**

their • its • her (x 2) • his • your

1   She's my sister. _*Her*_ eyes are blue.

2   It's Peter's tablet. _____ screen is broken.

3   Luis and _____ friend Maria are from Lima.

4   They're Spanish. _____ names are Javi and Ana.

5   That's Elena's phone. _____ phone is pink.

6   'How do you spell _____ name, Mia?' 'M-I-A.'

4 **Write a short text (50-60 words) about your brother or sister. Answer these questions to help you.**

1   Do you have brothers and sisters?

2   Is your sister pretty?

3   Does she have brown eyes?

4   What color hair does your brother have?

5   Is he tall?

Subject pronouns

I'm Alejandro.
You're Mexican.
They're in class 1B.

1 Underline the correct alternative.

Osman   Hi, ¹*I* /*you*'m Osman.
Amalia Are ²*you* / *he* Turkish?
Osman   Yes, I'm from Istanbul.
Amalia This is Adrian. ³*He* / *She*'s Mexican.
Osman   Hi, Adrian.
Adrian   Hi! ⁴*We* / *He*'re in the same class!
Amalia How old are you?
Adrian   ⁵*He* / *I*'m fifteen.
Amalia Fifteen? You're in class with Peter and Greta. ⁶*They* / *We*'re fifteen too.

Verb *to be*

2 Underline the correct alternative.

1 Britain *is* / *are* in Europe.
2 I *am* / *are* Spanish.
3 Brazil *is* / *are* in South America.
4 The star on the Turkish flag *is* / *are* white.
5 The British and American flags *is* / *are* red, white and blue.
6 The Polish flag *is* /*are* red and white.

3 Complete the sentences with *am*, *is* or *are*.

1 Canada __*is*__ in North America.
2 The Australian flag is blue with six stars. The stars _____ white.
3 Panama and Guatemala _____ in Central America.
4 The Japanese flag _____ white with a red circle.
5 I _____ Mexican.
6 The Russian flag _____ red, white and blue.

4 Complete the sentences with the correct form of *be*.

1 __*Are*__ you fifteen?
2 No, I _____ Peter, I'm Rikki.
3 Katie and Harry _____ from New York. They're from Los Angeles.
4 _____ Brad in our class?
5 _____ Jesus and Juan Brazilian?
6 You _____ from Istanbul; you're from Ankara!
7 _____ Joe your friend?
8 You and Kelly _____ in the same class. You're in class 1B and Kelly is in class 1A.

Possessive adjectives

5 Complete the text with the possessive adjectives from the box.

> her • my • his • our • their (x 2)

I have a sister and a brother. ¹____*My*____ sister Rachel and I have long, blonde hair and blue eyes. My mom has blonde hair too, but she has green eyes. ² _____ name is Lisa. My brother Josh has straight, black hair and freckles. My dad's hair is gray and he has a beard and glasses. ³ _____ name is Colin.
My grandad has short, gray hair and my granny has straight hair. ⁴ _____ names are Jim and Margaret. I also have an aunt and an uncle in Toronto in Canada. ⁵ _____ names are Louise and Richard. They have three children, Gemma, Mark and Joe. We love playing with ⁶ _____ cousins.

Plural of nouns

We add an *-s* at the end of nouns to form the plural.
eye → eyes   *sister → sisters*

Some nouns add *-es*.
potato → potatoes   *bus → buses*

Some nouns have irregular plurals.
*man → **men**   woman → **women***
*child → **children** *tooth → **teeth**   *fish → **fish***

6 Write the plurals.

1 door	_____	9 flag	_____
2 window	_____	10 sheep	_____
3 classroom	_____	11 glass	_____
4 kiss	_____	12 tomato	_____
5 tablet	_____	13 virus	_____
6 policeman	_____	14 phone	_____
7 schoolchild	_____	15 church	_____
8 firewoman	_____	16 chair	_____

Possessive *'s*

7 Write *'s* or *'* (apostrophe) in the correct place in the sentences.

1 It's Tom's Vespa.
2 Susie is Maria sister.
3 We're in my mother store.
4 They're the boys sneakers.
5 Jeanette is Luke wife.
6 The twins PlayStation is new.

1 Vocabulary & Listening

Countries and nationalities

1 Complete the sentences.

1 Hassan is from _____. He's Moroccan.
2 Anna is from Spain. She's _____.
3 Feng is from _____. He's Chinese.
4 Tara is from India. She is _____.
5 Laura is from _____. She's Italian.
6 Dylan is from the USA. He's _____.
7 Zeynep is from _____. She's Turkish.
8 Lien and Chi are from Vietnam. They're _____.
9 Akira is from _____. He's Japanese.
10 Pierre is from Paris. He's _____.

Appearance

2 🔊 3 Match the pictures to the words. Then listen, check and repeat the words.

1 [H] blonde hair   5 ☐ straight hair
2 ☐ curly hair   6 ☐ freckles
3 ☐ glasses   7 ☐ long hair
4 ☐ a beard   8 ☐ blue eyes

3 🔊 4 Write the words under the pictures. Then listen, check and repeat the words.

tall • short • slim • round • old
young • pretty • good-looking

1 _tall_ 2 _____ 3 _____ 4 _____

5 _____ 6 _____ 7 _____ 8 _____

The family

4 🔊 5 Complete Sophie's family tree. Then listen and check.

sister • cousin (x 3) • brother • aunt • grandmother
father • mother • grandfather • uncle

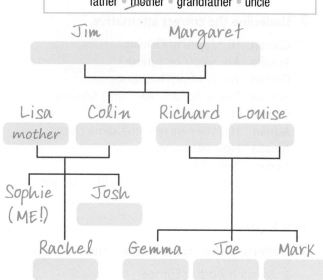

Expressions with the verb *to be*

Watch out!

We use the verb *to be* in the following expressions:

be afraid, be cold/hot, be hungry/thirsty, be in a hurry, be right/wrong, be sleepy

Listening

5 🔊 6 Listen to the conversations and complete them with one of the adjectives from the box above.

1 'Mom, I'm _____.'
  'Your sandwich is on the table.'
2 Are you _____? Would you like a drink?
3 My little brother is _____ of the dark.
4 I'm so _____. Can you close the door, please?
5 Please open the window. I'm so _____!
6 'So, Zurich is the capital of Switzerland. Am I _____?'
  'No, you're _____. It's Bern.'
7 I have no time for breakfast, I'm in a _____!
8 'Morning Paulie, time for school, wake up!'
  'Oh no please! I'm _____!'

▶ Words Plus 1 p. 132   DIGITAL BOOK ✓   ▶ Pronunciation Bank: /h/

Nadiya's family

1 ▶ **Watch the video without sound. Where is Nadiya from and where is her family from?**

Narrator Nadiya is a famous cook. She won *The Great British Bake Off*, a TV competition. She's British and lives in the UK with her husband and her children. Her parents are from Bangladesh, but she grew up in the UK, so she doesn't know Bangladesh well.

Nadiya I think I feel very British and sometimes I feel like I don't know the Bangladeshi side of me that much.

Narrator But her Bangladeshi side is an important part of her family life as well as her work as a chef. Nadiya has three sisters and two brothers. They all live nearby. They meet for important family celebrations. Nadiya is the chef in the family, but for family meals, everyone cooks.

Nadiya That is a mutton and potato curry that my big sister made.

Narrator This celebration is for Nadiya, who is going to Bangladesh. She wants to visit her family there, and learn more about the culture and the food. Her parents live in Bangladesh now, in a small village near Sylhet. At the airport, her dad picks her up. Together, they drive to the family village. Her mum is there to meet her. So are her uncles and aunts. And her cousins. And their children. They know she is a famous chef in the UK now, and are very happy for her.

Nadiya I did not think I was gonna cry. I thought I didn't miss them; it turns out I do.

Narrator Next, she goes to see her grandmother. She is very important to Nadiya. Nadiya stays in the village with her family for one week. She cooks with them, and learns from them, and is sad when it's time to say goodbye. She leaves her family, but continues her travels in Bangladesh. She will meet new people, try new things and learn all about her family's country.

2 ▶ **Watch the video again. Answer the questions.**

1 What is Nadiya's job?
2 How many brothers and sisters does she have?
3 Why is there a celebration for Nadiya?
4 Where are her mother and father?
5 Who is very important to Nadiya?
6 What will Nadiya learn about?

3 Pairwork Ask and answer questions about your family.

- Is your family nearby or in other countries? Where?
- Is your family important to you? If yes, why is it important?
- Why do you have family celebrations?

> **Life Skills: Respect others**
> - Value other cultures

Group work

4 Think about friends or family members from a different place or culture. Complete this table.

Things you learn from them	Things you try with them
local words	different food

5 Share your ideas with another group.

6 Make a class list of the important things you learn from other cultures.

Warm up

1 Who is the fanzine page about and who is it by?

Reading

2 🔊 7 Read and listen to the fanzine and complete the fact file.

About me

Hi, guys! I'm Becca, I'm sixteen, I'm from Suffolk and my hair is red (like Ed's).
And I'm a Sheerio (an Ed Sheeran fan)! Be one too!
We ♥ you, Ed!

Full name	
Nationality	
Birthday	
Star sign	
Favorite games	
Favorite food	
Important things in life	

Welcome to the Ed Sheeran fanzine!

His full name is Edward Christopher Sheeran, it's a very long name!

His parents are English and Irish, but he's from Suffolk, in England.

His birthday is on February 17th, so his star sign is Aquarius ♒

His favorite games are Monopoly and Lego - remember his song *Lego House*?

His favorite food is Oreo cookies and his favorite restaurant is Nando's, in London, where there is even a special 'Ed's Peri-Peri Sauce'.

There are tattoos all over his arms, including one of a cup of tea, a ketchup bottle and Van Gogh's *Starry Night*.

What's important to Ed in his life? Well, his friends: American singer Taylor Swift and the former British band One Direction. His wife Cherry (an old school friend) and their daughters: Lyra Antarctica and Jupiter.

Oh and his cats, Dorito and Calippo: there are more than 100,000 followers on their Instagram page.

And of course his music and: Lloyd, Felix, Cyril and Nigel (his guitars!)

♡ Like   ✏ Comment

3 Read the text again and answer the questions.

1 Where are Ed Sheeran's parents from?
2 Where are his tattoos and what are they?
3 Who are his famous friends?
4 What are Sheerios?
5 Who are Cyril and Nigel?
6 What are the names of his cats?

Learn to Learn / Listening strategies

Listening for specific information

- Look at pictures or information before listening to help you understand.
- Check what you are listening for: a name, a place, a time, yes/no, true/false etc.
- Try to predict the information you are going to hear (use the grammar to help you).
- Make notes of key words while you listen.
- Listen again and check your answers.
- Eliminate incorrect or impossible answers.

Listening

4 🔊 8 **Listen to the recording. Check (✓) the names of the authors you hear.**

Dan Brown ☐

Chimamanda Ngozi ☐

Jeff Kinney ☐

Toni Morrison ☐

5 🔊 8 **Listen again and choose the correct option (A, B or C).**

1 What's Bobby's full name?
 A Robert Gordon Morrison
 B Robert Luis Brown
 C Robert Luis Gordon

2 What's his nationality?
 A Colombian
 B American
 C British

3 How old is he?
 A 12
 B 18
 C 15

4 Who is Flaca?
 A his dog
 B his cat
 C an American author

Spoken interaction

6 Pairwork Choose a school club from the box and register. Ask and answer questions in turn.

> Book Club • Music Club • History Club • Sports Club

- favorite author
- favorite band / musician / singer
- favorite historic age
- favorite sport

A What's your name?
B My name's ...
A How old are you?
B I'm ...
A Who's / What's your favorite...

Writing

7 What's important in your life? Write a short paragraph about yourself.

> Hi, I'm ¹_____ from ²_____
> in ³_____.
> I ♥ ⁴_____ and my favorite school subject
> is ⁵_____. What's my favorite thing? It's
> my ⁶_____ (color) ⁷_____ (thing).
> Why is it my favorite? Because ⁸_____.

Choose the correct option (A, B, C or D).

1 'Where _____ from?' 'I'm from Spain'.
   A you are   **B** you   **C** are you   **D** you're   ☐

2 This is my brother. _____ name's David.
   A Her   **B** His   **C** He's   **D** Is   ☐

3 This is not my knapsack. It's _____.
   A Billy'   **B** Billys   **C** Billy's   **D** Billys'   ☐

4 Mary has two _____, a boy and a girl.
   A sons   **B** daughters   **C** children   **D** child   ☐

5 'I'm Tonya, nice _____ you'.
   A seeing   **B** to know   **C** to meet   **D** meeting   ☐

6 _____ are my new sneakers: do you like them?
   A This   **B** That   **C** These   **D** Those   ☐

7 Hi, Catherine. _____ Canadian?
   A Is she   **B** Are   **C** You are   **D** Are you   ☐

8 I'm thirteen. _____?
   A How are you old   **B** Are you how old   **C** How are you   **D** How old are you   ☐

9 Laura and I live in the same street. _____ go to school together.
   A We   **B** She   **C** They   **D** Us   ☐

10 Frances has _____ hair and _____ eyes.
   A brown / blonde   **B** red / green   **C** black / red   **D** black / blonde   ☐

11 Julian, Harry and Tom are brothers. _____ house is very big.
   A His   **B** Our   **C** Their   **D** Your   ☐

12 My friend Agnieszka is from Warsaw, Poland. She is _____.
   A French   **B** Polish   **C** American   **D** Turkish   ☐

13 _____ American, I'm from the UK.
   A I am   **B** Am I   **C** I am not   **D** I aren't   ☐

14 Look: in _____ picture there is our new puppy.
   A that   **B** these   **C** this   **D** those   ☐

15 My mother has a sister and a brother; they are my _____. I love them!
   A cousins   **B** aunt and uncle   **C** uncles   **D** grandparents   ☐

16 'Are they from Australia?' 'No, _____.'
   A they are   **B** no their   **C** they aren't   **D** aren't   ☐

17 I'm tired after this long walk. My _____ are sore.
   A foot   **B** foots   **C** feet   **D** feets   ☐

18 We are from Brazil. _____ African.
   A We are   **B** We aren't   **C** Us aren't   **D** We am   ☐

19 You're wrong. _____ aren't our bikes in the schoolyard! Ours are here.
   A That   **B** Those   **C** This   **D** These   ☐

20 Peru is in South America. _____ in Africa.
   A Is it   **B** It isn't   **C** They aren't   **D** Their   ☐

TOTAL _____ / 20

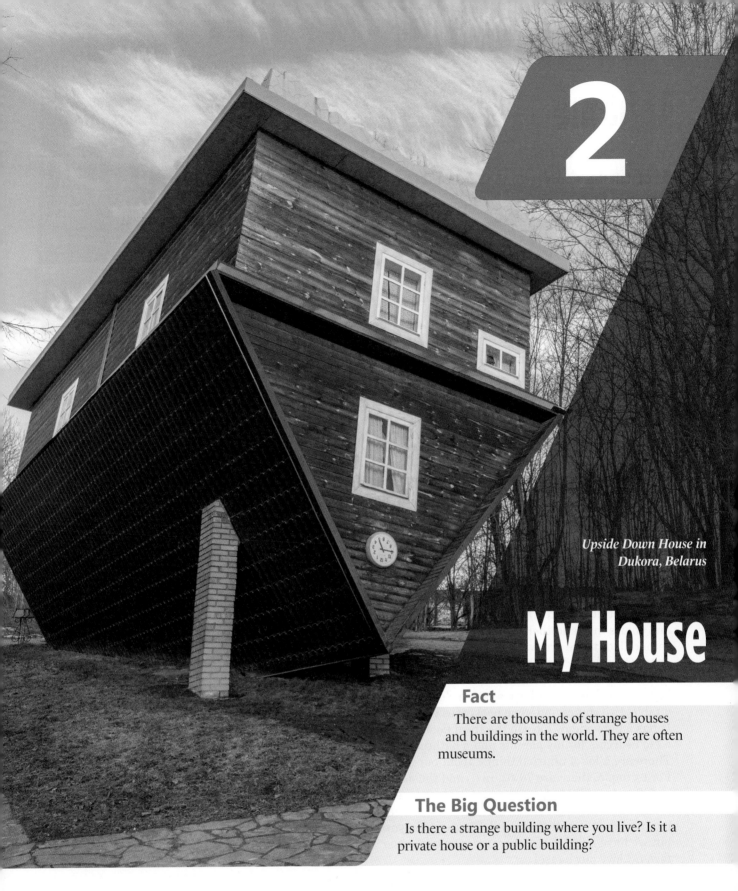

2

Upside Down House in Dukora, Belarus

My House

Fact

There are thousands of strange houses and buildings in the world. They are often museums.

The Big Question

Is there a strange building where you live? Is it a private house or a public building?

Unit Objectives

Vocabulary & Listening	Grammar	Language Skills	Video & Life Skills
• The house • Rooms and furniture	• *There is / There are* • Prepositions of place • Articles • Question words	Reading: A building with a past Listening: A girl and her house Writing: A historical building Speaking: Describing a house	▶ Homes on wheels Cultural awareness: • Learning about different lifestyles

At home

Vocabulary: Rooms in a house

1 Match the words (1-6) to the photos (A-F).

1. ☐D living room
2. ☐ bedroom
3. ☐ bathroom
4. ☐ kitchen
5. ☐ hall
6. ☐ yard

2 🔊 9 Now listen, check and repeat the words.

3 Read the text. Where is Martin's house?

A Tower House

Martin and his family have a new house. But it's not a normal house; it's very special. Their house is in a tower in the Highlands of Scotland.

This is my house. There are five floors and there are two rooms on each floor. On the first floor there's a big kitchen with a table and chairs in it and there's a living room. On the second floor there are two bedrooms, one for my sister Gemma and another room for me. There's also a small bathroom next to my bedroom. My bedroom isn't big but I have a bed, a closet, a table, two chairs and some bookcases in it. It has a big window too. On the third floor there's a big bedroom for my parents and a bathroom. There are a lot of unusual things about our house. For example, there are 70 stairs (!) and the door is 400 years old! My favorite place in the house is on the roof. It has an amazing view of the sea and mountains. It's really beautiful. There isn't a yard but we have a forest and there's a cave under the tower. I love our house!

4 Read the text again and answer the questions.

1. Why is Martin's house unusual?
   Because it is in a tower in the Highlands of Scotland.
2. Where is the living room?
3. Is there one bathroom in the house?
4. Who has a bedroom on the third floor?
5. What are the unusual things in Martin's house?
6. Where is his favorite place in the house?

> **Watch out!**
>
> We use *wh-* question words to make questions about:
>
> | people | → | *who* | place | → | *where* |
> | things | → | *what* | reason | → | *why* |
> | time | → | *when* | | | |

▶ Words Plus 2 p. 133

5 Match the questions (1-5) to the answers (a-e).

1 Where's my phone?
2 Who's that girl?
3 When's your birthday?
4 What's your name?
5 Why is the train late?

a ☐ My cousin Lola.
b ☐ Because of an accident.
c ☐ Juliet.
d ☐ In September.
e ☐ On the table.

Vocabulary: Furniture

6 🔊 10 Look at the picture of Jane's bedroom and match the furniture (A-H) to the words (1-8). Then listen, check and repeat the words.

1 ☑ bookcase
2 ☐ lamp
3 ☐ table
4 ☐ closet
5 ☐ bed
6 ☐ chair
7 ☐ window
8 ☐ door

Grammar: *There is/There are* – Affirmative and negative forms

There's a big kitchen.
There are two rooms on each floor.
There isn't a garden.

Find more examples of *there is* and *there are* in the text on page 22.

➡ Grammar reference p. 114

7 Underline the correct alternative.

1 There *is / are* a small living room in our house.
2 There *is / are* a girl from Hong Kong in my class.
3 There *isn't / aren't* two books in your bag.
4 There *is / are* five boys in my family.
5 There *is / are* a flag on the roof of the tower.
6 There *isn't / aren't* headphones on the table.

Prepositions of place

8 🔊 11 Match the prepositions (1-8) to the pictures (A-H). Then listen and check.

1 ☐ in
2 ☐ on
3 ☐ under
4 ☐ behind
5 ☐ next to
6 ☐ between
7 ☐ opposite
8 Ⓐ near

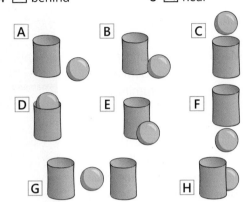

Speaking

9 Pairwork Look at the plan of the apartment. Take turns to ask and answer questions about where things are.

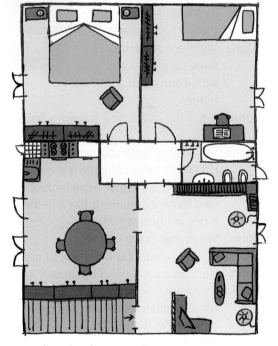

A Where's the stove?
B It's in the kitchen. It's next to the fridge.

Writing

10 Write a description of the apartment in exercise 9. Talk about the rooms and furniture. Use *there is/there are* and prepositions of place.

In the apartment there are five rooms. There's a living room...

A new home

1 Read the conversation. What does Maria have?

John Hi, Maria. How are you?

Maria I'm great, thanks. I have a room in an apartment!

John Fantastic! Where is it?

Maria It's in the city center. It's a big room and it has nice furniture. I have some photos of the apartment on my phone, look. This is my room. There's a bed and a table and chair...

John What are these here?

Maria They're lamps.

John Are there bookcases for all your books?

Maria Yes, there are. And there's a big closet for all my clothes too.

John It's lovely, Maria. Is there a living room?

Maria Yes, there is. And there's a kitchen too with a stove and a fridge.

John Is this the bathroom? Is there a bath in it?

Maria Yes, the big bathroom is next to the kitchen. It has a bath and a shower too. Then there's another small bathroom next to my bedroom. It has a shower but it doesn't have a bath.

John Who's that in the photo?

Maria My roommate, Candace. She's Canadian.

John She's very pretty. And the boys?

Maria Those are my friends, Mike and Neil. Mike's Candace's brother and Neil is my... well... we're friends...

John Maria!

2 Read the conversation again and check (✓) the things that are in Maria's room.

- ☐ bookcase
- ☐ lamp
- ☐ bath
- ☐ table
- ☐ shower
- ☐ closet
- ☐ bed
- ☐ stove
- ☐ chair
- ☐ fridge
- ☐ sofa
- ☐ window
- ☐ armchair
- ☐ door

3 Look at the pictures and match the furniture (A-F) to the words (1-6).

1 ☒ sofa
2 ☐ bath
3 ☐ shower
4 ☐ stove
5 ☐ fridge
6 ☐ armchair

Grammar: *There is/There are –* Interrogative form and short answers

Is there a living room?
Yes, *there is.*/No, *there isn't.*
Are there bookcases for all your books?
Yes, *there are.*/No, *there aren't.*

⊳ Grammar reference p. 114

4 Rewrite the sentences in the interrogative form, then write short answers.

1 There is a green bag. (✓)
   '*Is there a green bag?*' '*Yes, there is.*'
2 There are three boys in the classroom. (✗)
3 There is a bedroom next to the living room. (✓)
4 There are two armchairs in the living room. (✓)
5 There is a table under the window. (✗)
6 There is a man in the car. (✗)

There is / There are

1 Complete the table.

Affirmative	Negative
There [1]_____ a door.	There [3]_____ a yard.
There [2]_____ two lamps.	There [4]_____ two floors.
Interrogative and short answers	
Is there a bathroom? Yes, [5]_____ is. / No, there [7]_____.	
Are there three beds? Yes, [6]____ are. / No, there [8]_____.	

2 Underline the correct alternative.

1 There *is / are* a bathroom upstairs.
2 There *is / are* two new bookcases in the study.
3 There *is / are* four chairs in the kitchen.
4 There *is / are* two lamps in my bedroom.
5 There *is / are* a big yard with trees.
6 There *is / are* a TV in the living room.

3 Rewrite the sentences from exercise 2 in the negative form.

4 🔊 12 **Complete the conversation with the correct forms of *there is* or *there are*. Then listen and check.**

B&B   Hi, Henry, this is your room.
[1]_____ a double bed, a closet and a desk. [2]_____ also two lamps on the desk.

Henry   [3]_____ an internet connection?

B&B   Yes, [4]_____.

Henry   [5]_____ a password?

B&B   No, [6]_____. It's free Wi-Fi.

Henry   Excellent. Is that my bathroom?

B&B   Yes, it is. [7]_____ a shower but [8]_____ a bath...

Henry   No problem, I like showers!
[9]_____ other people in the house?

B&B   No, [10]_____.

a / an, the

5 Read the examples and complete the rule.

*There's **an** armchair and a sofa in **the** living room.*
*There isn't **an** apple in **the** fridge.*
*Jenny is **the** new student from **the** United States.*

We use [1]*a/an* with singular nouns beginning with consonant sound.
We use [2]*a/an* with singular nouns beginning with vowel sound.
We use *the* with unique and [3]*specific / non specific* nouns.

➜ Grammar reference & practice pp. 114-115

6 Complete the text with *a* or *an*.

My friend Emma is [1]_____ special person. She's very shy, but has [2]_____ very strong personality. She's [3]_____ only child. Her father's [4]_____ famous musician, and her mother's [5]_____ excellent architect. They live in [6]_____ big house with a yard on King's Street. Their house is full of music records and books. It's amazing! There's [7]_____ enormous aquarium in [8]_____ living room! Unfortunately, there isn't [9]_____ swimming pool, but [10]_____ sea is not too far.

7 Add *the* where necessary.

1 ____ Spain
2 ____ United Kingdom
3 ____ Brazil
4 ____ People's Republic of China
5 ____ Friday
6 ____ Empire State Building
7 ____ Prince George
8 ____ Miss Marple
9 ____ Andes
10 ____ Panama Canal
11 ____ Saudi Arabia
12 ____ Cayman Islands

Question words

8 Complete the sentences with the correct question word from the box. Then match the questions (1-6) to the answers (a-f).

when • why • what • where • how • who

1 ____ time is it?
2 ____ old are you?
3 ____ is your sister's birthday?
4 ____ is my phone?
5 ____ is that guy with a blue T-shirt?
6 ____ are you here? It's 8:30!

a ☐ Because I'm late!
b ☐ It's in the hall.
c ☐ September the 3rd.
d ☐ He's my brother Liam.
e ☐ Twenty past four.
f ☐ I'm sixteen.

In the house

1 Write the words from the box on this picture of houses in Melbourne, Australia.

> upstairs • balcony • fence • downstairs
> chimney • front yard

2 Write the words from the box under the pictures.

> cushions • rug • sink • recycling bins • mirror
> shelves • curtains • chest of drawers

1 _____

2 _____

3 _____

4 _____

5 _____

6 _____

7 _____

8 _____

3 Guess the piece of furniture!

1 _____

2 _____

3 _____

4 _____

5 _____

6 _____

Electrical appliances

4 Match the appliances (1-6) to a related word (a-f).

1 washing machine	a ☐	frozen foods
2 toaster	b ☐	roast turkey
3 oven	c ☐	bread
4 dishwasher	d ☐	glasses and plates
5 microwave	e ☐	clothes
6 stove	f ☐	pasta

Listening

5 🔊 13 Listen to this voice message from Tina to a friend. Check (✓) the words you hear.

☐ bath ☐ bed
☐ sofa ☐ closet
☐ bedroom ☐ washing machine
☐ chairs ☐ balcony
☐ table ☐ TV
☐ fridge ☐ window

6 🔊 13 Listen again and complete the sentences.

1 The new a_____ is in the center of town.
2 There's a f_____ in the kitchen.
3 There isn't a d_____ in the kitchen.
4 In the living room there's one large w_____.
5 There's a big c_____ in the bedroom.
6 There's also a s_____ in the bathroom.

▶ Words Plus 2 p. 133 | ✓ DIGITAL BOOK ▶ Pronunciation Bank: /ð/ vs /θ/

Homes on wheels

1 ▶ **Watch the video without sound. What kind of home is it?**

Theo	What's going on, guys? So, we have just arrived at the Colorado Tiny House Festival and this place is massive.
Narrator	Travel vloggers Bee and Theo are at The Tiny House Festival. They show us around. This motorhome is an interesting shape, and it's made of beautiful wood.

Inside it's got a sofa, and a bed. There's a bookcase for your books and all your things. There's also a window, so you've got a view of the places you visit. This one actually looks like a real house. It's got an air conditioner and lots of windows. It's also got tiles on the roof. Inside, there's even a staircase, that takes you up to a comfortable bedroom with a big bed.

Bee	So, we've just stopped for lunch.
Narrator	Now, it's time for some food. Small can also be beautiful. An unusual look outside, and really special inside. Great colors! And look at the bed by that big window. There's even a small stove. Bee and Theo have now got a lot of cool ideas for their own home on wheels.
Bee	So, thanks for watching, guys, and we'll see you on the next video.

2 ▶ **Watch the video again. Complete the sentences with words from the video.**

1 The motorhome has a bed and a _____.
2 This motorhome is made of _____.
3 This one is similar to a real _____.
4 It has a comfortable bedroom with a big
   _____.
5 This home has great _____.
6 Bee and Theo have lots of ideas for their own
   _____.

3 **Role play Choose Student A or B. You are at the Colorado Tiny House Festival. Do a role play. Follow the example.**

A *Hi, welcome to my mobile home!*
B *Hi, thank you. Is there a kitchen?*
A *Yes, there's a small kitchen with...*

Student A
• You live in a mobile home. Show Student B around your home.
• Talk about the furniture and objects inside your home.

Student B
• You want to see a mobile home. Ask the owner some questions.

> **Life Skills: Cultural awareness**
> • Learning about different lifestyles

Writing

4 **Think about your ideal home. Write a short text answering the questions.**

1 What type of home is it? (an apartment / a detached house / a cottage / a mobile home / a boat...)
2 Where is it? (in the city center / in a village / in the forest / by the sea...)
3 How many rooms are there?
4 Is there a garden / a terrace / a balcony?
5 Why is it special?

Warm up

1 **Look at the picture. What is that big building in the background?**

☐ an old castle
☐ a royal palace
☐ a hotel
☐ a private home

A building with a past

Opening in 1893 originally with 170 rooms, the Fairmont Le Château Frontenac in Québec's Old City is not only a hotel; it is an icon, designated a National Historic Site of Canada in 1981. Once the official residence of the French and British governors, there are objects from 400 years of history on display in the lobby. In summer, visitors can take a guided tour of the Saint-Louis Forts and Châteaux National Historic Site under Dufferin Terrace next to the Château.

Important visitors to the hotel, past and present, include: Queen Elizabeth II, Céline Dion, Leonardo DiCaprio, Paul McCartney and Charlie Chaplin. In 1943, British prime minister Winston Churchill and American president Franklin D. Roosevelt plan the allied invasion of occupied Europe there. In 1953, Alfred Hitchcock's films the movie *I Confess* with the hotel manager at the time, George Jessop, playing himself. Today the hotel has 18 floors, up to 80 meters high. There are 12 kilometers of hallways with 610 guest rooms and suites on them. And the hotel's 2,000 windows have spectacular views of the St. Lawrence River, the city and the interior gardens.

There is also a modern spa and fitness center, three restaurants, one coffee shop, two bars, several shops and banking services on site. As well as a terrace the rooftop garden is home to bees – hotel chefs get about 650 liters of honey from them every year.

Reading

2 🔊 14 **Read and listen to the text and check your answer. Then write what these numbers are about.**

3 _____	610 _____
12 _____	650 _____
18 _____	1893 _____
80 _____	1943 _____
170 _____	2,000 _____

3 Read the text again and write if the sentences are true (T) or false (F).

1 The Fairmont Le Château Frontenac is in France. ___
2 There are historic objects in the lobby. ___
3 There are lots of famous visitors to the hotel. ___
4 You can see the sea from some of the windows. ___
5 There are some shops in the hotel. ___
6 There is a farm on top of the hotel. ___

Listening

4 🔊 15 Listen to Julie talking about her house. Which one is it?

A

B

C

5 🔊 15 Listen again. Choose the correct option (A, B or C).

1 The house is ___.
 A big and modern
 B small and modern
 C small and old
2 The walls are ___.
 A gray
 B silver
 C white
3 Which of these sentences is true?
 A There is a big front door.
 B There is no front door.
 C There are lots of doors and windows.
4 The house is ___.
 A on one floor
 B on two floors
 C on the fourth floor
5 There are ___.
 A two bedrooms
 B three bedrooms
 C four bedrooms
6 Outside there is ___.
 A a chimney on the roof
 B a garden and a garage
 C furniture on the terrace

Writing

Learn to Learn / Writing strategies

Correct **punctuation** is important in all types of writing:
- **W**e always start a sentence with a **capital letter** and end it with a **full stop.**
- We also use capital letters for names of people and places, nationalities and languages, days of the week, months of the year and holidays (**C**hristmas).
- We should start a new paragraph on a line for each new idea.
- We use commas (,) to separate a list of words e.g. *There are two bedrooms, a bathroom, a living room, and a kitchen.*
- We use question marks (?) after questions and explanation marks (!) in informal writing for emphasis.
- We use apostrophes (') for possessive forms e.g. *This is Mark's house,* or for short forms *It's his house.*

6 Describe a historical building in your area, or that you have visited.

Speaking

7 Prepare a short oral presentation about your choice in exercise 6.

Choose the correct option (A, B, C or D).

1 _____ five people in my family.
   A They are   B There is   C Are there   D There are ☐

2 'Where are my keys?' 'They're _____ the table'.
   A at   B on   C in   D for ☐

3 We have _____ house in Malibu.
   A any   B a   C an   D the ☐

4 I'm in my bedroom playing the new video game; Dad is _____ in the kitchen.
   A upstairs   B down   C downstairs   D out ☐

5 I want to hang the poster of my favorite soccer team _____ my wall!
   A in   B at   C up   D on ☐

6 '_____ is your brother?' 'In his bedroom.'
   A When   B Where   C What   D How ☐

7 I want to buy some new _____ for the _____ in the living room.
   A cushions / bed   B curtains / table   C cushions / sofa   D chairs / sofa ☐

8 In our new house there's _____ armchair in _____ kitchen.
   A the / the   B an / the   C a / the   D the / a ☐

9 '_____ a garden in your house?' 'Yes, _____.'
   A Is there / there   B There is / there is   C Is / is   D Is there / there is ☐

10 There no fresh fruit _____ the fridge.
   A under   B at   C in   D on ☐

11 _____ time is the movie tonight?
   A How   B Where   C That   D What ☐

12 I have too many clothes: I need a new _____!
   A sofa   B closet   C shelves   D table ☐

13 _____ are you shouting?
   A Why   B When   C What   D Who ☐

14 My grandparents live _____ the capital city.
   A opposite   B behind   C on   D near ☐

15 _____ is the girl talking to your sister? I don't know her.
   A Where   B What   C Who   D How ☐

16 ... and the washing machine is just _____ the sink and the stove.
   A down   B between   C inside   D opposite ☐

17 Mom is hanging the new _____ for all my comics.
   A curtains   B shelves   C table   D bins ☐

18 Open the _____: there's fruit salad for dessert.
   A washing machine   B chest of drawers   C cupboard   D fridge ☐

19 I'm tired, I don't want to paint the _____!
   A fence   B sink   C garden   D chimney ☐

20 'Are there three bedrooms in their new house?' 'No, _____.'
   A theren't   B there aren't   C there not are   D aren't. ☐

TOTAL _____ / 20

3

Surfing competition in Portugal

Jobs & Sports

Fact
There are more than 40 water sports played professionally, including underwater rugby.

The Big Question
What's your favorite extreme sport? Can you play it?

Unit Objectives

Vocabulary & Listening	Grammar	Language Skills	Video & Life Skills
• Jobs • Sports	• *can / can't* for ability and possibility • Degrees of ability • Adverbs of manner • Object pronouns	Reading: It's women's work! Listening: A young athlete's day Writing: Writing about your sports skills Speaking: A conversation about sport	▶ Soccer in Soweto Employability Skills: • Working well as part of a team

I can drive very well

Vocabulary: Jobs

1 Match the words for jobs (1-12) to the photos (A-L).

1 [E] nurse
2 [ ] doctor
3 [ ] driver
4 [ ] teacher
5 [ ] architect
6 [ ] receptionist
7 [ ] journalist
8 [ ] waiter/waitress
9 [ ] businessman/ businesswoman
10 [ ] sales assistant
11 [ ] athlete
12 [ ] tennis instructor

 A
 B
 C
 D
 E
 F
 G
 H
 I
 J
 K
 L

2 🔊 16 **Now listen, check your answers and repeat the words.**

Watch out!

We talk about permanent jobs and temporary jobs in two different ways.

I'm a receptionist. (permanent job)
I work as a waiter. (temporary job)

3 Read the information from a jobs website. Write each person's job.

1 Katie _____
2 Lorant _____
3 Chati _____
4 Ellie _____

---

d

Ideal Jobs

Do you have an idea for your dream job? Hundreds of people find great jobs with *Dream Job* every week – this site really works! Send us your CV and post a message today! Posting a message is free – it doesn't cost money!

Name	Katie Brown
Age	19
City	Johannesburg
Job	receptionist

I'm Katie Brown! I live in Johannesburg now but I'm not South African, I'm British. I'm from Newcastle in the north of England. I work in a hotel in Johannesburg, The Red Palace. I'm a receptionist. I work in the mornings and the evenings but I don't work in the afternoons. Besides English, I can speak three languages (French, Italian and Spanish). I want to find a receptionist job on a cruise ship.

Posted by Katie, 24th March

Name	Lorant Kacsor
Age	21
City	Warsaw
Job	waiter

My name is Lorant and I'm a university student in Warsaw in the college of architecture. I work as a waiter in a café in the city center. I work late in the evenings and on weekends. I'm Polish but I can speak English and German very well. I want to find a job in London but I don't want to work as a waiter. I want to work as an architect.

Posted by Lorant, 25th March

Fast Finishers

Write about the jobs of five people you know.

My brother is an architect.

Name	Chati Kanokwan
Age	25
City	Bangkok
Job	teacher

Hi, I'm Chati. I'm twenty-five years old and I'm from Thailand. I work in a school. I'm a teacher. I teach math and science. This summer I want to find a job as a driver in the UK because I want to learn English. Sadly, I can't speak English very well, but I can drive very carefully!

Posted by Chati K, 24th March

Name	Ellie Estevez
Age	22
City	San Diego
Job	swimming instructor

Hi, I'm Ellie, I'm a true Californian from San Diego. My mom's American, from Oregon, but my dad's from Puerto Rico, a beautiful island in Central America. I work as a swimming instructor at my local swimming pool in the afternoons, but I want to work in tourism. I can speak Spanish as well as English, I can also scuba dive quite well. My dream is to be a tourist guide for marine wildlife.

Posted by Ellie E, 24th March

Grammar: *can / can't* for ability

I can drive very well.
I can't speak English at all.
Can you speak German?
Yes, I can. / No, I can't.

We use *can / can't* to talk about ability. To say how good we are at something we use *very well, well, quite well, (not) at all.*

▶ Grammar reference p. 116

5 Write sentences which are true for you.

1 speak French _____
2 ride a bicycle _____
3 ride a scooter _____
4 cook dinner _____
5 use an iPad _____
6 play the guitar _____

Speaking

6 In pairs, take turns to make true and false statements about the people from the Dream Jobs website. Can your partner remember which information is true or false?

A Lorant is a student.
B True!
A He can speak French very well.
B True?
A False! He can speak English and German.

4 CERT Read the text again and choose the correct option (A, B or C).

1 Katie is from __B__.
A South Africa   B the UK   C the USA
2 She can't speak _____.
A French and Italian   B Spanish   C German
3 Lorant is a student of _____.
A architecture   B medicine   C art
4 He's _____.
A an architect   B a waiter   C a teacher
5 Chati is a _____.
A student   B doctor   C teacher
6 He can _____ very well.
A drive   B speak English   C speak German
7 Ellie is from _____.
A Puerto Rico   B California   C Central America
8 She can _____.
A drive   B speak French   C swim

7 Read the information and use the prompts below to write correct sentences about Danny.

Name	Danny O'Sullivan
Age	28
Nationality	Australian
City	Los Angeles
Job	doctor
Languages	English, Mandarin Chinese

1 be / from Australia
2 be / 28 years old
3 live / in Los Angeles
4 be / a doctor
5 have a job / Cedars Hospital
6 can speak / two languages quite well

Danny is from Australia. He... He...

The life of a scuba diving instructor

1 **Read the interview with a scuba diving instructor. Do you think it's a dangerous job?**

Think about the Coral Reef, all the colorful fish, tropical beaches… Jessica has it all!

Jessica, tell us about your job. What is so special about it?
Well, I guess what's so special about being a scuba diving instructor is the element I work in, which is water. I'm always in the water, and that's why my hair is so dry!

But I guess working in exotic places can be very exciting…
I mainly work here in Melbourne, in swimming pools, which is where we do basic training. Some people can't even swim very well, you know, it can be very frustrating for them and for me. But I love my job so much.

What are the main challenges in your job?
First of all, trust. I'm very small and young, and sometimes big, adult men think I can't do my job very well because I'm too young and not experienced enough. But it's not

true. It can be difficult sometimes, but I can be very convincing because I'm absolutely the best instructor in town.

And a very modest one, too. What abilities do you need to scuba dive?
Anyone can scuba dive, but there are a lot of rules to follow. If you are pretty fit, with good muscular tone, if you're not afraid of water, if you can clear a scuba mask easily, well you too can scuba dive. And you'll love it!

Are you good at other sports too?
I love rugby, I'm a big fan of our national team but I can't play it. I also like yoga, but I can't do it often because I have no time, so I'm not really the best in my class…

2 **Read the text again and decide if the sentences are true (T) or false (F).**
1 Jessica is a professional swimmer. ___
2 Her place of work is in an exotic country. ___
3 Some of her students are not very good swimmers. ___
4 Some students think she's too young to be a good instructor. ___
5 Only very good swimmers can be good at scuba diving. ___
6 Jessica is very good at yoga. ___

3 **Complete the sentences with an object pronoun.**
1 I have a skateboard but I can't use _____.
2 Children love the beach. It can be very good for _____.
3 She's my schoolmate Annie. I study with _____.
4 Mark is so funny! I love _____!
5 Are you free tonight? Come with _____ to the movies.
6 You are new here, right? Can I help _____?

Grammar:
Object pronouns

Subject	Object
I	me
you	you
he	him
she	her
it	it
we	us
you	you
they	them

➜ Grammar reference p. 116

Speaking

4 **Pairwork** **What can you do very well or pretty well? What can't you do at all? Ask and answer questions using the prompts below.**

swim • speak a foreign language • teach others
babysit kids • ride a bike / scooter • dance • sing
use a computer • play an instrument • dive

can / can't

1 Complete the rule. Write *ability* or *possibility* next to the sentences.

1 My father can cook very well. _____
2 I can't watch a movie with you tonight. I have homework to do. _____

2 Complete the sentences with the correct form of *can*.

1 '_____ you ride a motorbike?' 'No, I _____.'
2 I understand him because I _____ speak French.
3 '_____ you cook paella?' 'Yes, I _____. I love Spanish food.'
4 Karen _____ only speak Polish, she _____ speak Italian too.
5 I _____ type quickly. I _____ type a hundred words per minute.
6 '_____ you start work next week?' 'I'm sorry, I _____. I'm very busy at the moment.'
7 George _____ go swimming tomorrow because he has a bad cold.
8 _____ you open that window? It's too hot in here.

3 Complete the interview. For each space (1–9) write *can* or *can't* and a verb from the box.

climb • sing • do • draw • play • speak (x3) • read

What can you do?
Alexis is 16 and she's from London.

Mr Jones What languages [1] _____ you _____, Alexis?
Alexis I [2] _____ _____ English and Greek. I'm bilingual. My mom is from Athens in Greece. We go there every summer.
Mr Jones [3] _____ your brothers _____ Greek too?
Alexis Yes, they can, but they [4] _____ _____ or write in Greek.
Mr Jones So, Alexis, what else are you good at?
Alexis Well, I'm very good at art. I [5] _____ _____ and paint really well.
Mr Jones [6] _____ you _____ an instrument?
Alexis No, I can't, but I [7] _____ _____ and dance. I'm the lead singer in a band.
Mr Jones Are you good at sports?
Alexis Not really, but I'm learning to climb and I really like it. There's a climbing wall at my local sports centre, but I [8] _____ _____ to the top yet. I [9] _____ _____ martial arts a bit, too.

Object pronouns

4 Underline the correct subject or object pronoun.

1 Andy Murray is my favorite tennis player. What do you think of *me/it/him*?
2 Is that pizza for *you/us/them*? Thank you!
3 This is Joe. *He/Him/It*'s my boyfriend.
4 Look! It's a photo of *you/them/he* and Simon!
5 Gal Gadot is a brilliant actor. I love *it/she/her*.
6 My parents and *me/I/we* always go to Greece in the summer.
7 Your old sneakers are ugly! I hate *them/they/it*!

Adverbs of manner

5 Look at the examples and complete the rules.

*I can run **quickly**.*   *She speaks very **fast**.*
*Paul sings very **badly**.*   *She can't swim **well**.*

To form an adverb from an adjective, we add the suffix [1] _____.
quick → quickly
[2] _____ and [3] _____ are irregular adverbs.
good → [4] _____   *fast →* [5] _____

6 Complete the sentences with the adverbs of manner.

1 Do your homework _____ (quiet).
2 I can't run very _____ (fast); I'm always late!
3 Lou can sing _____ (beautiful), he's in a choir.
4 I can't see very _____ (clear); it's too dark.
5 We can't speak English very _____ (good); we're new students.
6 _____ (unfortunate), I can't come to your party.

Round up

7 Complete the conversation with the words from the box.

it • quickly • can (x2) • her • you • brilliantly us • pretty • him

Katie Wow, Harry! I love your music! You [1] _____ play the guitar really well.
Harry Thanks! I really love [2] _____.
Katie So who's in the band with [3] _____?
Harry Well, there's my sister, Lizzie. Do you know [4] _____? She's the pianist, she can play the keyboards [5] _____. Clara Smith and her brother Jim are in the band, too.
Katie Really? [6] _____ they play too?
Harry Yes, they can. Their dad is a musician. I like [7] _____ very much; he's awesome.
Katie Wow! Well, I can sing [8] _____ well...
Harry Really? Then come sing with [9] _____!
Katie Are you sure? I can learn your songs very [10] _____. Let's do it then!

> **Grammar reference & practice pp. 116-117**

Jobs

21st-century jobs

1 🔊 17 **Write the jobs next the correct definitions. Then listen and check.**

> social media manager • app developer • influencer
> accountant • organic food producer • stylist
> personal assistant (PA) • psychologist
> sports manager • virtual assistant

1 A _____ works from home and assists customers online.
2 A _____ knows about fashion.
3 A _____ is good at organizing teams and competitions.
4 An _____ shows and suggests products online.
5 An _____ produces natural foods with no chemicals.
6 An _____ is good at creating apps for smartphones.
7 A _____ makes your posts catchy and visible to a lot of people.
8 A _____ helps you with your mental health.
9 A _____ is good at organizing other people's work.
10 An _____ manages your finances.

Workplaces

2 Write at least two jobs next to the places.

1 hospital _____
2 office _____
3 café _____
4 store _____
5 sports center _____
6 hotel _____

Sports

3 Write at least three sports in each group.

team sports	two-people sports
_____	_____
_____	_____
_____	_____

SPORTS

one-person sports
_____
_____
_____

4 🔊 18 **Write the sports from the box under the correct icon. Then listen and check.**

> ice skating • tennis • horseback riding • basketball
> baseball • volleyball • athletics • soccer
> martial arts • gymnastics • yoga • jogging

1 basketball   2 _____   3 _____
4 _____   5 _____   6 _____
7 _____   8 _____   9 _____
10 _____   11 _____   12 _____

play, go, do

5 🔊 19 **Complete the sentences with the correct form of the verbs *play, go* or *do*. Then listen and check your answers.**

1 I _____ ice skating in winter.
2 He _____ martial arts every Thursday.
3 We _____ yoga on the weekends.
4 They _____ football for the school team.
5 She _____ horseback riding on Saturday mornings.
6 We _____ volleyball at the beach.
7 He _____ athletics in the summer.
8 Do you _____ gymnastics at school?

Listening

6 🔊 20 **Listen to Josh applying for a summer job. Which job is it?**

☐ food delivery cyclist
☐ accountant
☐ app developer

7 🔊 20 **Listen again. What can he do? Check (✓).**

speak Spanish	☐	use a camera	☐
speak French	☐	ride a scooter	☐
speak German	☐	ride a bicycle	☐
speak Russian	☐	play soccer	☐
use a computer	☐	play tennis	☐

▶ Words Plus 3 p. 134   DIGITAL BOOK   ▶ Pronunciation Bank: Intonation in questions

Soccer in Soweto

1 ▶ **Watch the video. What is typical of South African soccer?**

Narrator	Welcome to Soccer City near Soweto in South Africa. It's the largest football stadium in Africa. Spain were the World Cup winners here in 2010. Today 90,000 people are here for a big match called the Soweto Derby. The match is between two local teams: Kaizer Chiefs and the Orlando Pirates. South Africa has a very special football culture and South African fans always make a lot of noise. The noise is very loud because of the vuvuzelas. You find these trumpets at all South African football matches. Today there are thousands of them. With the sound of the vuvuzelas it is like a big party. People love dancing and singing at the match. At half-time the fans get an extra show. Dan Magness, a famous British football freestyler, can do fantastic tricks with a football. Freestyle is very popular with young people in Soweto.
Dan	I've just performed a nearly perfect show in front of nearly 90,000 people. What a feeling!
Narrator	Dan goes into Soweto. He sees that even young children like doing freestyle. Freestyle is everywhere in Soweto. Chris is a South African champion freestyler. There is something different about freestyle in Soweto. It is almost like a dance. Lots of people say that this is because dancing is very popular in South Africa. These freestylers mix dancing and singing... with football skills. At this Soweto school the children do an 'African Warm-up' – singing and dancing before the match. You can see how football and dancing come together. Football and freestyle are international sports. People like playing them all over the world. But here in Soweto, football and freestyle are also a big part of South African life.

2 ▶ **Watch the video again. Underline the correct alternative.**

1 Soccer City is a *stadium / school*.
2 South African people can be very *quiet / noisy* at the stadium.
3 The noise comes from the *vuvuzelas / people singing*.
4 Dan Magness is a *football player / freestyler*.
5 Freestylers can *do tricks with a ball / make a lot of noise*.
6 Freestyle in South Africa is similar to *singing / dancing*.

3 Pairwork **Can you do any tricks with your hands or your feet? What are they? Tell your partner.**

> **Life Skills: Employability Skills**
> • Working well as part of a team

4 Read the sentences below with the help of a dictionary. Which ones are true about a good team player – in sports, at school or at work? Work in small groups.

A good team player
• has a positive attitude.
• works alone.
• is flexible.
• understands his / her role.
• is not very collaborative.
• respects others.
• never helps.
• listens actively.

5 Can you add other qualities of a good team player? Ask your teacher for help.

6 Share your ideas with another group.

Warm Up

1 Pairwork **Do you know any famous sportswomen from your country? Say their names and their sport.**

Reading

It's women's work!

1 At 23 American gymnast Simone Biles can't wear all her medals because she has 30 of them! She learns new gymnastic movements in just three days. There is even one called the Biles! After every competition she can eat her favorite food, pizza. She can't always go out with friends because of training. But she can laugh and have fun with the other gymnasts.

2 Federica Pellegrini is a swimming champion from Italy. She can swim very fast: 400m in under 4 minutes, and 200m in under 2 minutes! But at 32 she can't win more competitions, or can she? Federica is crazy about tattoos. You can see them on her body when she swims. She loves fashion and music too. You can buy her things on eBay. She often sells them there for charity.

3 28-year-old Liu Shiwen from China can play table tennis very well. She moves very quickly and can hit the ball very hard. She is a World Cup champion, a World champion, an ITTF World Tour champion and an Asian Cup champion. Champions can't often relax, but they can find time to try new clothes or make-up – two of her favorite hobbies!

4 Who can save a match, minutes before the end of her international soccer debut? Dalila Ippolito can! At 18 she can also say she is the first Argentinian woman to play in Italy, after signing with Juventus in 2020. To stop feeling homesick, she drinks maté, a traditional drink, listens to Latin American Reggaeton music, or she can pretend to be Lionel Messi on her PlayStation!

C

D

Listening

4 🔊 **22** **Listen to Theo talking about his daily routine. What is his sport?**

5 🔊 **22** CERT **Listen again and complete the sentences.**

A typical training day

6 a.m.	workout [1]_____
7 a.m.	a massage or spend time in [2]_____
8 a.m.	[3]_____
10 a.m.	classes where we can work on our [4]_____
12:30 p.m.	lunch (can't be too heavy)
2 p.m.	[5]_____ to become fit and strong, too
3 p.m.	[6]_____ if I can
4-6 p.m.	[7]_____ dance routines in the afternoon
7 p.m.	if there are no competitions you can [8]_____, then work on the music and creative moves

Writing

Learn to Learn / **Writing strategies**

An informal email

- Use an appropriate opening (Hi/Hello…).
- Use informal language and abbreviations.
- Write your message clearly and concisely.
- Ask a question or show interest in the other person.
- Use an appropriate close (Bye for now/Write back…).

6 **Write an email to a friend about a sport you do. Explain what you can and can't do well. Say where and when you can play this sport. Ask what sport your friend does.**

⚫⚫⚫

___ ___ ___ ___ ___   ⚪ ⚪ ⚫

_____

_____

_____

Speaking

7 Pairwork **Ask and answer questions about the sport in your email.**

2 🔊 **21** **Read and listen to the text about four professional athletes. Write their names, nationalities and sports. Then match the names (1-4) to the pictures (A-D).**

1 _____
2 _____
3 _____
4 _____

3 CERT **Read the text again. Write the name next to each question.**

1 Who can hit things hard? _____
2 Who has 30 medals? _____
3 Who has tattoos? _____
4 Who loves clothes and make-up? _____
5 Who loves pizza? _____
6 Who plays video games? _____
7 Who saves a match on an international debut? _____
8 Whose things can you buy online? _____

Choose the correct option (A, B, C or D).

1 Josh works in a _____. He's a doctor.
   A hotel   B hospital   C supermarket   D office   ☐

2 '_____ use your dictionary?' 'Sure. Here you are'.
   A Can I   B Can you   C Do I   D Am I   ☐

3 Steve can meet _____ at the swimming pool.
   A us   B we   C our   D I   ☐

4 I love computers and all about IT. I want to be an _____!
   A accountant   B app developer   C influencer   D virtual assistant ☐

5 Snowboarding is my new sport, I can't do it very _____.
   A good   B goodly   C well   D bad   ☐

6 My sister loves drawing buildings. She's studying really hard to become an _____.
   A architect   B app developer   C accountant   D influencer   ☐

7 _____ speak two languages: English and Portuguese.
   A I can't   B I can   C Do I   D Can I   ☐

8 Marc Jacobs is my favorite _____: his suits are the best!
   A psychologist   B influencer   C personal assistant D stylist   ☐

9 Miss Greyson is our new English teacher. I like _____ very much.
   A him   B she   C them   D her   ☐

10 I have a new part-time job for the weekend as a _____ at Pink boutique.
   A teacher   B sales assistant   C journalist   D nurse   ☐

11 We are barefoot when we do our _____ training.
   A football   B martial arts   C running   D baseball   ☐

12 '_____ Sarita come out and play?' 'No, she _____: she's doing her homework.
   A Can / can   B Can / can't   C Can't / can't   D Can't / can   ☐

13 Careful! You can hurt yourself quite _____ with your hockey stick.
   A badly   B bad   C well   D good   ☐

14 I love the countryside. It's where I can go _____.
   A ice skating   B swimming   C horseback riding D skiing   ☐

15 My little sister is starting talking: she _____ say just a few words, but she's cute.
   A cans   B can   C can't   D does can   ☐

16 My friends always take me with _____ when they go out.
   A him   B it   C they   D them   ☐

17 On the weekend, I love playing _____ with my friends in the park!
   A yoga   B gymnastics   C volleyball   D ice skating   ☐

18 Jason's mom's a famous _____ and she's often away for work.
   A sales assistant B receptionist   C businesswoman   D waitress   ☐

19 Our new classmate is great at sports: she can run very _____.
   A quick   B fastly   C quickly   D slow   ☐

20 In the winter we go _____ on the small frozen lake in the forest.
   A swimming   B ice skating   C horseback riding D running   ☐

TOTAL _____ / 20

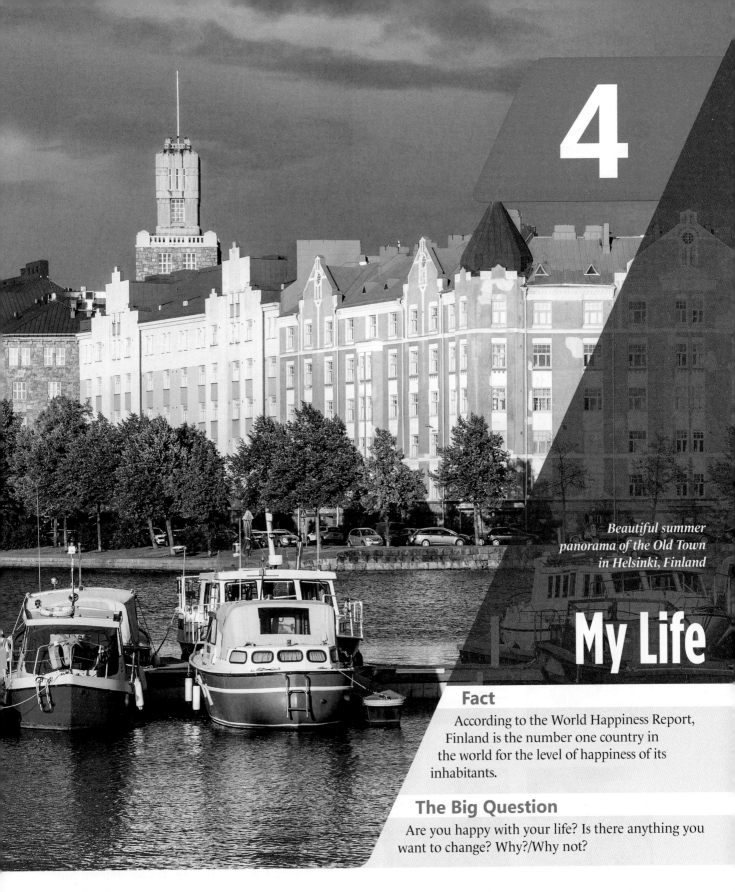

4

Beautiful summer panorama of the Old Town in Helsinki, Finland

My Life

Fact

According to the World Happiness Report, Finland is the number one country in the world for the level of happiness of its inhabitants.

The Big Question

Are you happy with your life? Is there anything you want to change? Why?/Why not?

Unit Objectives

Vocabulary & Listening	Grammar	Language Skills	Video & Life Skills
• Routine and free-time activities • Parts of the day • Quality adjectives and their opposites	• Present simple • Prepositions of time • Adverbs and expressions of frequency	Reading: A typical day in space Listening: A woman and her job Speaking: Talking about routine at work Writing: Describing a routine	▶ Making friends Social skills: • Meeting new people

Vocabulary: Daily routine activities

1 🔊 23 **Write the correct verb under the pictures. Then listen and check.**

> do my homework • have lunch • wake up
> get dressed • go to bed • take a shower
> catch the bus • get to school

1 _____

2 _____

3 _____

4 _____

5 _____

6 _____

7 _____

8 _____

2 **Pairwork Write other activities that you do every day.**

3 **Read the text and underline all the verbs of routine you can find.**

My life in the mountains

My name's Helga Fischer and I'm 16 years old. I don't live in a big city, but in a small town in an area called Styria in the south of Austria. I love it because it has lots of mountains, forests and lakes, but my home isn't very near my school. I go to a very small school in the mountains – it only has 49 students!

On weekdays, in the morning, I always wake up at 6:30 a.m. I don't like getting up early, so I stay in bed as late as I can but then mom calls me and I hurry up! I usually take a shower and get dressed very quickly, and I leave home at 7:00 a.m. I don't have breakfast at home, so I take some bread and fruit with me. I usually meet my friends in town and we catch the bus together. On the journey to school, I usually chat with my friends, so it isn't boring.

Our school is very high up in the mountains, and we travel along small, winding roads to get to it. We never walk or cycle because the journey is all uphill! In spring and summer it's quicker than in the winter. That's because it snows a lot and we have to drive very slowly because of the ice.

We usually get to school at about 8:15 a.m. and we

start classes at 8:45. We have three classes in the morning and then we have a break. We always have lunch at noon. After that, we have two hours of lessons. I finish classes at 2:30 p.m., and I get home around 3:30. After school I always do my homework (boring!), but I read books and play with my younger brother, too.

On Tuesday afternoons I play basketball. In the evening, I sometimes help my mom with the cooking, even though she doesn't think I'm a great cook! At 8:00 p.m., we have dinner. Finally, I go to bed at about 10:00 p.m.

4 **CERT** **Read the text again and complete the sentences.**

1 Helga likes Styria because _____.
2 Her school has only _____.
3 She doesn't eat breakfast at home because _____.
4 The journey to school isn't boring because she _____.
5 The journey to school is slower in the winter because _____.
6 At 12:00 p.m. the students _____.
7 At three thirty Helga _____.
8 After school she _____.

> ### Watch out!
>
> We use the verb *have* in a lot of idiomatic phrases, such as *have breakfast/lunch/dinner*, *have a break*, *have a rest*.

Grammar: Present simple – Affirmative and negative forms

5 Read the sentences and complete the table.

*I **start** classes at 8:30.*
*I **don't have** breakfast at home.*
*My mom **calls** me.*
*She **doesn't think** I'm a great cook.*

+	I start She ¹_____	classes at 8:30.
–	You don't catch He ²_____	the bus in the mornings.

➡ Grammar reference p. 118

6 Complete the sentences with the Present simple of the verbs in parentheses.

1 Lily _____ (have) breakfast at 7:30 in the morning.
2 I _____ (not leave) for school before 8 a.m.
3 After school, Max _____ (relax) on his bed and listens to music.
4 Heather and Emma _____ (not wake) up early on Sundays.
5 Yvonne _____ (not do) her homework before school.
6 We _____ (finish) school at 3:30 p.m.
7 The children _____ (not have) dinner early on the weekend.
8 John always _____ (get) to school before his classmates.

Grammar: Prepositions of time

*I always get up **at** 6:30 a.m.*
*We have three classes **in** the morning.*
***On** Tuesday afternoon I play basketball.*

➡ Grammar reference p. 118

Speaking

7 Pairwork Have a look at Helga's routine again. Take turns to say when you do the following activities.

> get up • have breakfast • have lunch
> do homework • play (a sport) • go to bed

I get up at 7 every morning.
I play football on Wednesday afternoon.

Life at Boarding School

In the UK, some schools are called 'boarding scools'. A boarding school is a school where you also eat and sleep. Today, we are here with Sam Jacobs, 15, an exchange student attending a boarding school in the southwest of England.

Interviewer Hi, Sam. So, my first question is: do you like boarding school?

Sam I do now, yes, but at first, no! I have lots of friends here and we do lots of things.

Interviewer Sam, tell us about your typical day… What time do you get up?

Sam Well, I usually get up at 7 a.m., take a shower and get dressed. We wear a uniform to school every day. Then I have breakfast at 8 a.m. Classes always start at 9 a.m.

Interviewer And where do you have your lunch?

Sam We always have lunch and dinner in the dining hall. It's a big room where everybody eats together.

Interviewer And what do you do after school?

Sam Well, my homework first. Here in the UK, they call it *prep*. Then I usually do sport. This year I'm on the soccer and swimming teams.

Interviewer Do you have any free time?

Sam Oh yes, of course! Before bed at 10 p.m., I watch TV, listen to music or just hang out with my friends.

Interviewer It sounds fun!

Sam It is, but I love going home too. And my mom misses me a lot.

Interviewer Does she ever come and visit?

Sam She doesn't come because it is too far away, but I go home for long holidays.

1 Read the text. Would you like to attend boarding school?

2 Read the text again and answer the questions.

1 Do you sleep at boarding school?
2 How old is Sam?
3 What does Sam wear to school?
4 What time does Sam have breakfast?
5 Where does he have dinner?
6 What sports does he do?

Grammar: Present simple – Interrogative form

> *Do you like boarding school?*
> *What time do you get up?*
> *Where do you have your lunch?*
> *How often does she come and visit?*
>
> ▸ Grammar reference p. 118

3 Complete the questions with the Present simple of the verbs from the box.

| play • have • do • use • go • finish |

1 Where _____ Anna _____ to school?
2 What time _____ the lesson _____?
3 _____ you _____ lunch at school?
4 When _____ you _____ your homework?
5 _____ Max _____ rugby after school?
6 _____ they _____ the science lab during the chemistry class?

4 Critical thinking In pairs, discuss the following questions.

• Do you think boarding school is a good idea for all students?
• List three positive and three negative aspects of boarding schools.
• Compare your list with another pair. Are there points in common?

Present simple

1 Complete the rules.

1 To form the Present simple with **he/she/it** we add _____ to the base form of the verb.
2 To form the negative and to ask questions, we use the auxiliary verb _____ with **he/she/it** and _____ with **I/you/we/they**.

2 Complete the sentences with the Present simple affirmative or negative of the verbs in parentheses.

1 Hannah and Louis _____ (go) to school by bus.
2 After school Tom _____ (relax) on the sofa in the living room.
3 My sister _____ (not take) a shower in the morning.
4 We _____ (wake up) early on weekdays.
5 Samantha and her brother _____ (not have) lunch at school.
6 We _____ (not watch) TV before we do our homework.

3 Write questions from the prompts using the Present simple.

1 Jay and Lucy / leave home together in the morning / ?
2 you / do your homework in the evenings / ?
3 Charlie / get dressed before or after breakfast / ?
4 Greg / have lunch at home or at school / ?
5 Martin / always / catch the 7:45 a.m. bus / ?
6 Sarah / get home before her parents / ?

Prepositions of time

4 Complete the sentences with the words from the box.

> in (x 3) • from • at (x 2) • to • on (x 2)

1 We start music class _____ nine o'clock.
2 They go on vacation _____ the summer.
3 _____ Sundays I get up late.
4 The meeting is _____ seven _____ nine.
5 I hate the cold _____ January.
6 I have lunch _____ noon.
7 What do you do _____ the weekends?
8 Come and have a coffee _____ the afternoon.

Adverbs and expressions of frequency

5 Read the examples and underline the correct alternative.

I'm **often** in the library after school.
I **always** wake up at 7 o'clock on weekdays.
Do you **often** play football?
I take the bus to school **every day**.

We put adverbs of frequency [1] before / after the verb _be_ and [2] before / after other verbs.
We put expressions such as **every day/week/month/year** at the [3] beginning / end of the sentence.

6 Rewrite the sentences using the adverbs and the expressions in parentheses.

1 He's in his bedroom after he comes home from school. (always)
2 When Ali is sick, he eats sweets. (never)
3 We have dinner all together in the evenings. (usually)
4 I turn on the TV if there's nothing interesting. (never)
5 Before you leave for school, do you make your bed? (every day)
6 Dad works in the garage on Saturdays. (often)

7 Answer the questions so that they are true for you.

1 How often do you take a shower?
2 How often are you late for school?
3 How often do you have lunch at home?
4 How often do you go to the movies?

Round up

8 Online interaction **Sosuke wants to know about Lenny's family. Read the email and underline the correct alternative.**

New Message   – ✗ ✕

Dear Sosuke,
My mother is a receptionist in a big hotel. She only [1]_work / works_ in the morning from 8:30 to 12:30.
My father is a businessman. He [2]_gets / get_ home [3]_at / in_ the evening before dinner but he [4]_does / doesn't_ work on Saturdays or Sundays.
[5]_Do / Does_ your parents work? What do they do?
My sister is a student at the university. She [6]_want / wants_ to be a vet because she loves animals. She [7]_have / has_ lessons [8]_on / in_ Mondays, Wednesdays and Thursdays and she works in the lab [9]_in / on_ the afternoons.
My mother makes dinner and we eat together during the week but we are all free [10]_on / in_ the weekend! She [11]_doesn't / don't_ make lunch or dinner [12]_in / on_ Saturdays and Sundays!
Write soon!
Lennie

Send   ▪ | ▾

⊳ Grammar reference & practice pp. 118-119

Verbs of routine

1 Complete the expressions under the pictures with the words from the box.

> dinner • work (x 3) • Internet
> breakfast • up • television (TV) • bed

1 get _____

2 have _____

3 go to _____

4 start _____

5 finish _____

6 make _____

7 watch _____

8 surf the _____

9 go to _____

Free-time activities

2 Which of these activities do you do at home? Which do you do outside? Write them in the correct group in the diagram.

> swimming • drawing • playing video games
> reading • listening to music • cooking
> dancing • playing chess

At home | Both | Outside

3 Look at some other expressions for free-time activities. Add them to the diagram in exercise 2.

> studying • taking the dog for a walk • playing cards
> surfing the Internet • cleaning the house
> making lunch/dinner • chatting online

The time

4 🔊 24 Listen and write the times from the box in the watches.

> 12:30 • 5:15 • 9:45 • 10:00 • 8:10 • 6:40

1   2   3

4   5   6

Adjectives and their opposites

5 Match each adjective (1-6) to its opposite (a-f).

1 late
2 small
3 happy
4 boring
5 quick
6 calm

a ☐ interesting
b ☐ excited
c ☐ slow
d ☐ sad
e ☐ early
f ☐ big

Listening

6 🔊 25 Listen to a radio program. What does Rashid do on the weekends?

7 🔊 25 **CERT** Listen again and choose the correct option (A, B or C).

1 Rashid _____ wakes up at 7 o'clock.
  A often   B usually   C always
2 He leaves the house at _____.
  A 8:00   B 8:15   C 8:45
3 At school, he _____ at 1:30 in the afternoon.
  A has a break   B starts classes   C has lunch
4 On _____, he has his favorite class at school.
  A Wednesdays   B Thursdays   C Fridays
5 He always _____ after school in his bedroom.
  A watches TV   B eats   C does his homework
6 He sometimes goes surfing with _____.
  A his friends   B his brother   C his sister

➡ **Words Plus 4** p. 135

✓ **DIGITAL BOOK** ➡ **Pronunciation Bank: 3rd person -s**

Making friends

1 ▶ **Harry meets Darsha. Watch the video. What's Harry's weekend job?**

Harry	Great place, isn't it?
Darsha	Yeah, the coffee is fantastic! Hi, I'm Darsha.
Harry	Good to meet you, Darsha. I'm Harry.
Darsha	Are you a student?
Harry	I am, yes, but I'm also a musician in a reggae band.
Darsha	A band? That's so cool! Do you practise every day?
Harry	No, we don't. We play on Thursdays and at the weekends.
Darsha	Do you play gigs?
Harry	Sure, sometimes. Music is my life, my future... What do you do, Darsha?
Darsha	I'm an actress.
Harry	Really? Are you in films?
Darsha	No, I'm not. Not yet! I do commercials... I go to the Arts college around the corner.
Harry	Me too. Do you live in this part of London?
Darsha	Yes, I do, but I'm from Manchester.
Harry	Cool! Darsha, are you free after class on Thursday afternoon?
Darsha	In the afternoon? Yes, I am. Why?
Harry	Why don't we go for a coffee before I go to the gig? And listen to my band's CD?
Darsha	Yes, I'd love to. Thanks.
Harry	Great! Here at 6?
Darsha	Fine by me.
Harry	OK! See you on Thursday, then.
Darsha	Bye.

2 ▶ **Watch the video again. Answer the questions.**

1 Where are Harry and Darsha?
2 Is it the first or the second time they meet?
3 Does Harry play on Saturday?
4 Do you think Harry likes Darsha? Why?
5 Does Darsha want to be a singer?
6 What does Harry want to do on Thursday?

3 Underline the correct alternative.

1 **Meet an old friend**
   A Hi, Jeremy, how are you?
   B *Great, thanks. / Good to see you. / See you later.*

2 **Meet a new person**
   A Hi, I'm Matt.
   B *Fine, thanks. / Good to meet you. / Bye.*

3 **Saying goodbye**
   A See you tomorrow.
   B *Yes. / Thanks. / Bye.*

Useful language

Hi, I'm Darsha.
Good to meet you.
Are you a student?
Do you like... ?
What do you do?
Do you live in... ?
Why don't we... ?
See you on Thursday.

Life skills: Social skills

• Meeting new people

4 Pairwork You meet a new friend. Follow the steps and practice the conversation.

• Introduce yourself.
• Ask where your friend lives.
• Ask what he/she does after school.

5 Complete the mind map with the key language for interaction from the conversation.

Breaking the ice
Great place, isn't it?

Reacting/Showing interest
That's so cool!
1 _____
2 _____
3 _____

KEY LANGUAGE FOR INTERACTION

Inviting a friend out
4 _____

Accepting an invitation
5 _____

6 Pairwork Take turns to reply to the following situations.

1 Break the ice at a concert.
2 Your friend invites you to a theater show. Accept.

An unusual job

Warm up

1 Look at the photos and read the title of the article. Where are the men? What do you think is unusual about their day?

A Life in the Stars

On a typical day in space astronauts have a lot of different jobs to do. A work day on the International Space Station isn't eight hours, it's twelve hours!

The astronauts get up when it's morning at Mission Control in Houston, Texas. They don't have a bathroom on the Space Station and water is difficult to use because there's no gravity. The astronauts wash with gel soap and then they put on their clothes. They have breakfast in the 'kitchen', then they look at their list of jobs for the day. They talk to Mission Control about any problems they have, and then they start work.

The Space Station is the astronauts' laboratory. It's also their office and their home. In the afternoon they work on experiments with the scientists at Mission Control. They write about their experiments on their computers and they look at data and they clean the Space Station. It's very important to keep healthy in space too, so the astronauts also exercise for two hours every day. This helps them prepare for space walks. They put on their special spacesuits and helmets and they practice walking in them.

In the evening, the astronauts sit down to have dinner and talk about their day. They don't make dinner, or cook any of their meals because their food comes in packets. It's not delicious but it is healthy. They go to bed when it's night in Houston, but they don't have beds. They sleep in special chairs!

Reading

2 🔊 26 **Read and listen to the text. Put the events in the astronauts' day in the correct order.**

- ☐ talk to Mission Control
- ☐ have dinner
- ☐ start work
- ☐ exercise
- ☐ go to bed
- ☐ work on experiments
- ☐ 1 put on their clothes
- ☐ clean the Space Station

3 CERT **Read the text again and answer the questions.**

1 Do astronauts work for eight hours a day on the Space Station?
2 What do they do in the morning?
3 What do they do in the afternoon?
4 Why is exercise important in space?
5 Do they make dinner in the evening?
6 Where do they sleep?

Listening

4 🔊 27 CERT **Listen to the interview. Which picture shows the woman's job? Check (✓).**

1 ☐ a photographer

2 ☐ a zoo keeper

3 ☐ a vet

5 🔊 27 **Listen again and write if the sentences are true (T) or false (F). Then correct the false ones.**

1 Stella works with gorillas. ___T___
2 She gets up early every day. _____
3 She makes food for the animals. _____
4 The gorillas exercise for an hour every week. _____
5 In the afternoon Stella cleans the gorillas' homes. _____
6 Stella doesn't like her job. _____

Learn to Learn / Writing strategies

Taking notes

- Use a list with bullet points for your notes.
- Write key words and phrases (nouns, verbs, adjectives).
- Don't write grammar words (pronouns, prepositions, auxiliary verbs, etc.).
- Use abbreviations; don't write full words.

Speaking

6 Pairwork **Look at the pictures of the other two jobs in exercise 4. Choose one of them. Ask and answer questions about the jobs. Use the words from the box and the questions below to help you. Take notes of your partner's answers.**

> take photographs • watch animals
> give animals medicine • help animals

1 work in an office/hospital/hotel?
2 get up early?
3 work in the morning/afternoon/evening?
4 work on weekends?
5 finish work early/late?
6 put on special clothes for your job?

A Do you work in a hospital?
B No, I don't.

Writing

7 **Use your notes from exercise 6 to write a paragraph about your partner's job.**

> Pablo is a photographer. He doesn't work in a hospital or in an office. He works outside. He...

4 Quick Check

Choose the correct option (A, B, C or D).

1 School _____ at 8:10 a.m. and _____ at 3 p.m.
   A start / finish   B starts / finish   C starts / finishes   D starts / finishs ☐

2 My brother _____ chemistry at the university.
   A study   B studys   C studies   D studyes ☐

3 I _____ at 7 in the morning.
   A get up   B get   C gets up   D go to bed ☐

4 I _____ French; I _____ Spanish.
   A don't study / studies   B study / don't study   C doesn't study / study   D doesn't study / don't study ☐

5 My English teacher _____ in the city center.
   A don't live   B live   C lives   D doesn't lives ☐

6 Jeremy and Sara _____ a uniform.
   A wear   B wears   C doesn't wear   D don't wears ☐

7 Do you like our language lab?
   A Yes, I do.   B Yes, I does.   C Yes, I don't.   D No, I doesn't. ☐

8 In the morning she _____ breakfast and then _____ to school.
   A have / go   B has / goes   C has / go   D have / goes ☐

9 _____ your homework at school?
   A You do   B Do you do   C Does you do   D You don't ☐

10 My cousin _____ in the cafeteria.
   A don't have lunch   B don't has lunch   C doesn't has lunch   D doesn't have lunch ☐

11 _____ tennis?
   A You play   B Does you play   C Do you play   D You don't play ☐

12 Do you like sports?
   A Yes, I don't.   B No, I do.   C No, I don't.   D No, I doesn't. ☐

13 Does your father teach history?
   A Yes, he teaches.   B Yes, he does.   C Yes, he do.   D No, he don't. ☐

14 Where does your best friend play football?
   A Yes, she does.   B Yes, he does.   C In the park.   D At 6 p.m. ☐

15 _____ to bed?
   A When do you go   B When do you   C You go when   D When you go ☐

16 Our friends _____ to Spain on vacation.
   A don't go   B doesn't go   C not go   D not goes ☐

17 She never _____ video games.
   A plays   B doesn't play   C not play   D not plays ☐

18 '_____ go to the movies?' 'Every weekend.'
   A How often do you   B Where   C What   D Do you ☐

19 What time do you do your homework?
   A At 7 in the evening.   B At 7 a.m. in the evening.   C At 7 p.m. in the morning.   D At the evening. ☐

20 What time do you have lunch?
   A At midday.   B At home.   C In the cafeteria.   D Yes, I do. ☐

TOTAL _____ / 20

Students throw their hats during graduation ceremony at Portsmouth University.

Education

Fact

Around the world, more than 72 million children don't attend school and 759 million adults are illiterate.

The Big Question

Why do you think it is important to get an education? What are the risks for those who do not have one? What are the risks for a country with a high percentage of illiterate people?

Unit Objectives

Vocabulary & Listening	Grammar	Language Skills	Video & Life Skills
• School subjects • School equipment • School people and places	• Present continuous: all forms • Present simple vs Present continuous • State verbs • *whose* • Possessive pronouns	Reading: The Khan Academy Listening: Learning abroad Speaking: Talking about learning English Writing: A report	▶ Asking for and giving opinions Respect others: • Talking about preferences

A School Exchange

Here are some of the pictures from this year's Spanish exchange trip between Redland High School and the Evolis Centro de Formación in Barcelona, Spain. The Spanish students are staying in Bristol this week with our students' families and they are doing lessons with us here at Redland. In the afternoons they go on trips to visit interesting places in the local area.

The Spanish Exchange is a fantastic experience for all our students!
Do you want to visit a Spanish school and then host a Spanish student in your home?
Would you like to try studying in Spain for one week? We're collecting names for next year's trip now.
Register in Mr O'Connor's classroom, 2F1, in the English department, or click on the link to register online.

Exchange trip dates
Spanish students' trip to Bristol – March 11th-18th
Redland students' trip to Barcelona – May 21st-28th

Vocabulary: School subjects

1 🔊 28 **Match the words from the box to the pictures for school subjects. Then listen and check.**

> math • history • geography
> physical education (PE) • art • science • English
> information technology (IT) • drama • music

1 _____ 2 _____ 3 _____ 4 _____

5 _____ 6 _____ 7 _____

8 _____ 9 _____ 10 _____

2 Look at the pictures on pages 52-53. Check (✓) the school subjects mentioned in the captions.

- ☐ math
- ☐ history
- ☐ geography
- ☐ physical education
- ☐ music
- ☐ science
- ☐ English
- ☐ information technology
- ☐ drama
- ☐ art

3 Read the information on the school website. Match the pictures (A-F) to the captions (1-6).

4 CERT **Read the text again and choose the correct option (A, B or C).**

1 The exchange trip is between a British school and a school in _____.
  A Mexico   B Spain   C Argentina

2 This week the Spanish students are in _____.
  A Barcelona   B London   C Bristol

3 The Spanish students are staying _____.
  A in a hotel   B in a school   C with British families

4 In the mornings the students _____.
  A go on trips   B stay with families   C have classes in the British school

5 The British students' trip to Spain is _____.
  A now   B in May   C in March

6 For next year's exchange trip students can _____.
  A register online   B register in the library   C register in the office

Watch out!

We use *why* to ask the reason or explanation of something. In the answers we use *because*.

*... **because** she wants to improve her English pronunciation.*

▶ Words Plus 5 p. 136

1 ☐ Here we're chatting in the student lounge with our Spanish friends before classes start on Monday morning.

2 ☐ Manuela and Simon are working on a project in the information technology classroom.

3 ☐ In this picture we're all playing basketball in physical education class, Spain vs England!

4 ☐ Amalia understands English very well, but her pronunciation is not good. Here she is studying in the library. She's listening to audio tracks because she wants to improve her English pronunciation!

5 ☐ Don't worry, we aren't making a bomb. We're just doing an experiment in science class!

6 ☐ In this photo we're singing old Beatles songs, but we aren't singing in English. We're singing in Spanish!! Raoul is playing the guitar; Brian is on the trumpet and Francisco is playing the tamborine. You're awesome, guys!

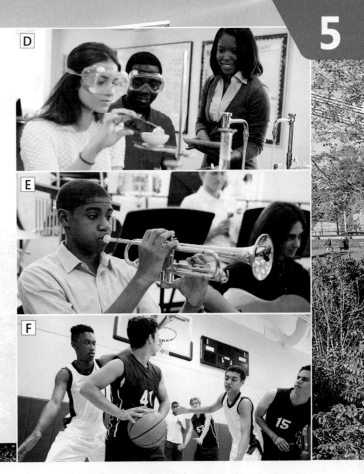

Grammar: Present continuous – Affirmative and negative forms

*The Spanish students **are staying** in Bristol this week.*
*We **aren't singing** in English. We're **singing** in Spanish.*

➡ **Grammar reference p. 120**

Watch out!

We don't usually use **state verbs** such as *feel, hear, know, understand, like, want, belong, be* in the progressive (continuous) form.
*Amalia **understands** English very well.*

5 Complete the sentences with the Present continuous of the verbs in parentheses.

1 Tamsin _____ (do) her homework in the living room.
2 We _____ (visit) the museum – it's really interesting.
3 My mom _____ (cook) chili con carne in the kitchen.
4 Take your umbrella – it _____ (rain) outside.
5 Ben _____ (not work) today. He's on holiday.
6 The children _____ (not play) in the garden. They're in their room.

6 Look at the picture and write what the people are doing. Use the words from the box.

play • study • cook • read • sleep • listen to

1 Mr Thompson _____.
2 Mrs _____.
3 Sally _____.
4 Luke _____.
5 The twins _____.
6 The dog _____.

Speaking

7 Pairwork What are the people you know doing now? In pairs, talk about your friends and family.

A *My dad is working in his office.*
B *My dad isn't working today. He's playing tennis with his friend Miguel.*

Let's do a project together!

Today, we're talking to two students from class 2B, Heidi Jackson and Max Williams, about a special school project.

Interviewer Hello, Heidi and Max. Thanks for talking to us today.

Heidi Thanks for the invitation!

Interviewer So, Heidi, what type of projects do you usually do at school?

Heidi Well, we often do science or English projects.

Max Yeah, I really like the science experiments but the English projects are a bit boring.

Interviewer So, are you working on a project at the moment?

Heidi Yes, we are. Every year we do a sports project, like learning about a new sport or doing a competition, but this year we're organizing a sponsored run for The Wilcox Children's Hospital.

Interviewer That's amazing! Whose idea is it?

Max Mine! We're planning a 5-mile run around the city on May 14th. Students are registering online and they are adding their sponsors.

Interviewer Fantastic! So, how is it going?

Heidi Really well! So far, 70 students are planning to do the run… but the deadline is on Saturday so there's still time to register. We hope to raise $1,000 for the hospital.

Interviewer Well good luck! And remember to register before Saturday…!

1 **Heidi and Max are talking about a school project. Read the interview.**

2 **Read the interview again and answer the questions.**

1 What kind of projects does Max not like?
2 What kind of project do they do every year?
3 What are they organizing?
4 When are they planning the event?
5 How much money do they hope to raise?
6 What is the last day to register online?

Grammar: Present continuous – Interrogative form

A *Are* you **working** *on a project at the moment?*
B *Yes, we are.*
A *How* **is** *it* **going**?

➡ Grammar reference p. 120

3 **Put the words in the correct order to make questions.**

1 doing / the / who / is / experiment
   Who is doing the experiment?
2 Nadya / what / studying / are / Liam / and
3 using / Internet / project / are / for / you / the / your
4 everyone / class / same / doing / in / is / your / the / project
5 you / the / project / history / enjoying / are
6 starting / the / they / when / project / French / are

Speaking

4 **Pairwork Take turns to ask and answer the following questions.**

- Are you doing a school project at the moment?
- What type of projects do you prefer?
- Do you think school projects are useful? Why?/Why not?

Present continuous

Spelling rules		
regular verbs	+ -ing	work → work**ing**
verbs ending in consonant + -e	cut -e + -ing	have → hav**ing**
verbs ending in vowel + consonant	double the consonant + -ing	stop → stop**ping**

1 Read the spelling rules and write the -ing form of the verbs.

1 eat _____
2 give _____
3 cut _____
4 become _____
5 meet _____
6 get _____
7 see _____
8 talk _____
9 make _____
10 study _____

2 Complete the sentences with the Present continuous of the verbs from the box.

ask • do • eat • have • open • watch

1 We _____ Tina's birthday cake.
2 Dad _____ a TV program about cars.
3 I _____ the window because it's hot.
4 Sally _____ the teacher a stupid question.
5 Mom _____ breakfast in a café.
6 The students _____ their homework in the library.

3 Use the words in parentheses to correct the sentences.

1 Peter's playing basketball. (tennis)
   Peter isn't playing basketball. He's playing tennis.
2 Joe and Sarah are cooking dinner. (lunch)
3 The baby is sleeping in the car. (in his bed)
4 Denise's writing an email. (letter)
5 My dad's driving to the beach. (to the city)
6 They are chatting online. (on the phone)

4 Put the words in the correct order to make questions. Then write short answers.

1 he / is / listening / the / to / teacher / ? (✓)
2 going / to / are / they / the museum / ? (✗)
3 Sally / wearing / hat / is / a / ? (✓)
4 your dad / writing / a book / is / ? (✗)
5 a test / students / the / doing / are / ? (✓)
6 listening / rap music / my sisters / to / are / ? (✓)

Present simple and Present continuous

5 Complete the table with the time expressions from the box.

never • on the weekend • often • today • this month in the afternoon • these days • every year

Present simple	Present continuous
always, usually, [1]_____, sometimes, rarely, [2]_____; every day, every month, [3]_____; in the morning, [4]_____, in the evening; on Mondays, on Tuesdays, [5]_____	(right) now; at the moment, at present; [6]_____, this morning, this week, [7]_____, this year; [8]_____

State verbs

6 Which of the following are state verbs? Which are action verbs? Write S or A.

1 understand __
2 believe __
3 go __
4 travel __
5 know __
6 do __
7 want __
8 make __
9 hate __
10 prepare __
11 like __
12 study __

Possessive pronouns and *whose*

7 Write answers using the possessive pronoun.

1 Whose project is this? (Sheila) *It's hers.*
2 Whose notepads are these? (we)
3 Whose chair is this? (Tim)
4 Whose books are these? (the teachers)
5 Whose phone is that one? (you)
6 Whose jacket is this? (I)

Round up

8 Online interaction Complete the message with the words from the box.

mine • doing • searching • don't • never training • I'm • are

Hi Pete, I'm [1]_____ math, but I [2]_____ understand the exercises! [3]_____ you studying now or are you [4]_____ at the gym? I need help! I have a book here, but it's not [5]_____. Maybe it's from the library, I don't remember! Anyway, [6]_____ reading the rules but I can't do the exercise. I'm also [7]_____ the Internet for more examples, but I [8]_____ find what I'm looking for! Please call me ASAP!

Grammar reference & practice pp. 120-121

School equipment

1 Complete the words for school equipment.

1 p ___ c ___ ___   c ___ ___ ___
2 n ___ ___ e ___ ___ o ___
3 l ___ ___ ___ ___ ___
4 e ___ ___ s ___ ___
5 ___ u l ___ ___
6 ___ a ___ ___ ___ ___ a ___ ___ ___
7 m ___ ___ ___ ___ ___
8 ___ ___ n ___ ___ ___ ___

2 Read the definitions for four of the things in exercise 1 and write the words.

1 It's for doing math problems.   _____
2 It's for drawing lines.   _____
3 They're for underlining words and phrases.   _____
4 It's for putting all your pencils and pens in.   _____

3 Now write definitions for the other four things from exercise 1.

School people and places

4 Read the text below and look at the words in bold. Then match the questions to the answers.

Hi, my name is Gloria and I'm a student at Pringle High International School. I'm 16 and I'm in my final year. Mr Manson is our school's **principal**. He is responsible for everything in the school. He has four **secretaries** working for him and they answer the phone and emails, organize events at the school and help us when we have problems.
My **classmates** are from all over the world. Mr Kearney is our laboratory **technician**. He helps us in the laboratories with our science and information technology projects. Mr Blair is the **school janitor**. He cleans the classrooms after school.
My favorite thing at school is our mascot – it's a black cat and his name is Meo. He lives in the school garden!

1 What is a principal's job?
2 What does a secretary do?
3 What does a teacher do?
4 Where does a technician work?
5 What is a janitor's job?
6 What does a classmate do?

a ☐ In the science lab and computer room.
b ☐ He/She teaches the students.
c ☐ He/She is responsible for the school.
d ☐ He/She cleans the school.
e ☐ He/She answers the phone and emails and organizes events.
f ☐ He/She sits in the same class as you.

5 Match the words (1-8) to the pictures (A-H). Use a dictionary to help you.

1 ☐ gym
2 ☐ classroom
3 ☐ laboratory
4 ☐ principal's office
5 ☐ library
6 ☐ student lounge
7 ☐ computer room
8 ☐ cafeteria

A

B

C

D

E

F

G

H

Listening

6 🔊 29 Listen to the names of the subjects and write them in the correct place on the timetable.

	Monday
9:00-10:00	English
10:00-11:00	
break	
11:15-12:15	
12:15-13:15	
lunch	
2:00-3:00	
3:00-4:00	

▶ Words Plus 5 p. 136   ✓ DIGITAL BOOK   ▶ Pronunciation Bank: /n/ vs /ŋ/

Asking for and giving opinions

1 ▶ **Watch the video. What is Harry doing?**

Darsha	Oh! So you can read! That's incredible Harry!
Harry	Very funny. I love reading, and you?
Darsha	Me too, but I never read paperback books, I read on my Kindle.
Harry	I can't read ebooks, they're so... cold.
Darsha	I don't agree. I always carry my Kindle in my bag, see? It's so practical, and light. Books are heavy, and my bag is small! Anyway, books belong in the past: they're old stuff!
Harry	How can you say that? Books are living creatures! Here, touch it. Smell it! What do you think?
Darsha	Yeah... you're right, it smells like paper. So what? Anyway, what are you reading?
Harry	*Slam*, by Nick Hornby.
Darsha	Oh yes, I know it. It's also a film.
Harry	What do you think of it?
Darsha	The film? It's nice. I prefer films to books.
Harry	I don't. Would you like to read it? You can borrow my book.
Darsha	Thanks, but on my Kindle it's only £1.99!
Harry	Well, I agree it's cheap but... it doesn't smell so good.
Darsha	Yeah... you're certainly right.

Useful language

I love reading, and you?
Me too.
I don't agree.
How can you say that?
What do you think (of it)?
I prefer films to books.
I agree it's cheap, but…

Life Skills: Respect others

• Talking about preferences

2 ▶ **Watch the video again. Write if the sentences are true (T) or false (F).**

1 Harry is reading an ebook. ___
2 Darsha has a big bag. ___
3 She thinks ebooks are practical and light. ___
4 Harry likes smelling paper books. ___
5 He likes the movie *Slam*. ___
6 Buying the book on a Kindle is cheap. ___

3 Underline the correct alternative.

1 I really like soul music.
   How can you say that? / Me too.
2 What do you think of the new French teacher?
   I think she's nice. / Her name's Mrs Dufour.
3 I prefer math to English.
   I don't! / And you?
4 London is a beautiful city.
   I agree, but it's very expensive. / I don't.

4 Complete the mind map with the key language from the conversation.

Giving your opinion
I love reading.
I prefer 1 _____.

Asking for people's opinion
What do you think (of it)?
What's your opinion about...?
I love (reading). 2 _____?

KEY LANGUAGE FOR CONVERSATION

Agreeing
3 _____.
I agree.
You're (certainly) right.

Disagreeing
How can you say that?
I don't think so.
I don't 4 _____.

5 Pairwork Choose a movie, a song, a book or a subject you really like. Exchange opinions about them.

A *I really like the Star Wars saga. I'm a huge fan!*
B *I think it's really boring!*
A *How can you say that? It's simply fantastic!*

Online Learning

Warm up

1 **Look at the pictures below. Where are the students? What are they doing?**

Reading

2 🔊 **30** **Read and listen to the text. Match the pictures (A-C) to the paragraphs (1-3).**

3 **CERT** **Read the text again and answer the questions.**

1 What is Salman Khan's job?
2 What does the Khan method use to teach students? Check (✓).
☐ a television channel
☐ an interactive YouTube channel
☐ books
3 What subjects do the Khan videos teach?
4 What subject is Kalinda studying?
5 Why does she like the method?
6 What subject is Peter studying?
7 Why does he like the method?

1 Salman Amin Khan (born October 11, 1976) is an American teacher and the founder of the Khan Academy, a free, online education service. The academy started with a YouTube channel in 2004 to teach math online to his young cousin. Today the Khan Academy has over 6,500 interactive video lessons on YouTube and around 4 million people around the world use it. Its video lessons teach school and university subjects at different levels, from English and history, to math and science. A lot of successful students are saying they get great exam results because they use the Khan Academy method. Why do users love this digital teaching method?

2 Hi I'm Kalinda. I'm revising math for my school exams. I'm using the Khan Academy videos on YouTube. I'm watching an interactive lesson now. Salman Khan is writing the problem on the interactive screen. Now he's explaining the steps we need to do to solve it, and he's writing the results. I like the Khan Academy videos because I can work at my own speed. I can stop the video when I'm not sure about something and I can play it again and again.

Posted by Kalinda, USA

3 Hello, I'm Peter. I'm studying history on YouTube with Khan Academy. I like this method because it uses pictures and diagrams and small paragraphs of text, so the information is easy to remember. Khan breaks down the topic into small steps and he can explain things very clearly. He makes difficult subjects seem easy! There are also great practice exercises to do after the lessons. You complete them and send them to the Khan Academy and they correct them for you, so you can see where you still have problems.

Posted by Peter, Canada

Listening

4 🔊 **31** **Listen to the interview. Where is Clint studying now?**

5 🔊 **31** **Listen again and write if the sentences are true (T) or false (F).**

1 Clint is studying alone this year. ____
2 His parents are his teachers. ____
3 This method doesn't use books. ____
4 Clint studies in the morning with his parents. ____
5 In the afternoon he meets his friends. ____
6 Clint and his family visit places to see things they are learning about. ____

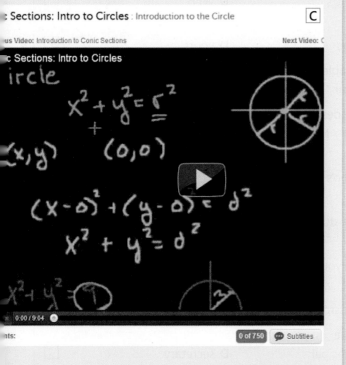

Speaking

6 Pairwork Ask and answer questions about your experience of learning English. Ask about where and how you study and your likes/dislikes.

A Where are you studying English now?
B I'm studying English at the EnglishFast center in Beijing.
A What does your teacher use to teach English?
B She uses videos, books, audio CDs...
A Do you like it?
B Yes, I do./No, I don't.
A Why do you like it?
B I like it because...

Learn to Learn / Writing strategies

Using *because* in your writing

We can use *because* to give a reason for a statement. *Because* adds information to a short sentence. This makes your writing more fluent.

*I like the Khan Academy videos **because** I can work at my own speed.*
*I like this method **because** it uses pictures and diagrams and small paragraphs of text.*

7 Add information to these sentences. Use *because* and the expressions from the box.

> it isn't cool • I want to study in the USA • it's difficult
> he likes Chelsea • ~~it's interesting~~ • we love movies

1 Marcia likes history...
   Marcia likes history because it's interesting.
2 Jacob doesn't like science...
3 My brother always wears a blue T-shirt...
4 I'm studying English...
5 We often watch DVDs on the weekend...
6 Sam doesn't listen to classical music...

Writing

8 CERT Write a paragraph about your experience of studying English. Use your answers from exercise 6 and the text on page 58 to help you. Think about the things below and give reasons for your likes/dislikes.

- Where you are studying now.
- What things you use to study.
- Why you like it/don't like it.

I'm studying English at the Green Park Language School in Tulum at the moment. In our classes we use a Student's Book and some CDs...

Choose the correct option (A, B, C or D).

1 Where _____ you going?

   A is   B am   C are   D do ☐

2 I _____ my homework because I can't find the book!

   A do   B 'm doing   C 'm do   D 'm not doing ☐

3 Are you listening to me?

   A Yes, I do.   B Yes, I listen.   C No, I can't.   D Yes, I am. ☐

4 What _____ saying?

   A is she   B is you   C are he   D she is ☐

5 What _____?

   A you are doing   B are doing   C you doing   D are you doing ☐

6 'Is Carlos eating?' 'No, _____ a smoothie.'

   A he drinking   B drinking   C he drinks   D he's drinking ☐

7 No, we _____ math, we _____ art!

   A are studying /   B aren't studying /   C don't study /   D play /
      study   are studying   are studying   don't studying ☐

8 _____ the lesson?

   A Do you understand B Are you understanding C You understand D Are you understand ☐

9 Who _____?

   A are you to talking B to are you talking C are you talking to D are talking you ☐

10 Where are you going?

   A Home.   B Yes, I am.   C No, I'm not.   D Yes, I'm going. ☐

11 Why are you crying?

   A Yes, I can.   B Because I can't   C I'd like to but I can't. D Sure! ☐
                 do this test!

12 '_____ books are these?' 'They're Amelia's.'

   A Whose   B Whoses   C Who's   D Who ☐

13 'Is this Penny's bag?' 'Yes, it's _____.'

   A her   B she   C hers   D yours ☐

14 These are our tickets; _____ are over there, on the table.

   A them   B they   C their   D theirs ☐

15 Don't use that bottle, it's _____. _____ is on the desk.

   A mine / You   B my / Your   C her / Mine   D mine / Yours ☐

16 '_____ is this backpack?' '_____!'

   A Who / My   B Whose / Mine   C Who's / Mine   D Whose / Me ☐

17 I usually _____ history in the library.

   A studying   B study   C am studying   D not study ☐

18 What _____ at the moment?

   A are you reading B you are reading C do you read   D you reading ☐

19 I like hanging out in the _____.

   A library   B gym   C classroom   D student lounge ☐

20 The person responsible for everything in the school is the _____.

   A technician   B school janitor   C principal   D secretary ☐

TOTAL _____ / 20

6

Asian street food stand in Camden Market, London

Food & Drink

Fact

Street food is becoming the new trend. People are always looking for new and exciting food experiences, which is what food stands offer: tasty, international, informal, easy-to-eat food.

The Big Question

TV shows, celebrity chefs, social media posts and pictures, new restaurants opening every day: why are people so obsessed with food?

Unit Objectives

Vocabulary & Listening	Grammar	Language Skills	Video & Life Skills
• Food and drink • Menus	• Countable and uncountable nouns • *some, any* • *a lot/lots of, a little, a few, much, many* • Imperatives • Verbs of preference	Reading: The Slow Movement Listening: An interview Writing: A questionnaire Speaking: Reporting data to the class	▶ Ordering food and drink Respect others: • Consider other people's needs

Vocabulary: Food and drink

1 🔊 32 **Match the pictures (A-R) to the words (1-18). Then listen and check.**

'Alfresco' dining

Share: Facebook Twitter Pinterest 8+

The sun doesn't always shine in the summer in North America or Britain, so people can't often eat 'alfresco', or outside – but when the weather is good, they love having a barbeque or a picnic!

In the US, people usually have barbeques in their backyard, and they sometimes make a special place there to cook the barbeque. These places are called barbeque pits or BBQ areas. At the beach and in local parks, there are often BBQ areas for people to come and cook their food on. These are free for everyone to use. But what are American people's favorite barbeque foods? Hamburgers seem to be the number one barbeque meat in the US, followed by hot dogs, steak and chicken. For those who don't eat any meat, the alternative is the always popular corn on the cob, or any other vegetable like tomatoes, eggplants, zucchini or barbeque potatoes. You can also grill some *s'mores*: they are chocolate, roasted marshmallows sandwiched between two graham crackers.

1 ☐ water	___	10 ☐ cola	___
2 ☐ strawberries	___	11 ☐ pasta	___
3 ☐ sandwich	___	12 ☐ chicken	___
4 ☐ salad	___	13 ☐ bread	___
5 ☐ cheese	___	14 ☐ lentils	___
6 ☐ fish	___	15 ☐ soup	___
7 ☐ peppers	___	16 ☐ eggs	___
8 ☐ rice	___	17 ☐ butter	___
9 ☐ cake	___	18 ☐ grapefruit	___

2 Nouns can be countable (= have the plural form) or uncountable (= only have the singular). Look at the list above and write C or U next to each word.

3 Read the text. What does the title of the article mean? Check (✓).

☐ eating good food   ☐ eating outside
☐ eating at home   ☐ eating healthy

4 CERT **Read the text again and answer the question**

1 Where do American people usually have barbeques?
2 What can you grill on the barbeque?
3 Where do British people go to have a picnic?
4 Name three ingredients of the perfect picnic.
5 What is typical picnic food?
6 What does the Picnic in the Park service offer?

▶ Words Plus p. 137

to cook

Create an account | Sign in ▾

Search

Despite the cold, the changing weather and the bees, British people love picnics. 70% of them go on a picnic in the summer. Popular places are at the beach or next to a river. In cities people often have picnics in local parks too, where they can find some tables and benches.
But what makes the perfect picnic?
The location is very important. Parks with lakes and a playground for children are families' favorite spots. Then comes the food. Some people buy ingredients at the supermarket and make their own sandwiches and potato salad, or shop at the local deli for typical British food such as Scotch eggs, Cornish pasty and shepherd's pie. But those who don't have any time or don't want to waste a day cooking can order a gourmet picnic basket already full of delicacies, or call the Picnic in the Park service. In this case, they don't need to do much. Just show up at the park and a butler will do the rest. The last thing to remember for the perfect picnic is the company. You can be at the best spot with great food, but it can't be a perfect day without your best friends.

Grammar: *some, any*

> You can also grill **some** fruit on the barbeque.
> But those who don't have **any** time…
>
> ➡ **Grammar reference p. 122**

5 Complete the sentences with *some* or *any*.

1 Is there _____ milk in the fridge?
2 I need _____ eggs for the cake.
3 We don't have _____ coffee.
4 For Sunday's barbeque we're having _____ hamburgers and _____ zucchini.
5 There isn't _____ cheese, I'm afraid.
6 We usually have _____ fish for dinner.

Grammar: Quantifiers

	countable	uncountable
affirmative	a lot of / lots of	
	many, a few	a little
negative	many	much
questions	How many…?	How much…?

➡ **Grammar reference p. 122**

6 Complete the sentences with the correct quantifier.

1 Not _____ people have a big breakfast in the morning.
2 We have _____ pasta for lunch every day. (*a large quantity*)
3 _____ bottles of cola do we have?
4 I want a pizza with _____ cheese on top. (*a small quantity*)
5 _____ sugar do you put in your coffee?
6 We don't have _____ money. Let's just have a sandwich.
7 There are _____ people I know at the picnic. (*not a lot*)

7 Get ready for a picnic! Write a list of what you put in your basket.

sandwiches, a packet of chips, some fruit…

Speaking

8 Pairwork Talk about your lists and prepare a basket together.

A *I have some cheese and tomato sandwiches. What do you have?*
B *I have tuna and tomato sandwiches.*
A *OK. Then I have…*

Kitchen work!

In this special interview, we talk to Lucas Graham, head chef at the five-star hotel City Inn in Miami.

Interviewer	Lucas, tell us, why are you a chef?
Lucas	Because I love food!
Interviewer	What type of food do you like cooking most?
Lucas	Definitely desserts. I like all sweet things and I just love making new cakes and desserts for my clients.
Interviewer	What do you not like about working in a kitchen?
Lucas	Oh, I hate washing the dishes!
Interviewer	Oh yes, me too! So, what are your rules for a successful career as a chef?
Lucas	Keep a good routine and be organized. Keep your kitchen clean and make sure the people working with you are doing their job correctly.
Interviewer	How many people work in your kitchen?
Lucas	Well, the kitchen is quite big. So, at the moment there are about 20 chefs in the kitchen.
Interviewer	Wow, that's a big kitchen and a lot of chefs!
Lucas	Yes, but I prefer working on my own because I like a quiet space when I work.
Interviewer	Any other hints for someone who wants to become a chef?
Lucas	Yes, be disciplined… work hard and be friendly to your colleagues, of course!

1 **Read the text. What is Lucas's favorite food?**

2 **Read the text again and underline the correct alternative.**

1 Lucas works in a five-star *hotel / restaurant*.
2 He works as a chef because he loves *cakes / food*.
3 He doesn't like *making desserts / washing the dishes*.
4 Routine and organization are the rules for a successful *career / hotel*.
5 *There are / There aren't* many chefs in the City Inn kitchen.
6 He likes working *alone / with 20 chefs*.

Grammar: Verbs of preference

*I **like** sweet things.*
*I **love** making new cakes.*
*I **hate** washing the dishes.*
*I **prefer** working on my own.*

Verbs of preference can be followed by a noun or by a verb in the *-ing* form.

▶ Grammar reference p. 122

3 **Use the prompts to make sentences.**

1 Andrew / like / play / video games
2 Francis and Jack / not like / do / homework / on the weekends
3 My mom / love / go / shopping
4 Carla / hate / cook / fish
5 My cousins / not like / walk / to school
6 Sue / prefer / work / at home

Speaking

4 **Pairwork Answer the questions.**

- Do you like cooking? What dishes can you cook?
- Do you prefer eating at home or eating out? Why?
- Do you like watching TV programs about food and chefs? Why?/ Why not?

Verbs of preference

1 Complete the sentences with the *-ing* form of the verbs from the box and the verbs in parentheses.

> run • do • use • go • play • read • eat • walk

1 I _____ (love) to the movies.
2 _____ you _____ (like) Minecraft?
3 I _____ (not like) pudding.
4 _____ Syd _____ (prefer) magazines?
5 Peter _____ (not like) to school.
6 Paul _____ (hate) experiments.
7 We _____ (prefer) social networks.
8 She _____ (love) in the park in the early morning.

Countable and uncountable nouns

2 Complete the table with the words from the box.

> milk • cookies • peas • bananas • pasta • oranges
> coffee • rice • carrots • eggs • fruit juice • butter

Food & Drink

Countables	Uncountables

some / any with countable and uncountable nouns

3 Read the sentences and complete the rule.

*There's **some** butter in the fridge.*
*I need **some** eggs for the cake.*
*There isn't **any** milk.*
*There aren't **any** oranges.*
*Do you have **any** money?*

We use ¹_____ and ²_____ with uncountable nouns and countable nouns in the plural. We use ³_____ in positive sentences, ⁴_____ in negatives and questions.

4 Underline the correct alternative.

1 Here's *some / any* coffee for you, Mom.
2 Do we have *some / any* cereal for breakfast?
3 My brother doesn't want *some / any* salad.
4 There are *some / any* DVDs on the teacher's desk.
5 I don't have *some / any* brothers or sisters.
6 Is there *some / any* fruit?

How much? / How many?

5 Complete the sentences with *How much / How many*.

1 _____ meals do you have each day?
2 _____ tea do you usually drink?
3 _____ movies do you watch in one week?
4 _____ cereal do you usually eat?
5 _____ pens do you have?
6 _____ money is there in your wallet?

much/many, a lot of/lots of, a little, a few

6 Underline the correct alternative.

1 Do you have *much / a few* homework this week?
2 I don't have *many / lots of* friends.
3 Phil watches *a lot of / a little* movies.
4 I'm not rich, but I have *a little / a few* money in the bank.
5 There are only *many / a few* mistakes on my English test. I'm happy!
6 Not *many / much* people like broccoli.

Imperatives

7 Complete the instructions with the words from the box.

> don't talk • use • write • don't copy • complete
> don't use

This is your first English test. Listen carefully. ¹_____ the sentences with the correct form of the verb. ²_____ the words in the gaps. ³_____ only a black pen. ⁴_____ during the test. ⁵_____ a dictionary. ⁶_____ from your friend.

Round up

8 Complete the conversation with *some, any, How much* and *How many*.

Amy I want to make a cheese omelette. Do we have ¹_____ eggs?
Rob Yes, we do.
Amy ²_____ are there?
Rob Let me check, er... six.
Amy Great. And is there ³_____ cheese?
Rob Yes, there's ⁴_____ parmesan and ⁵_____ mozzarella.
Amy And ⁶_____ olive oil do we have?
Rob Oops! There isn't ⁷_____ olive oil.
Amy Look, there's ⁸_____ butter in the fridge. Let's start then!

▶ **Grammar reference & practice pp. 122-123**

Food and drink

1 Complete the mind map with at least three words in every box.

meat and fish
_____
_____

carbohydrates
_____
_____

dairy products
_____
_____

FOOD

vegetables
_____
_____

sweet food
_____
_____

drinks
_____
_____

fruit
_____
_____

Containers and quantities

2 🔊 **33** Match the words (1-8) to the words (a-h). Then listen and check.

1 a carton of   a ☐ bread
2 a slice of   b ☐ chocolate
3 a bag of   c ☐ milk
4 a can of   d ☐ cake
5 a bar of   e ☐ cereal
6 a loaf of   f ☐ flour
7 a bowl of   g ☐ cola
8 a packet of   h ☐ chips

Verbs about cooking

3 🔊 **34** Match the verbs (1-8) to their definitions (a-h). Then listen and check.

1 mix   a ☐ to cook food in very hot water
2 add   b ☐ to cook in an oven or over a fire
3 bake   c ☐ to mix an ingredient into a liquid by moving a spoon
4 fry   d ☐ to put something with something else to make it bigger
5 stir   e ☐ to cook food by heating it in steam from boiling water
6 boil   f ☐ to put two or more foods together so they become one
7 roast   g ☐ to cook food in hot oil or fat
8 steam   h ☐ to cook in the oven

4 Complete the recipe with the verbs from the box.

mix • add (x2) • bake • stir • press • use • give

To make delicious cookies, you need very simple ingredients: flour, eggs, sugar, butter and vanilla extract. First, ¹_____ 250g of butter and 140g of sugar together in a large bowl with a wooden spoon, then ²_____ 1 egg yolk (the yellow part) and 2 teaspoons of vanilla extract. ³_____ 300g of plain flour and ⁴_____ until the mixture is well combined. ⁵_____ your hands in the end to ⁶_____ everything a good mix. ⁷_____ the dough, give the cookies your favorite shape and ⁸_____ in the oven at 180°C.

Listening

5 🔊 **35** Listen and complete the order at the Park Café for the two people.

TABLE _12_		TIME
Food		
- 1 (1) <u>cheese sandwich</u>		
- 1 (2) _____		
- 1 (3) _____		_with fruit_
- 1 (4) _____		
Drinks		
- 1 (5) _____		
- 1 (6) _____		

6 Look at the pictures and write what these people are having for breakfast.

Marcia

Jake

Susie

1 Marcia's having some _orange juice,_ _____
2 Jake _____
3 Susie _____

➡ Words Plus 6 p. 137 ✓ DIGITAL BOOK ➡ Pronunciation Bank: /a/, /ʌ/ and /əu/

Ordering food and drink

1  **Darsha and Harry are eating out. Watch the video. Why isn't Darsha eating meat?**

Darsha	Hello. Sorry I'm late.
Harry	Never mind. What are you having? Hamburger? Hot dog? Toast?
Darsha	No, thanks. I'm not eating much meat these days.
Harry	Why not?
Darsha	I'm trying to be a vegetarian.
Harry	A vegetarian? Really? Not me, I can't live without meat.
Waiter	Hi. Are you ready to order?
Harry	Yes. I'm having a ham and cheese sandwich with mayonnaise.
Waiter	Anything else?
Harry	Yes, I'd like a portion of chips and a coke, please.
Waiter	I'm afraid we haven't got any chips at the moment. How about some onion rings?
Harry	Onion rings are fine, thanks.
Waiter	And for you?
Darsha	I'd like a Margherita pizza with a lot of cheese. And an orange juice.
Waiter	So that's one Margherita, one ham and cheese sandwich, one portion of onion rings and two cokes.
Harry	Yes, that's right!
Darsha	No, it isn't right. It's one coke and one orange juice.
Waiter	OK.
Darsha	And can I pay by credit card?
Waiter	Sure. We accept all credit cards.
Darsha	OK, great thanks. Onion rings? Don't talk to me after lunch!

Useful language

What are you having?
Are you ready to order?
I'm having…
I'd like…
And for you?
Anything else?
Can I pay by credit card?

Life Skills: Respect others

- Consider other people's needs

2  **Watch the video again. Answer the questions.**

1 Is Harry upset with Darsha because she's late?
2 Is Darsha having a hot dog?
3 What does Harry order to drink?
4 Why is Harry having onion rings?
5 Who is having pizza?
6 Does the restaurant accept credit cards?

3 **Role play** **Student A you are the customer. You want to order Japanese food. Look at the menu and decide what you want to order. Student B you are the waiter/ waitress. Perform the conversation, then swap roles.**

Fuji Delight
Favorites

Chicken teriyaki	$7.99
Mixed sashimi	$11.49
Salmon with sesame seeds	$8.99
Sushi plate	$10.99
Salmon & avocado rolls	$4.49
Cucumber & shrimp roll	$3.99
Salad	$5.99
Noodle soup	$4.99

Take it Slow

Warm up

1 Look at the people in the pictures (A-C). Who do you think is stressed? Why?

Reading

2 🔊 36 **Read and listen to the text. Which of these things are part of the Slow Movement? Check (✓).**

- ☐ fast-food restaurants
- ☐ yoga and t'ai chi classes
- ☐ exams and tests
- ☐ spending time with your family/friends

In the world today we do everything fast. A lot of us are stressed and tired because we work long hours and travel long distances to get to work. We don't spend time with our families and friends. We never feel relaxed. For people in the Slow Movement, this is crazy. They want to change things.

They want us to slow down and enjoy our lives more. And other people are starting to listen. There are now Slow Movement groups in many cities around the world and people are choosing different lifestyles. Maria from Italy and Nancy from Singapore, are fans…

Maria, Rome – Slow Food

Maria is cooking dinner for her family at home. She's making pasta with fish. She goes out to the market every morning to buy food, and then she spends two hours in the evening cooking dinner. Her family always eats together at the table. They chat about their day and they eat Maria's delicious food.

'The Slow Movement is about changing the way we live. It helps us to have less stress in our lives,' says Maria, 'Slow Food is part of the movement. We think it's important to cook real food and for families to eat the food together. It takes more time to do this, but in my family we never eat in front of the television. We share food and we share conversation. It means we are close in the family.'

3 **CERT** **Read the text again and answer the questions.**

1 Why are people stressed in the world today?
2 What do people in the Slow Movement want to do about this?
3 What is Maria doing in the picture?
4 Why does she think cooking dinner every day is important?
5 What is Nancy doing in the picture?
6 What sports do people in the Slow Exercise Movement do? Why?

Listening

4 🔊 37 **Listen to an interview with David, a fan of the Slow Movement. What part of the movement is he talking about? Check (✓).**

☐ Slow Driving
☐ Slow Cities
☐ Slow Food

5 🔊 37 **Listen again and write if the sentences are true (T) or false (F).**

1 In a Slow City people choose a slow lifestyle. _T_
2 People in London and New York are relaxed. ___
3 Ludlow is very noisy. ___
4 People in Ludlow drive to work in other cities. ___
5 Offices close at half past 8 in Ludlow. ___
6 David is taking English lessons this month. ___

Writing

6 **Are the people in your class stressed? How do they relax? Use the prompts below to prepare a questionnaire about their routines and free time.**

- live in the city?
- travel long distance to school / work?
- study / work long hours?
- what sports / play?
- go walking?
- what free-time activities / do?
- what / usually / eat?
- when / cook?
- eat with your family / friends?
- what / do / this week / to relax?

1 *Do you live in the city?*

Speaking

7 Pairwork **Ask and answer the questions from your questionnaire in exercise 6. Then ask four other people in your class your questions. Make a note of their answers.**

8 **Report back to the class about your classmates' answers.**

Four people live in the city and one person doesn't.

Nancy, Singapore – Slow Exercise

Nancy, a student from Singapore, is practicing t'ai chi in her local park. She's learning to do slow exercises and meditation to help her to relax. 'Students' lives are crazy. We run from science lectures to English classes, to music lessons, and then to the gym. Often we also have evening jobs!' she says, 'In the Slow Exercise Movement we don't play competitive sports like tennis or football and we don't go cycling or running. I'm learning to do gentle exercise like yoga or t'ai chi instead. I do t'ai chi every morning before I go to university. It relaxes me and helps me slow down. I don't get stressed now and I have more energy.'

Quick Check

Choose the correct option (A, B, C or D).

1 There aren't _____ people in the room.
   A any   **B** some   **C** a lot   **D** a little   ☐

2 There's _____ milk in the fridge.
   A some   **B** the   **C** a   **D** any   ☐

3 Would you like _____ fish for dinner?
   A some   **B** often   **C** the   **D** a   ☐

4 We _____ homework at all for the vacations!
   A don't have no   **B** have any   **C** don't have any   **D** have some   ☐

5 We _____ sandwiches for lunch.
   A don't never have   **B** never have   **C** doesn't never have   **D** don't have never   ☐

6 I love ice cream! I _____ one in the evening.
   A never have   **B** rarely have   **C** don't have   **D** always have   ☐

7 We need _____ eggs and _____ butter for the cookies.
   A some / any   **B** any / some   **C** any / any   **D** some / some   ☐

8 _____ water in the fridge?
   A Is there some   **B** Is there any   **C** There is some   **D** There is any   ☐

9 I _____ fruit for dinner, but I have some dessert.
   A have any   **B** don't have some   **C** have some   **D** don't have any   ☐

10 I _____ coffee; I don't like it.
   A never drink any   **B** always drink some   **C** often drink any   **D** drink some   ☐

11 What do you have in your bag?
   A I have some breads.   **B** I have any bread.   **C** I don't have some breads. **D** I have some bread.   ☐

12 _____ are drinks.
   A Tea, juice and chips   **B** Tea, juice and milk **C** Tea, carrots and milk   **D** Peas, juice and milk   ☐

13 In the UK, people often have _____ for breakfast.
   A pizza with milk   **B** milk and chips   **C** tea and chicken   **D** porridge   ☐

14 For dessert there's _____.
   A ice cream, chocolate   **B** ice cream, eggs   **C** ice cream, chocolate   **D** meat, chocolate cake   ☐
      cake and fish   and porridge   cake and apple pie   and apple pie

15 _____ are there on the table?
   A How much banana   **B** How bananas   **C** How many bananas   **D** How much bananas   ☐

16 '_____ sugar do we need?' 'Not much, just _____.'
   A How many / any   **B** How much / a little **C** How many / some   **D** How much / any   ☐

17 Don't buy too _____ apples, there are _____ at home.
   A much / a few   **B** many / a few   **C** many / a little   **D** much / a few   ☐

18 Anything to drink?
   A Some cola, please.   **B** Yes, I do.   **C** A big portion, please.   **D** Sorry, I'm not hungry.   ☐

19 _____ your credit card! They don't accept cash.
   A Forget   **B** Don't forget   **C** Not forget   **D** You don't forget   ☐

20 Do you want some dessert?
   A Yes.   **B** No, thanks.   **C** In the fridge.   **D** Five, please.   ☐

TOTAL _____ / 20

7

YouTube Gaming

A view of YouTube Gaming Space at the Thailand Game Show big festival in Bangkok. Thailand is a big market for video games in Asia.

Entertainment

Fact

The video game industry is a cultural phenomenon. It is worth $100 billion, which is more than the music and movie industries combined together.

The Big Question

Teenagers are broadcasting live online, playing video games and even making them: is this really healthy and safe entertainment?

Unit Objectives

Vocabulary & Listening	Grammar	Language Skills	Video & Life Skills
• Entertainment, leisure and media • Music genres	• *was / were* • *be born* • Past simple: regular and irregular verbs, affirmative form	Reading: Entertainment before social media Listening: ebooks Writing: A description Speaking: Describing an object	▶ Talking about a past event Know yourself: • Understand feelings

Vocabulary: Entertainment and leisure

1 🔊 38 **Match the activities (1-8) to the pictures (A-H). Then listen and check.**

1 ☐ play video games
2 ☐ watch YouTube or Netflix
3 ☐ hang out with friends
4 ☐ go out on my hoverboard
5 ☐ go to a music festival
6 ☐ listen to music
7 ☐ watch a theater show
8 ☐ go to the movies

A

B

C

D

E

F

G

H

2 **Pairwork Which of these activities do you like doing? Take turns to ask and answer about how often you do them.**

I like playing video games. I usually play after lunch.

VIDEO-G MILLIONAIRES

The first commercial video games appeared in the early 1970s. In the 1980s there were the first reports of video game addiction. Nowadays, teenagers spend hours playing video games. Some of them are also becoming millionaires by making video games, something that only a few years ago just wasn't possible.

We often hear the negative stories of the video gaming phenomenon: it isn't healthy; kids spend too much time in front of a screen; it can have negative effects on their school work and social life; there is too much violence and kids can become aggressive. But there are positive aspects, too.

It's 2017 and Alex Balfanz is turning 18. He is a high school student and he is a normal teenager. He studies hard and plays video games. But he doesn't just play them. Alex makes video games. His adventure game,

3 **Read the text. Does it talk positively or negatively about video gaming?**

4 **Read the text again and write if the sentences are true (T) or false (F).**

1 There weren't video games before 1980. ___
2 Teenagers are becoming rich by selling their video game ideas. ___
3 Some teenagers are angry and aggressive because they spend too much time playing video games. ___
4 *Jailbreak* only became a success a few weeks ago. ___
5 Alex Balfanz works at the university. ___
6 It was possible to earn money by making video games when Alex Balfanz was a child. ___

Jailbreak, was an immediate success. In a couple of months, he earned a seven-figure salary, enough to pay for all four years of his college tuition. A few weeks ago a kid played the game for the umpteenth time!

Opportunities like this were just a dream. Was this possible just five or seven years ago? No, it wasn't. But now, thanks to online sales platforms, anyone with a good idea can be successful.

Another way of making money is simply by playing video games. Ten years ago, the professional video game player didn't exist but now it is a sport attracting 600 million viewers. Even the International Olympics Committee is thinking about adding it to their events list. So, perhaps video gaming does have its positive side too!

Grammar: *was, were*

His game **was** an immediate success.
A few years ago it **wasn't** possible.
Opportunities like this **were** a dream.
Was this possible five or ten years ago?

➲ Grammar reference p. 124

5 Rewrite these sentences using *was* and *were*.

1 She's at school today.
   _____ yesterday.
2 My parents are in Spain now.
   _____ in 1998.
3 I'm not afraid of flying.
   _____ when I _____ a child.
4 Are you at the movies?
   _____ last week?
5 There aren't any yellow taxis in London.
   _____ when we _____ kids.

Grammar: Past simple – Regular verbs

The first video games **appeared** in the 1970s.
A few weeks ago a kid **played** the game.

To form the Past simple we add *-ed* to the base form of regular verbs.

➲ Grammar reference p. 124

6 Complete the sentences using the Past simple of the verbs from the box.

| create • start • enjoy • work • walk • live |

1 Martin _____ in a bar in Barcelona last summer.
2 Mark Zuckerberg _____ Facebook when he was at college.
3 Elena _____ in Milan in 2010.
4 The concert _____ at 8 p.m.
5 Tanya and Karen _____ for 5 kilometers two days ago.
6 We really _____ the movie yesterday evening.

Speaking

7 Make sentences which are true for you using the verbs in the Past simple and the expressions in the word pools.

Last week I started a new puzzle.

create • start
enjoy • work
finish • live

last week
yesterday • last year
five years ago

1 Read the text. Do you know Sacha Baron Cohen?

Not the usual celebrity!

British actor, comedian and producer, Sacha Baron Cohen was born in London in 1971. He attended the University of Cambridge, where he studied history. He is famous worldwide because he created fictional characters such as Ali G. and Borat.

Sacha Baron Cohen began to work as a model before he worked as a presenter on a satellite television station. On television, people usually forget he is playing a role because his shows are in a documentary style. Guests do not realize they are part of a comic situation. His first successful character was the ignorant and impolite Ali G. on the *11 O'Clock Show* in 1998. He also appeared as Ali G. in Madonna's music video *Music* in 2000. Another character is Borat, a naïve, anti-Semitic and controversial Kazakh journalist who visits the UK and the USA. In the film *Borat*, set in the United States, Baron Cohen used satire to reveal how simple it is to be a racist or a sexist. Sacha Baron Cohen uses alter egos to expose people's ignorance and prejudice with obvious satire.

In addition to TV, he also appeared in a number of movies. He voiced King Julien in *Madagascar*, had a role in *Les Miserables*, *Alice Through the Looking Glass* and *Hugo*, and wrote and starred in the British comedy *Grimsby* as an English football hooligan.

2 Read the text again and complete the sentences.

1 Sacha Baron Cohen was born _____.
2 He created a number of _____.
3 Before he worked in TV, he _____.
4 As Ali G., he appeared on _____.
5 He uses his alter egos to _____.
6 In addition to TV programs, he also _____.

Grammar: *was born*

*Sacha Baron Cohen **was born** in London in 1971.*

> ⊵ Grammar reference p. 124

3 Complete the sentences with *was/were born*.

1 Jake and his brother _____ in Minnesota.
2 Where _____ you _____?
3 Alice _____ three months before her cousin.
4 Joseph _____ in 2002.
5 I _____ on a hot summer day in 2000.
6 Jack, Laura and Diana _____ on the same day in 1999.

4 Critical thinking Take turns to ask and answer the questions.

1 Do you think it was correct of Sacha Baron Cohen to use his fictional characters to ridicule public figures?
2 Do you think it is appropriate that actors and comedians earn so much money?
3 Do you think Baron Cohen's comedy is real entertainment?
4 What is the role of comedians? Discuss the ideas below.

> to entertain • to make people laugh • to make people think • to criticize society • to comment on politics

Past simple – *be*

1 Read the sentences and complete the rules.

*His first success **was** Ali G.*
*It **wasn't** possible.*
*There **weren't** any websites.*
***Were** you born in May?*

1 With *I/he/she/it*, we use _____.
2 With *we/you/they*, we use _____.
3 The negative of *was* is _____.
4 The negative of *were* is _____.

2 Use the prompts to write sentences and questions using the Past simple of the verb *to be*.

1 Hannah / not / at the library / this afternoon
2 you / at the festival / in Lima / last week?
3 Tom and Charlie / at the swimming pool / at 7 a.m. this morning
4 the book / helpful for your project?
5 I / on the same airplane / as Greg / last night
6 Liam / not / at the concert / yesterday

3 Read the questions and write the short answers in the Past simple.

1 Was Chris at the movies with Meg last night? (✓)
2 Were you both tired after the festival? (✗)
3 Were you home late again last Friday? (✓)
4 Was Mr. Hawkins angry that you were late? (✗)

Past simple – Regular and irregular verbs

4 Read the sentences and underline the correct alternative.

*Cohen **began** to work as a model.*
*He **voiced** King Julien in Madagascar.*
*He **had** a role in Les Miserables.*
*He **wrote** the comedy Grimsby.*

You add *-ed* to the base form of the verbs to form the Past simple of *regular / irregular* verbs.

5 Complete the sentences using the Past simple of the regular verbs in parentheses.

1 My dog _____ (escape) from home yesterday.
2 They _____ (agree) with me about what to see at the movies.
3 He _____ (try) to start the car but it didn't have any gas.
4 I _____ (carry on) working late last night.
5 Paul _____ (fail) his driving test again.
6 She _____ (stop) at the crosswalk before crossing the street.

6 Complete the table with the Past simple of the irregular verbs.

Base form	Past simple	Base form	Past simple
begin		hit	
drink		cost	
swim		put	
run		cut	
break		send	
forget		mean	
speak		keep	
wake		meet	
bring		do	
buy		have	

Past time expressions

7 Look at the table and complete the sentences.

yesterday	yesterday morning/afternoon/evening
last	last Monday/Tuesday/night/month
ago	two minutes/hours/days/months ago
in	in 2016

1 _____ night we saw *Star Wars*.
2 I met Patsy _____ morning.
3 Shakira was born _____ 1977.
4 I started swimming two months _____.

8 Rewrite the sentences using the Past simple.

1 He writes a lot of emails every day. (yesterday)
2 We go to Brasilia to visit my aunt. (last week)
3 Emma makes video games for her job. (a new video game last month)
4 I meet my friends online. (yesterday evening)
5 She runs for 30 minutes. (last Monday)
6 The concert begins at 8 p.m. (yesterday evening)

Round up

9 Complete the conversation with the most appropriate verb in the Past simple.

Lucy   Where ¹_____ you during the summer, Mark?
Mark   I ²_____ in London.
Lucy   Oh, cool! ³_____ you there to work or to see the sights?
Mark   A bit of both! I ⁴_____ as an intern at a software company.
Lucy   Wow! ⁵_____ it fun?
Mark   Yes, it ⁶_____ a great experience.

▶ Grammar reference & practice pp. 124-125   ▶ Irregular verbs pp. 142-143

Entertainment and media

1 🔊 39 **Write the words from the box in the correct column. Then listen and check.**

> performance • reporter • comedian • sitcom
> audience • stage • theater • documentary
> presenter • award • reality show • studio
> producer • episode • filmmaker • playwright
> set • costumes • soundtrack • script

Job	Place	Other

2 Complete the text with words from exercise 1.

Fringe Festival

The Fringe Festival started in 1947. It takes place in Edinburgh every year in August. Everybody can participate with any kind of ¹performance. So, if you are a dancer, an actor, a singer or a ²c_____, you are welcome! In fact, comedy is the largest section of the festival. You can find a ³s_____ anywhere in the city: in church halls, theaters, and even in a public toilet! Sometimes members of the ⁴a_____ offer their own homes as a stage for performances. Performers come to Edinburgh with their own instruments and ⁵c_____. Many also receive an ⁶a_____ at the end of the festival!

Music genres

3 🔊 40 **Complete the types of music. Then listen and check.**

1 punk
2 hip ____
3 new ____
4 cou_____
5 bl____
6 grun__
7 go_____
8 ja____
9 ro____
10 heavy m_____
11 ra__
12 clas_____

Listening

4 🔊 41 **Listen to the conversation and answer the questions.**

1 What type of music is Julie listening to?
2 Does David like it?

5 🔊 41 **Listen to the conversation again and complete the sentences.**

1 David prefers hip hop and _____ music.
2 David and Jacob went to a music festival last _____.
3 Julie likes new age and _____ music.
4 David thinks new age music is too _____.
5 David didn't pass his _____ exam.
6 David invites Julie to a _____ concert next weekend.

Verbs followed by prepositions

6 Match the verbs (1-8) to the prepositions (a-h).

1 stay
2 go
3 be
4 be interested
5 be mad
6 be keen
7 be hopeless
8 meet

a ☐ in
b ☐ about
c ☐ at
d ☐ on
e ☐ out
f ☐ about (something)
g ☐ up with
h ☐ in

7 Complete the sentences with the correct form of some of the verbs from exercise 6.

1 I was tired on Saturday. All my friends went out, but I _____ in.
2 When I was a kid I _____ about *Harry Potter*'s books!
3 I _____ at math. I can't do fractions or multiplications!
4 Last weekend, I _____ with my old friend, Isabel.
5 My sister _____ on horses at the moment.
6 I _____ in history when I was at school. It was my favorite subject.

8 Write six sentences about your last weekend. Use the verbs from the box or other verbs of your choice.

> chat • walk • watch • listen • study

Last weekend I watched six episodes of Riverdale.

➡ Words Plus 7 p. 138 | ✓ DIGITAL BOOK ➡ Pronunciation Bank: *-ed*

Talking about a past event

1 ▶ **Watch the video. How does Harry feel about Darsha going to the cinema with Peter?**

Harry	Oh here you are. I called you yesterday evening. Where were you?
Darsha	I'm sorry Harry, I was at the cinema. I saw *Bohemian Rhapsody*.
Harry	That film about Freddie Mercury and Queen? What was it like?
Darsha	It was interesting. I'm not a big fan of Queen, but the music was great and the actors played quite well, I think.
Harry	That's good to know. And where was it?
Darsha	At the Odeon, in Leicester Square.
Harry	What time?
Darsha	At seven. Why all these questions, Harry? You sound like a policeman!
Harry	Me? I'm just curious. Peter saw the same film yesterday.
Darsha	I know, I went with him.
Harry	Oh, so you two went together.
Darsha	Yes. Is that a problem?
Harry	Of course not.
Darsha	Good. And after the cinema, we had dinner together.
Harry	Dinner? Where?
Darsha	At the Cabbage Corner, the new vegetarian bistrot in King's Street.
Harry	Was it good?
Darsha	What?
Harry	The cabbage.
Darsha	We had cous cous and it was delicious. Harry Davies, are you jealous?
Harry	Me? Jealous? No! Ha ha ha!

Useful language

Where were you?
What was it like?
What time was it?
Where was it?
Was it (any) good?
Who were you with?

I was at… / I went to…
I was / went with…
It was interesting / great / wonderful / cool / awful…

Life Skills: Know yourself

• Understand feelings

2 ▶ **Watch the video again. Underline the mistakes in the sentences and correct them.**

1 Harry called Darsha yesterday morning.
2 Darsha loves Queen.
3 Harry went to the movies at seven last night.
4 Peter and his mom went to the movies together.
5 Darsha had lunch at a vegetarian bistrot.
6 Darsha thinks Harry is funny.

3 Pairwork Use the prompts to make the conversation.

You

Ask where your friend was on Saturday evening.

Ask what it was like.

Ask where the exhibition was.

Ask what time he/she was there.

Ask who he/she was with.

Ask what the food was like.

Your partner

Say you were at the new modern art exhibition.

Say that you really liked it.

Say that it was at the City Exhibition Centre.

Say what time you were there.

Say you were with your sister. You went to the new Mexican restaurant in Bridge Street later.

Say the food was great.

Entertainment before social media

Warm up

1 Look at the pictures (A-C) and match them to the years when they first appeared. Do you have any of these objects in your house?

1979 • 1985 • 1989

Reading

2 🔊 42 Now listen and read the article. Check your answers to exercise 1.

Everybody loves social media. Social networking sites like TikTok and Instagram are the new form of entertainment. Lots of people also multitask while watching TV – they check their socials accounts, surf the Net or post something about the program they're watching. Others listen to music on their phones while uploading something onto Instagram. But what were some of the most popular forms of entertainment before social media?

Before the iPod arrived in the shops in the early 2000s, there were portable cassette players called Walkmans. Sony Corp introduced the Sony Walkman in July 1979. It had chunky buttons, headphones and a blue and silver case. The 1980s was definitely the Walkman decade. People listened to music everywhere, and in 1986 the word 'Walkman' entered the Oxford English Dictionary.

3 What do these dates and figures refer to? Read the text again and write your answers.

1 1979 _____
2 1980s _____
3 1989 _____
4 300,000 _____
5 1985 _____
6 9,000 _____

Listening

4 🔊 43 **Listen to Helen talking about her hobbies. What three types of entertainment does she mention at the beginning?**

5 🔊 43 **Listen again and write if the sentences are true (T) or false (F). Then correct the false ones.**

1 Helen likes watching documentaries in the evening. ____
2 She doesn't think reading is boring. ____
3 She started her hobby when she was seven. ____
4 She got a Kindle from her aunt on her 11th birthday. ____
5 She loves science fiction books. ____
6 She read two *Hunger Games* books last night. ____

Speaking

6 Pairwork Choose two objects from the past. Then describe the objects to your partner. Use the Internet to help you. Use the questions below to help you with your description.

● When did it first appear in stores?
● Was it big or small?
● Was it for children or adults?
● What color was it?
● What was it for?

Learn to Learn / Writing strategies

Organizing ideas

Before writing about a topic, you need to *organize* your ideas. The best way to do this is to write your ideas under a selection of headings. For example, if you are writing about your last holiday, you could write ideas under the following headings:

When	Where	Who	What	Why

Add your ideas to the table with as many details as possible. Then you can use these ideas to write your paragraph.

Writing

7 Use your ideas from exercise 6 to write a short paragraph describing one of your two objects. Make sure you organize your ideas before writing your paragraph.

Video games and consoles are also very popular forms of entertainment. The Nintendo Game Boy, released in Japan in April 1989, started the success story. Nintendo sold the entire stock of 300,000 units in the first two weeks!

Then, of course, there was the VHS revolution long before DVDs, downloading films and Netflix. People watched films on VHS tapes and rented them from places like Blockbuster. The first Blockbuster store opened in Dallas, Texas in 1985 and 9,000 more then followed around the world. Today, however, Blockbuster is virtually extinct – just one effect of the digital influence on entertainment and media.

Choose the correct option (A, B, C or D).

1 I _____ in 2009.

   A was borned   **B** were born   **C** born   **D** was born   ☐

2 The flowers _____ white roses.

   A were   **B** was   **C** is   **D** where   ☐

3 '_____ you born?' 'In January.'

   A When were   **B** When are   **C** When where   **D** Where were   ☐

4 Where _____ at 10 a.m. yesterday?

   A you were   **B** you   **C** was you   **D** were you   ☐

5 Were you and Sally at the party last weekend?

   A Yes, I was.   **B** Yes, you were.   **C** Yes, we were.   **D** No, she wasn't.   ☐

6 I was a student at middle school two _____.

   A days ago.   **B** years ago.   **C** last years.   **D** Sunday ago.   ☐

7 Were _____ on vacation in this photo?

   A your parents   **B** your sister   **C** I   **D** your dad   ☐

8 We _____ all day yesterday.

   A travel   **B** traveled   **C** traveld   **D** travels   ☐

9 She _____ her first book when she _____ five.

   A read / were   **B** reads / was   **C** readed / was   **D** read / was   ☐

10 My parents _____ in France when they _____ young.

   A lived / are   **B** lived / were   **C** lived / was   **D** live / were   ☐

11 Mr Fletcher _____ at school at 9:30 a.m. _____ Monday.

   A arrives / last   **B** arrived / past   **C** arrived / last   **D** arrived / ago   ☐

12 Yesterday evening my mom's car _____ under the snow!

   A stops   **B** stop   **C** stopped   **D** stoped   ☐

13 When Leila _____ at primary school she _____ to sleep at 8 p.m.

   A was / goed   **B** was / went   **C** were / go   **D** were / went   ☐

14 I _____ drinking coffee last weekend and I didn't like it at all!

   A try   **B** tried   **C** tryed   **D** tryd   ☐

15 When she was a child, Jennifer Lopez _____ two languages at home: English and Spanish.

   A speaks   **B** speak   **C** speaked   **D** spoke   ☐

16 Yesterday I _____ a new pair of jeans.

   A buyed   **B** bought   **C** buy   **D** buied   ☐

17 I _____ you a letter last month.

   A wrote   **B** wroted   **C** writed   **D** write   ☐

18 Dakota Fanning _____ an actress when she _____ very little.

   A become / was   **B** become / is   **C** became / was   **D** becomed / was   ☐

19 When she was a child, she _____ London was in the USA!

   A thinked   **B** thoughted   **C** thought   **D** thinks   ☐

20 I _____ to the store and I _____ a new coat.

   A goed / bought   **B** went / buyed   **C** went / bought   **D** go / buy   ☐

TOTAL _____ / 20

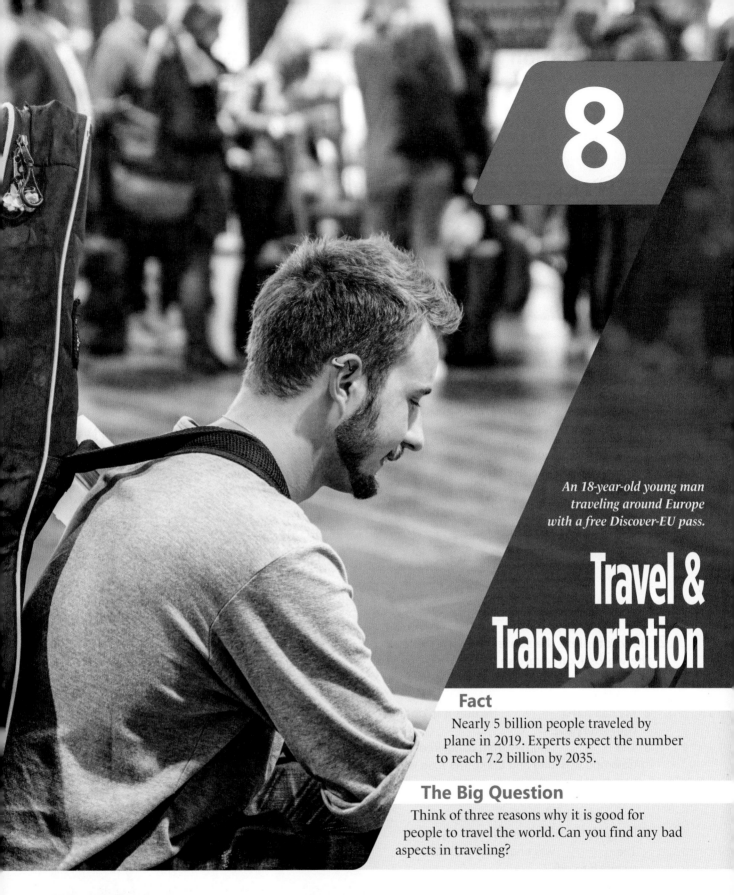

8

An 18-year-old young man traveling around Europe with a free Discover-EU pass.

Travel & Transportation

Fact

Nearly 5 billion people traveled by plane in 2019. Experts expect the number to reach 7.2 billion by 2035.

The Big Question

Think of three reasons why it is good for people to travel the world. Can you find any bad aspects in traveling?

Unit Objectives

Vocabulary & Listening	Grammar	Language Skills	Video & Life Skills
• Travel and transportation • Vacations • Places in town • Directions	• Past simple: negatives and questions • *could*	Reading: London Transportation Listening: Four travel stories Writing: The story of black cabs Speaking: Talking about the Tube	▶ Asking for and giving travel information Solving problems: • Doing a phone reservation

Vocabulary: Transportation

➤ Words Plus 8

1 🔊 44 **Complete the table with the words from the box. Then listen and check.**

> bus • airplane • ferry • train • scooter • ship
> tram • subway • taxi • helicopter • truck
> glider • motorbike • bicycle • car

By air	By land		By sea
	By rail	By road	

2 Now complete the sentences with some of the words from exercise 1.

1 We took a black _____ when we were in London.

2 My dad has a _____. He uses it to go to work every day.

3 The _____ journey from Bangalore to Colombo was long and tiring. The road was very bumpy.

4 In New York City they call it the _____ but in England they call it the Underground.

5 Last year I went on a cruise with my family. The _____ was enormous and there was so much to do!

6 When we go to France, we usually take the _____ from Dover to Calais.

7 I prefer cycling in the city. My _____ is fast and comfortable.

New Yorkers call their underground train system "the Subway", whereas Londoners call theirs "the Tube".

3 Pairwork Do you like traveling? Tell your partner about your last vacation.

Last summer I went to... with my family. We traveled by...

Watch out!

Travel is important to learning about the world.
*We had a two-day **trip** to Oxford.*
travel – the act of traveling
trip – to go to another place for a short time and return

A vacation
that went wrong...

4 **Read the text and find six things that went wrong.**

Teenagers love traveling and they are visiting more and more exotic places around the world. Travel is so easy these days – you can go anywhere by land, by air, by train and even by sea, if you don't suffer from seasickness, of course! But sadly, not all trips are a fantastic experience.

Rachel and Yukiko went to Acapulco for a week to celebrate Rachel's 18th birthday and their vacation was terrible! They booked everything online. They found a great offer and paid just $200 per person for their flight and accommodation. The offer was perfect and they were very excited.

But when they got to the airport the flight was late... seven hours late! They didn't have travel insurance, so they didn't get any help. They just waited and waited. Then when they finally arrived in Acapulco, what did they do? They looked for a bus to take them to their hotel. But at 1 a.m. there were no buses. There were only taxis and the trip cost $150! When they finally got to the hotel, there was nobody at the reception and they waited for two hours. And what time did they get into their room? At 4 a.m.! But the room was awful! There were cockroaches; it was dirty and there was only one bed! Yukiko didn't like the food and Rachel had food poisoning for three days. So, as you can see, not all vacations go to plan...!

5 **CERT** **Read the text again and answer the questions.**

1 Why did Rachel and Yukiko go to Acapulco?
2 Where did they buy their vacation?
3 How late was their flight?
4 Did they take a bus or a taxi to their hotel?
5 How long did they wait at the reception desk?
6 What happened to Rachel?

Grammar: Past simple – Negative and interrogative forms

> They **didn't have** travel insurance.
> What **did** they **do**?
>
> We use the auxiliary *did* to form the negative and interrogative forms of the Past simple.
>
> ➡ **Grammar reference p. 126**

6 **Complete the sentences with the Past simple of the verbs in parentheses.**

1 _____ your sister _____ (go) to the same primary school as you?
2 Where _____ Brian and Sue _____ (meet)?
3 Alicia _____ (not buy) any milk yesterday.
4 What time _____ Harry _____ (arrive) last night?
5 We _____ (not want) to go to school this morning.
6 I _____ (not know) who she was.

7 **Write questions or negative sentences using the Past simple.**

1 Owen went to Rome. (-)
_____

2 My sister traveled by plane. (?)
_____

3 We stayed in a luxury hotel. (-)
_____

4 Paul and Amy took the subway to the party. (?)
_____

5 I flew to New York from London. (?)
_____

6 Holly and Ed enjoyed their vacation. (-)
_____

Speaking

8 **Pairwork Take turns to ask and answer about a vacation or an event which went wrong.**

- When did it happen?
- Where was it?
- Why did it go wrong?
- What didn't go as planned?

Doing the Grand Tour

Nowadays, young people often travel around Europe –, 1____ while others fly with low-cost airlines like Ryanair and easyJet. Between 1660 and about 1840, hundreds of rich young men also traveled around Europe on the so-called *Grand Tour*, when they came of age.

2____, perhaps a family member or a good friend, and they could afford to visit many places although the itinerary was fairly standard. Starting in France, where 3____, they then went to Switzerland and Italy and they often stayed a few months in Florence. Rome and Venice were also on the itinerary, but southern Italy and even Greece were only for a few. 4____ and often spent a few weeks in small cities and up to several months in the main cities. Guidebooks and tour guides also developed as a result of the Grand Tour.

The main aim of the Grand Tour was to learn about classical and Renaissance art and architecture, while 5____. Although the Grand Tour was an educational trip, many travelers spent time in more frivolous activities such as drinking and gambling.

6____ Historians say that it could last from a few months to several years! They didn't have a round-trip ticket.

Not surprisingly, the Grand Tour still influences tourist destinations today and shapes the idea of the culture and sophistication of traveling.

1 Pairwork Do you know what the Grand Tour was in the 17th and 18th centuries? Talk to your partner.

2 `CERT` Read the text. Match the sentences (A-F) to the gaps (1-6) in the text.

A And how long did the Tour last?
B They usually traveled with a chaperon
C many see its capital cities by train
D some travelers went to Naples to study music
E The Grand Tourist traveled from city to city
F they obviously visited Paris

Grammar: *could*

> They **could** afford to visit many places.
> It **could** last several years.
>
> *could* is the Past simple of *can*. It expresses ability and possibility or permission in the past.

> **➲** Grammar reference p. 126

3 Complete the sentences with *could* and the verbs in parentheses.

1 Jake _____ (not swim) when he was four.
2 _____ your grandfather _____ (speak) Spanish when he was at school?
3 I _____ (not find) my cell phone yesterday evening.
4 Lucy _____ (ride) a horse when she was two!
5 _____ you _____ (read) when you were at nursery school?
6 Lara _____ (stay out) late before she was 18.

Speaking

4 Pairwork What could and couldn't you do when you were a child? Use the prompts to help you.

Possibility or permission
● travel on the bus
● spend the night at a friend's place
● spend money on your interests
● watch TV after dinner

Ability
● speak a foreign language
● ride a bicycle
● buy a train ticket
● play a musical instrument

Past simple – Negative and interrogative forms

1 Read the sentences and underline the correct alternative.

*They **didn't** have a round-trip ticket.*
*She **didn't** like the food.*
*'**Did** you visit the Uffizi?' 'Yes, I **did**.'*
The negative and interrogative forms of the Past simple are *different / the same* for all persons.

2 Rewrite the sentences using the words in parentheses.

1 Amy and Jo went to Paris last week. (Berlin)
  Amy and Jo didn't go to Paris last week. They went to Berlin.
2 They traveled by train. (bus)
3 They visited Check Point Charlie. (the Reichstag)
4 They stayed at a B&B. (youth hostel)
5 Jo wanted to eat Indian food. (German food)
6 Amy bought a CD by Mozart. (Beethoven)

3 Correct the sentences so that they are true for you. Use the Past simple affirmative or negative.

1 I _____ (visit) Rome when I was a child.
2 I _____ (learn) to ride a scooter last summer.
3 My parents _____ (travel) to the UK when they were students.
4 I _____ (win) a medal in a sports competition last year.
5 My best friend _____ (give) me a book for my birthday.
6 I _____ (take) a ferry two years ago.

4 Use the prompts to write questions and short answers.

1 Steph / take / bus / yesterday ? (✗)
  A *Did Steph take the bus yesterday?*
  B *No, she didn't.*
2 they / come / with you / last Sunday ? (✓)
3 you / pay for / bus ticket / last night? (✓)
4 Denise / give / you / birthday present? (✗)
5 I / leave / my keys / school / yesterday? (✗)
6 Tom / visit / Malaysia / in 2018? (✓)
7 you / see / Lana / party / last Saturday (✗)
8 Philip and Jonathan / win / first prize / Math Olympics (✓)

5 Read the answers and write the questions.

1 A *When did you go to Japan?*
  B I went to Japan last summer.
2 A _____?
  B I parked my scooter in the main square.
3 A _____?
  B We went to Lima by bus.
4 A _____?
  B I went to sleep at 11 p.m. last night.
5 A _____?
  B I bought two: one ham sandwich and one tuna salad sandwich.
6 A _____?
  B I watched *The X Factor* on TV yesterday evening.
7 A _____?
  B I met Alison and Flora at the party yesterday.
8 A _____?
  B I bought a black T-shirt because I didn't have one.

could

6 Use the prompts to write sentences with *could*.

1 My sister / swim / when / be / three
2 I / meet / a Mexican girl / but / she / speak not / English
3 we / ride a bicycle / be / six
4 Pete / stay up late / last night
5 I / play the piano / be / primary school
6 they / see not / the stage / concert

Round up

7 CERT Online interaction Sue writes to Nick about a change of plans. Complete the message with the correct option (A, B, or C).

Hi Nick, we're in London, at last! We ¹ _____ at 7 p.m. because the train ² _____ late, so we missed the 7:15 bus to Greenwich.
We ³ _____ take a taxi because we didn't ⁴ _____ any money, so we walked to the hostel.
We were there at 8:30 but they ⁵ _____ have any room for us! In the end we found a B&B on the same street. Jane sent you a voice message.
⁶ _____ you get it?

	A	B	C
1	A did arrive	B did arrived	C didn't arrive
2	A were	B did	C was
3	A couldn't	B could	C did
4	A had	B have	C haved
5	A could	B didn't	C couldn't
6	A Did	B Do	C Were

Vacations

1 🔊 **45** **Complete the sentences with the words from the box. Then listen and check.**

> excursion • tour • campsite • city vacation
> sightseeing tour • B&B (bed & breakfast)
> youth hostel • trip

1 We only had three days and we decided to go on a _____ to Paris. It was short, but we had a great time!
2 The best _____ of London is on board the hop-on-hop-off bus.
3 We went to Dublin – Joseph, Mike and I. There wasn't much money, so we stayed in a _____.
4 When I travel, I prefer _____ accommodation because I love meeting the local people.
5 The return _____ was a nightmare because our flight was delayed.
6 The best part of the vacation was a one-day _____ to the small islands by boat.
7 The guided _____ of the Transport Museum wasn't that interesting.
8 As soon as we put up the tent in the _____ it started to rain!

Places in town

2 **Write the places from the box under each icon.**

> bus stop • hospital • tourist information center
> restaurant • museum • train station • cathedral
> stadium • police station

1 _____ 2 _____ 3 _____

4 _____ 5 _____ 6 _____

  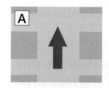

7 _____ 8 _____ 9 _____

Travel verbs

3 **Match the verbs (1-8) to their opposite (a-h).**

1	check in	a ☐	get off
2	miss	b ☐	pull out
3	drop off	c ☐	check out
4	get in	d ☐	land
5	leave	e ☐	get out of
6	pull over	f ☐	arrive
7	get on	g ☐	pick up
8	take off	h ☐	catch

Directions

4 🔊 **46** **Match the directions (1-6) to the pictures (A-F). Then listen and check.**

1 ☐ go straight on
2 ☐ turn left
3 ☐ go past
4 ☐ cross the road
5 ☐ take the second road on the right
6 ☐ turn right

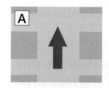 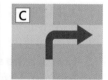

Listening

5 🔊 **47** **Listen to Phil, a tourist, asking for directions. Where does he want to go?**

6 🔊 **47** **CERT** **Listen again and complete the sentences with one or two words.**

1 Phil forgot his passport on _____.
2 He's looking for the _____.
3 The woman told him to walk for about _____ meters.
4 Past the cathedral there's a _____.
5 The police station is on Queen's _____.
6 The _____ is opposite the bank.

Speaking

7 **Pairwork In turns, give directions to go from your school to**

- the train / bus station
- the hospital
- a hotel
- the police station

➡ Words Plus 8 p. 139   ✓ DIGITAL BOOK ➡ Pronunciation Bank: /ɪ/, /iː/

Asking for and giving travel information

1 ▶ **Watch the video. Ally is calling Greyhound Lines to buy a ticket. Why can't she buy it online?**

Operator	Greyhound Lines, how can I help you?
Ally	Hello, I'm trying to buy a ticket online but the system isn't working. Can you help me?
Operator	Sure. Where are you going to?
Ally	Baltimore.
Operator	Leaving from?
Ally	New York.
Operator	OK, let me see. Right, the next bus leaves at 3:45 p.m.
Ally	Great, and what time does it arrive in Baltimore?
Operator	It arrives at 8:15 p.m.
Ally	Great. Can I buy the ticket, please?
Operator	Sure. Single or round-trip?
Ally	Round-trip, please. Is there an early morning bus from Baltimore to New York tomorrow?
Operator	Yes, there's a bus at 8:20 a.m.
Ally	Thank you very much. How much is a round-trip to Baltimore?
Operator	Do you have a Student Advantage Discount Card?
Ally	Yes, sure.
Operator	Can I have your Card number, please?
Ally	It's 04MK1061.
Operator	Right, then it's 65 dollars. Can I have your credit card details, please?
Ally	Sure. The name is Alison Jennings, and the number is 518 71...

Useful language

Can you tell me what time...?
Can I have a ticket...?
What time does it arrive / leave?
How can I get (back) to...?
How much is a single / return ticket to...?
Can I pay by...?

Life Skills: Solving problems

• Making a phone reservation

2 ▶ **Watch the video again. Answer the questions.**

1 Did Ally try to buy the tickets online?
2 Where does she want to go?
3 How long does it take to get to Baltimore?
4 Is it possible to buy tickets on the phone?
5 How long is Ally staying in Baltimore?
6 Can Ally have a special price? How do you know?

3 Underline the correct alternative.

1 A How can I help you?
  B *Sure. / Hello, I'd like... / Yes, I can.*
2 A Where are you going to?
  B *Quito. / One way, please. / Can I buy the ticket, please?*

3 A *Leaving from? / One way or round-trip? / How can I help you?*
  B Round-trip, please.
4 A When would you like to leave?
  B *Tomorrow morning at 9 o'clock. / I'd like a ticket to Shanghai, please.*

4 Role play You are at the train station. Ask about travel information. Practice the conversation in pairs.

You	Your partner
Ask when the next train to Detroit leaves.	Say at 4:45 p.m.
Ask when it arrives.	Say at 7:25 p.m.
Ask about the price of a round-trip ticket.	Ask if he / she has a railcard.
Say yes.	Say $26.50.
Ask to pay by credit card.	Say yes.

Out and about in London

Warm up

1 Match the types of London transportation (1-5) to the pictures (A-E).

1 ☐ Docklands Light Railway
2 ☐ The Tube
3 ☐ Black cab
4 ☐ Emirates Air Line
5 ☐ Double-decker bus

Reading

2 🔊 48 **Pairwork**
Read and listen to the text. How would you like to travel around London? Why? Tell your partner.

Moving around London

Getting around London can be fun, chaotic, confusing at times, but never boring! There are so many different ways to travel around the capital that a visitor can literally be spoilt for choice. London is famous for its bright red double-decker buses, its black taxis and underground Tube, but you'll be surprised by how many other types of transportation there are too.

London's distinctive **red buses** run day and night through the city. The first bus service began in 1829 from Paddington and now the iconic double-decker buses are a quick and cheap way to get around the city. You can also do lots of sightseeing from the top deck!

Then of course, there's the **Tube**, the underground rail network. The first underground railway opened in the 1860s. There are 11 different Tube lines, which run between 5 a.m. and midnight. In addition, there's the **Docklands Light Railway** (DLR) which opened in 1987 and serves the redeveloped Docklands area of London. Significant improvements were made to the DLR ahead of the Olympic Games in 2012 and during the Games it carried double its normal number of passengers.

Many people just walk or cycle around the city. Otherwise, the classic **black taxi** is another way of getting from A to B in London. You can catch a taxi in the street and there is a minimum charge of £3.20. The first motor cabs arrived in London in 1897 and are now a distinctive part of London life. People get in and out of them night and day.

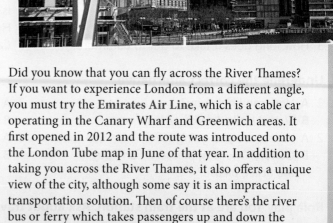

Did you know that you can fly across the River Thames? If you want to experience London from a different angle, you must try the **Emirates Air Line**, which is a cable car operating in the Canary Wharf and Greenwich areas. It first opened in 2012 and the route was introduced onto the London Tube map in June of that year. In addition to taking you across the River Thames, it also offers a unique view of the city, although some say it is an impractical transportation solution. Then of course there's the river bus or ferry which takes passengers up and down the River Thames on a daily basis.

There are many ways to pay for your trip around London – by cash, credit card or simply by Oyster card, a plastic smartcard that can hold credit to pay for trips on the Tube, DLR, Emirates Air Line, buses, river bus or tram. So why not visit London…? Getting around is easy; it's just a question of choosing how!!

Learn to Learn / Reading strategies

Open-ended questions

When you have to answer open-ended questions, look for the paragraph in the text which refers to the question. Write the number of the question next to the paragraph, or underline the sentences which contain the answer to help you.
Write a complete answer using your own words. Try not to copy the whole answer from the text.

3 CERT **Read the text again and answer the questions.**

1 When do London buses run?
2 Where can you do sightseeing?
3 How many Tube lines are there in the city?
4 When did the DLR open?
5 How can you travel across the River Thames?
6 How can you pay for your trip?

Listening

4 🔊 49 CERT **Listen and choose the correct option (A, B or C).**

1 What time does the next bus to Camden leave?

 A B C

2 How do Katy and Jack decide to go to the party?

 A B C

3 Where was Ella when she saw the accident?

 A B C

4 How did Tom's grandad get to work in London?

 A B C

Speaking

5 Pairwork **Ask and answer questions about the history of the London Tube. Use the following information to help you.**

- Metropolitan Railway (1st underground railway) – opened in 1863
- first underground signs – appeared in the early 20th century
- World War II – people used Tube stations as shelters
- Victoria Line – opened in 1969 with automatically-driven trains
- Oyster card – first on sale in 2003

1 when / first underground railway / open?
   A *When did the first underground railway open?*
   B *It opened in 1863.*
2 when / first underground signs / appear
3 what / happen / during World War II?
4 when / the Victoria Line / open?
5 when / the Oyster card / first / go on sale?

Writing

6 CERT **Read the text about the history of London's black cab and complete it with one word for each space.**

THE BLACK CAB

The history of London's famous black cab is long and interesting. The first cab ¹_____ the hackney coach in the 17th century. At this time, there ²_____ only 20 available for hire in the whole of London. The first taxi rank appeared ³_____ 1636 outside the Maypole Inn in The Strand. One of the many stories about the origins ⁴_____ the taxi meter says that Wilhelm Bruhn invented ⁵_____ in 1891, and that the word 'taxi' comes ⁶_____ the German word *taxe* meaning 'charge'.
⁷_____ you know that London's first motor cabs date back to 1897? But they ⁸_____ the first real black cabs. These, the FX3 Austin, arrived in 1947. They weren't the ones we can see today, but they ⁹_____ very similar.

7 **Now write a similar text about the history of the London Tube. Use the information in exercise 5 to help you.**

Quick Check

Choose the correct option (A, B, C or D).

1 I _____ a tablet for my birthday, I _____ a scooter.
   A don't get / got   B didn't get / got   C didn't got / get   D don't got / get ☐

2 She _____ a book yesterday night, she _____ a magazine.
   A don't read / readed   B didn't read / readed   C read / don't read   D didn't read / read ☐

3 _____ your father _____ in a band when he was young?
   A Did / play   B Did / played   C Does / play   D Does / played ☐

4 We _____ to the sea but we _____.
   A did go / swim   B didn't go / swam   C went / didn't swim   D went / swam ☐

5 I _____ when I was 3 years old!
   A could swim   B can swim   C could swam   D could swimmed ☐

6 Could you ride a bicycle when you were 4?
   A Yes, I could.   B Yes, I can.   C Yes, I couldn't.   D No, I can't. ☐

7 Yesterday evening my mom _____; we _____ pizza.
   A cooked / ordered   B didn't cooked / ordered   C didn't cook / ordered   D not cooked / ordered ☐

8 We went to the concert last weekend but we _____ you.
   A see   B saw   C didn't saw   D didn't see ☐

9 Why _____ you _____ your homework? Now it's too late!
   A did / finish   B didn't / finish   C didn't / finished   D do / finished ☐

10 Did you like the music show?
   A Yes, I do.   B Yes, I like.   C Yes, I did.   D No, I don't. ☐

11 Did your best friend buy you a present for your birthday?
   A No, she doesn't.   B No, she didn't.   C Yes, she didn't.   D Yes, I did. ☐

12 Did your teacher show you a video?
   A No, he doesn't.   B No, he don't.   C No, he did.   D Yes, he did. ☐

13 We _____ a car at the rental place, so we _____ the train.
   A could find / took   B couldn't found / took   C could find / take   D couldn't find / took ☐

14 We went to the _____ to catch the train.
   A airport   B seaport   C train station   D coach station ☐

15 Last week I went to school _____.
   A by bicycle   B on bicycle   C by cycling   D on cycling ☐

16 You need a _____ to travel outside Europe.
   A driving licence   B passport   C visa   D credit card ☐

17 _____ a souvenir in Lahore last summer?
   A Do you buy   B Did you buy   C Did you bought   D Do you bought ☐

18 'Did Sandy and Tom land in Tokyo?' 'No, _____. They landed in Osaka.'
   A they didn't   B you didn't   C they did   D they don't ☐

19 She _____ when she arrived in Chicago and her parents _____ very worried.
   A called / were   B didn't call / were   C called / were   D did call / were ☐

20 We _____ the exam. It was horrible.
   A did pass   B didn't passed   C didn't pass   D pass ☐

TOTAL _____ / 20

A model on the catwalk during New York Fashion Week.

Fashion

Fact

The fashion industry is the product of the modern age. It is a global business which includes designer fashion and everyday clothing.

The Big Question

Are there too many fashion victims in this world? Are you a slave to fashion or do you not really care about what you put on in the morning?

Unit Objectives

Vocabulary & Listening	Grammar	Language Skills	Video & Life Skills
• Fashion and style • Clothes and accessories • Fabric and materials • Money	• Comparative and superlative adjectives • *too, (not) enough, very, extremely* • *(not) as... as*	Reading: Eco-clothing Listening: Vegan shoes Writing: An article about eco-clothing Speaking: Talking about fashion habits	▶ Making suggestions Get organized: • Be careful with money

Vocabulary: Fashion and style

1 🔊 50 **Write the words from the box next to the correct definition. Then listen and check.**

> must-have • vintage • timeless • old-fashioned
> designer label • popular retail stores
> fashion victim • catwalk

1 _____: a famous company that makes expensive clothes, bags or other accessories

2 _____: clothes shops you find in every town or city

3 _____: something highly fashionable and in demand

4 _____: the place where models walk during a fashion show

5 _____: clothes in a style from the past

6 _____: clothing that never goes out of fashion

7 _____: somebody who wears fashionable clothes that sometimes make him/her look silly

8 _____: clothes that are no longer in style

2 Pairwork What type of clothes do you wear? Take turns to ask and answer about what you like and what you don't like wearing.

▶ Words Plus 9 p. 140

3 Read the text. Would you like to go to a fashion show?

Catwalks around the world

Are you crazy about fashion or do you hate it? Do you shop in popular retail stores or do you think designer labels are the best? Fashion is everything from clothes, shoes and accessories to make-up and hairstyles, and is now one of the biggest industries in the world.

One of the most important events in the fashion world's calendar is Fashion Week, when fashion designers show off their newest collections in fashion shows. There are four very important fashion weeks – in Paris, New York, London and Milan, and others in Copenhagen, Berlin and lots of other cities around the world, so if you are a real fashion lover there is always something to see!

Everyone likes getting dressed up, but there are some people who really dress to kill and love the latest fashion styles. These people often sit in the front row of catwalks watching models wear must-have designer labels. In February 2018, even Queen Elizabeth II made a visit to London Fashion Week!

Then there are also Teen Fashion Weeks in America where teen models walk the catwalk and designers sell their teen collections. These are smaller but just as important as the big shows for everybody involved. Models want to be taller, thinner and more beautiful than everyone else, while designers want to produce the best show of the year with video backdrops, extravagant lighting shows, live streaming and the coolest music. Some say it is the best business in the world; others say it's the worst, but it's definitely more exciting than many others!

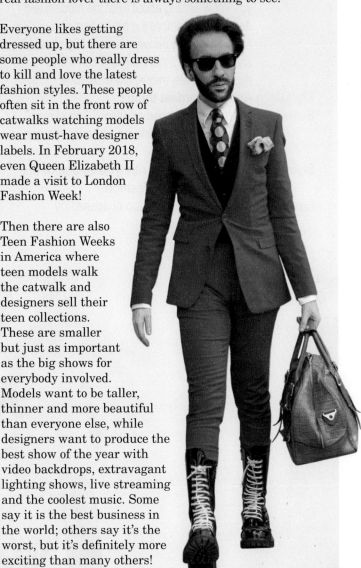

4 Read the text again and write if the sentences are true (T) or false (F). Then correct the false ones.

1 Fashion is the biggest industry in the world. ___
2 The New York Fashion Week is one of the most popular fashion shows in the world. ___
3 Copenhagen Fashion Week is as important as Milan Fashion Week. ___
4 People who watch fashion shows are usually fashion lovers. ___
5 Queen Elizabeth II appeared on the catwalk at the 2018 London Fashion Week. ___
6 A 15-year-old model can walk the catwalk in America. ___
7 Fashion designers compete to give the best fashion show. ___
8 Fashion isn't as exciting as other industries. ___

Grammar: Comparative and superlative adjectives

*These are **smaller** but just **as important as** the big shows.*
*Fashion is one of **the biggest** industries in the world.*
*Some say it is **the best** business in the world.*

➡ Grammar reference p. 128

5 Complete the sentences using the comparative or superlative form of the adjective in parentheses.

1 I think the Marc Jacobs fashion show was _____ (good) than the Stella McCartney one.
2 Alison was the _____ (short) model in the show.
3 Andrew's designer suit is _____ (expensive) than Richard's.
4 I think those pants are _____ (nice) than the blue ones.
5 My designer shoes aren't as _____ (comfortable) my sneakers!
6 That was the _____ (bad) fashion show ever!

Speaking

6 Pairwork Answer the questions.

1 Which is the best place in your town for shopping?
2 Which is the cheapest?
3 Which is the coolest item of clothing in your wardrobe? Describe it to your partner.

1 Read the article. Do you follow any fashion bloggers?

2 CERT **Read the article again and answer the questions.**

1 Are fashion blogs serious sites?
2 What did Susie Lucas do when she was a child?
3 Why did she start writing her blog?
4 How does she help people on her blog?
5 What does she find hard?
6 Does she agree with her description?

Grammar: *very, extremely, not enough, too*

> I was **extremely** interested in clothes.
> There **wasn't enough** space to write.
> They're **too** expensive.
> It's **very** difficult to find new beauty tips.
>
> ➡ Grammar reference p. 128

3 Underline the correct alternative.

1 Daniel hates anything to do with fashion.
He thinks it's *extremely / enough* boring.
2 My clothes are so old-fashioned but I don't have *very / enough* money to buy anything new.
3 There aren't *enough / extremely* fashionable clothes shops in my town.
4 It's really *enough / very* difficult to become a top model.
5 We're *extremely / enough* excited about the launch of the new fashion magazine.
6 These designer shoes are *too / enough* expensive for me. I can't buy them.

4 Critical thinking In pairs, discuss which statements you agree and disagree with.

1 Fashion bloggers are essential to fashion journalism.
2 Fashion blogs are just full of stupid, useless fashion gossip.
3 Too many fashion bloggers promote clothes that real people can't afford.

MEET THE FASHION BLOGGER

Fashion blogs offer incredible style advice and give you inspiration about what to wear for any occasion with a mix of serious and fun fashion articles. StyleM@g talked to **Susie Lucas**, one of the most influential fashion bloggers in the US, about why she started her blog.

StyleM@g **Hi Susie. So, why are you a fashion blogger?**

Susie Well, when I was a little girl I was extremely interested in clothes. I always dressed up in my mom's dresses. Then I got my first job as a fashion writer on a vintage fashion magazine. There wasn't enough space to write all the articles I wanted, so I started *Lifestyle*, and it quickly became the most exciting blog around.

StyleM@g **What's the best thing about being a fashion blogger?**

Susie Well, I love doing behind-the-scenes pieces, you know, writing about what the models and designers do before the big fashion shows. But I also like telling people where to buy cheaper, stylish clothes… not everyone can afford designer labels, they're too expensive!

StyleM@g **And the hardest thing?**

Susie Mmm, that's a good question. Sometimes it's very difficult to find new beauty tips and fashion advice.

StyleM@g **Some people describe you as one of the coolest women in fashion.**

Susie I'm not cool, I'm just too obsessed by fashion!

Comparative and superlative adjectives

1 Read the sentences and underline the correct alternative.

*Models want to be **taller**, **thinner** and **more beautiful** than everyone else.*
*Designers show off their **newest** collections in fashion shows.*
*Some say it is **the best** business in the world, others say it's **the worst**.*
*These are **as important as** the big shows.*

1 We use *comparative / superlative* adjectives when we compare two or more people or things.
2 Comparative adjectives are often followed by the word *than / most*.
3 To form the superlative of longer adjectives, we use the word *more / most*.
4 We use *as ... as* to compare two things which are *different / the same*.

2 Complete the table with the comparative and superlative forms.

Adjective	Comparative	Superlative
big		
important		
new		
late		
small		
tall		
thin		
beautiful		
good		
cool		
bad		
exciting		

3 Complete the sentences with the comparative form of the words in parentheses.

1 The name Suzie is _____ Joanna at the moment. (popular)
2 Mark's jacket is _____ Justin's coat. (expensive)
3 The blonde model is _____ the brunette. (tall)
4 Milan is _____ Athens. (fashionable)
5 That shirt is _____ the gray one. (big)
6 Sometimes the quality of ready-to-wear clothes can be just _____ designer labels. (good)

4 Use the prompts to write sentences using the superlative.

1 Tokyo / expensive capital city / the world
2 Russia / big country / the world
3 I / young child / my family
4 Elon Musk / rich person / the world
5 mosquitoes / dangerous insects / the world
6 the Burj Khalifa / tall building / the world

5 Use the prompts to write sentences using (not) as ... as.

1 Nora / tall / Suzie
2 Rome / not big / New York
3 Aunt Mary / not old / granny
4 my scooter / not fast / yours
5 your jacket / not cool / mine
6 Sandra / good / Paula / at volleyball

very, extremely, not enough, too

6 Complete the sentences using very, extremely, (not) enough or too.

1 My grandmother gave me $100, so I have _____ money to buy a new pair of jeans.
2 When I was a child, I was _____ interested in TV commercials. I watched them for hours.
3 It's _____ difficult to be successful in the fashion industry, almost impossible sometimes.
4 There wasn't _____ space in the store to see the clothes. There were _____ many people!
5 Eve's collection wasn't good _____ to win the first prize.
6 That dress is _____ big for her. She's very small.

Round up

7 Complete the text about a designer's career with the words from the box.

enough • more • in • than • most • extremely • best

When I was a child, I loved my dad's suits. I thought they were the ¹ _____ elegant clothes ² _____ the world. That's how I started drawing my own suit designs. I was ³ _____ interested in fashion ⁴ _____ in football! After university, I got my first job as an apprentice designer in a suit store in London, but it wasn't ⁵ _____ for me. I wanted to have my own fashion label, and I did it. It was the ⁶ _____ thing for me. I feel ⁷ _____ happy that I can just follow my dreams!

▶ Grammar reference & practice pp. 128-129

Clothes and accessories

1 🔊 51 **Write the words from the box in the correct column. Then listen and check.**

flip flops • pants • cardigan • beanie • dress
pullover • gloves • earrings • necklace • belt
watch • scarf • boots • sneakers • skirt • jacket
shoulder bag • top

Clothes	Accessories

Fabric and materials

2 **Look at the pictures and complete the text with the words from the box.**

silk • wool • cotton • leather • plastic • linen

This year for Christmas I bought clothes and accessories for everybody: a yellow ¹ _____ belt for my older brother Freddy; an orange pullover for Dad (he loves ² _____); a pair of beige ³ _____ shorts for my younger sister Flora; a colorful ⁴ _____ scarf for Granny; a flowery ⁵ _____ T-shirt for my younger brother Philip and pink ⁶ _____ smartphone cases for me and Mom!

Money

3 🔊 52 **Write the correct words under each picture. Then listen and check.**

cash machine / ATM • credit card • coins • bills
cash register • wallet • savings • tip

1 _____ 2 _____

3 _____ 4 _____

5 _____ 6 _____

7 _____ 8 _____

Listening

4 🔊 53 **Listen to the conversation. Underline the correct alternative.**

1 Emma, Hannah and Liam are at *the movies / a restaurant / a shopping center*.
2 *Hannah / Emma / Liam* has a credit card.
3 *Hannah / Emma / Liam* loves shopping.

5 🔊 53 **Listen again and write if the sentences are true (T) or false (F). Then correct the false ones.**

1 You don't pay your bill at the cash register. ___
2 They all want to leave a tip. ___
3 Liam says he doesn't have much money. ___
4 Liam offers to pay the bill for everyone. ___
5 Hannah asked her uncle for some money. ___
6 Liam thinks Hannah spends too much money. ___

▶ Words Plus 9 p. 140   ✓ DIGITAL BOOK   ▶ Pronunciation Bank: /ə/

Making suggestions

1 ▶ **Watch the video. What's wrong with the hairdresser's gift card idea for Mother's Day?**

Harry	Hey there. What's up?
Darsha	I'm looking for a present for my mum but I can't find anything good.
Harry	Oh, is it her birthday soon?
Darsha	No Harry, it's Mother's Day tomorrow!
Harry	Tomorrow?! Oh no! I forgot! Quick, quick! Let's find something.
Darsha	OK. What about something to wear? Like a silk scarf.
Harry	No, I gave her a silk scarf last year.
Darsha	Right. How about buying perfume?
Harry	My mum hates perfume. I bought her some for Christmas and she gave it to her sister for her birthday.
Darsha	OK, no perfumes. Why don't we buy our mums some music? What kind of music does your mum listen to?
Harry	Apart from what my band plays, I think she likes jazz. But I have no idea which musicians...
Darsha	Hmm, that's a good point. I don't know what my mum likes either.
Harry	Well, maybe we could buy them books.
Darsha	No! I've got a better idea! How about a gift card for the hairdresser's? They'll love it!
Harry	This is the greatest idea of all! Our mums deserve the best! Quick, let's find something.
Darsha	Right. Let me see... It's 80 pounds.
Harry	80 pounds for two?
Darsha	No, it's 80 pounds each.
Harry	Oh... Well, I still think a book is a pretty good idea.
Darsha	Me too.

Useful language

What about…?
How about buying…?
Why don't we buy…?
We could buy…
Let's buy…

Life Skills: Get organized

- Be careful with money

2 ▶ **Watch the video again. Underline the mistakes in the sentences and correct them.**

1 Darsha is looking for a present for her grandma.
2 It's Mother's Day next week.
3 Darsha gave her mother a silk scarf last year.
4 Harry's mom loves perfume.
5 His mom likes rock music.
6 It costs 80 pounds for two gift cards.

3 Pairwork Make suggestions for the following situations.

1 It's your mother's birthday. Decide on a gift.
2 It's Saturday afternoon. You and your friend are bored.
3 You want to go to the movies but the bus is really late.
4 It's your birthday and you want to throw a theme party. Decide on the theme.

4 Pairwork Use the prompts to make the conversation.

You	Your partner
Ask your friend what he/she is doing.	Say you are looking for a present for your friend, Lola's birthday.
Ask when her birthday is.	Say that it is next Saturday.
Ask if she likes jewelry.	Say that she does but that it is a very personal present.
Suggest buying a book.	Say that you think it's a boring present.
Suggest buying a ticket to New York Fashion Week.	Say that is a great idea and that you might buy two tickets!

Waste is one of the biggest problems in our modern world. The world's oceans are full of plastic and we are producing three per cent more waste every year.

In some areas, microplastics from tires and synthetic textiles are a bigger source of marine pollution than larger plastic waste. So, recycling is more and more important than ever before. The fashion industry, too, is looking for solutions to the problem of pollution caused by plastic materials.

We know a lot about vintage fashion and recycling our old clothes in charity shops. Now designers are recycling materials to make clothes. Some are experimenting with plastic bottles by dissolving them and using the polyester in them to make new fabrics – and Emma Watson's dress is an amazing example of the use of technology in fashion. Other designers are using bicycle inner tubes to make leather-style jackets and T-shirts. London Fashion Week 2018 saw a lot of different examples, including a new kind of leather made from the skins of chestnuts.

Emma Watson at the Ziegfeld Theatre in New York

Boots produced using old seats of buses

Eco-clothing

Warm up

1 **Read the text quickly. Find the name of these objects and write it under each picture.**

1 _____   2 _____

3 _____

Reading

2 🔊 54 **CERT** **Read and listen to the article. Then answer the questions.**

1 Why is material recycling so important?
2 How are some designers making leather-style jackets?
3 What did designers use to make Emma Watson's dress?
4 What innovative material was used at London Fashion Week in 2018?
5 Are only designer labels producing clothes from recycled materials?
6 What material was used to make the USA 2015 Women's World Cup uniforms?
7 What can you make out of old seats of buses and trains?
8 What kind of recycling does *Worn Again* use?

But it isn't just designer labels that are producing environmentally-friendly clothing. Big, ready-to-wear brands are also thinking about sustainability in their clothes. *Nike*, for example, made socks and shorts from recycled plastic bottles for the USA 2015 Women's World Cup uniforms. Other companies recycle old car tires to produce sneakers and sandals. *Above+Below London*, a British shoe company, produces boots and Converse-style basketball shoes made from the old seats of buses and metro trains!

But some say that this method of recycling is just a way of making the lifetime of material longer and longer. One fashion company aims to eradicate all textile waste. *Worn Again* uses chemical recycling to dissolve materials and remake them into new clothes, so creating a 'circular' fashion industry. Sounds easy? No, it is very difficult but definitely the future for textiles.

A worker polishes a bag made with two car tires

Maasai warriors at the London Marathon wearing sandals produced with old tires

100% VEGAN

Listening

3 🔊 55 **Megan is shopping online. What does she want to buy? Listen to the conversation.**

4 🔊 55 **CERT** **Listen again and complete the sentences.**

1 Megan didn't stop _____.
2 She says that leather shoes aren't very _____.
3 The shoes come in lots of different _____.
4 Grant prefers the _____.
5 Grant thinks the hiking boots are _____.
6 Grant takes a size _____.

Learn to Learn / Writing strategies

Making vocabulary lists

A good way to learn vocabulary is to make vocabulary lists on different topics. For example, if your topic is fashion, then list all the words you already know first. Then add to the list new words.

fashion
vintage
designer
...
Add as many words as you can.

Speaking

5 **Pairwork Discuss the following questions together. Use your fashion vocabulary lists to help you.**

1 How often do you buy clothes?
2 Where do you usually buy them and how much do you pay for them? Give examples.
3 When it comes to fashion, what is your style?
4 Which is the most expensive clothing item in your wardrobe? Which is the cheapest? Which is the most important for you?
5 Where do you put your old clothes? Do you recycle them? How?

Writing

6 **Internet research What do you think about using recycled materials to make clothes? Do you think it is possible or just too expensive? Would you buy vegan shoes? Write a short article. Use the prompts below and the Internet to help you.**

- Say what kind of recycled materials are used to make clothes.
- Talk about how expensive the process is.
- Give your opinion.

Quick Check

Choose the correct option (A, B, C or D).

1 Your jacket is _____ mine.
A bigger   B bigger than   C more bigger than   D big than ☐

2 I can't wear your jeans, you're taller _____ me!
A as   B of   C that   D than ☐

3 My friend's smartphone costs a fortune, it's _____ than mine.
A more expensive   B expensive   C cheaper   D bigger ☐

4 Mum found a mysterious box in the attic: it's _____ than our house!
A old   B oldest   C more old   D older ☐

5 Main Street is always full of people: it is the _____ place in town!
A more big   B busiest   C noisy   D more small ☐

6 Sheldon Cooper is _____ character on TV.
A most intelligent   B the more intelligent   C the most intelligent   D more intelligent ☐

7 The Flash is _____ of all superheroes.
A the faster   B the most fast   C the most faster   D the fastest ☐

8 Lorna has found a black kitten: it is _____ in the world!
A cuter   B cutest   C the cutest   D cutest than ☐

9 The headmaster's speech was the _____ thing on earth!
A more boring   B most boring   C as boring as   D boriest ☐

10 A frog is _____ a beetle.
A as not as small as   B not as small   C not as small as   D as smaller than ☐

11 This is _____ film of the year.
A the worse   B the baddest   C the worst   D as bad as ☐

12 Thanks grandma: your cakes are always _____!
A the goodder   B the better   C the worst   D the best ☐

13 China's population is growing very fast: it's _____ country in the world.
A the more populated   B the most populated   C as populated   D the many populated ☐

14 My essay was good, but yours was _____!
A much better   B much best   C the better   D best ☐

15 Tim is only 14, but he's already _____ his father.
A taller than   B taller as   C more tall than   D more tall as ☐

16 Mosquitos can be _____ dangerous for people.
A extremely   B not enough   C more   D most ☐

17 It's very cold outside, don't forget your _____.
A skirt   B scarf   C shirt   D shoes ☐

18 I like comfortable clothes. I usually wear a _____.
A suit   B swimsuit   C tracksuit   D dress ☐

19 You need a pair of _____ to go jogging.
A sandals   B boots   C trousers   D sneakers ☐

20 You go to a _____ to withdraw money.
A cash machine / ATM   B savings   C change   D credit card ☐

TOTAL _____ / 20

10

*Exchange students
from all over the world
meet at a college in London.*

Language

Fact

Over 700 million people in the world speak English as a second language and a billion speak English as a foreign language.

The Big Question

Why are you learning English? Do you think it is important for your life? Why?

Unit Objectives

Vocabulary & Listening	Grammar	Language Skills	Video & Life Skills
• Language learning • Education • Word formation	• *be going to* • Present simple and Present continuous for the future • Future time expressions	Reading: A text about endangered languages Listening: A person describing a trip to India Writing: Online research Speaking: A short presentation	▶ Asking for and offering help School skills: • Dealing with pressure

The Future of English

English is presently one of the most widely spoken and written languages in the world. There are about 380 million native English speakers, and millions more who are learning English as a second language. English is just everywhere – in cinema, music, science, on TV and of course the Internet. Whether you are a beginner, intermediate or advanced learner, English is such an important language that everyone wants to learn it and use it to communicate with others. But what is the future of English?

There are around 60-70 new 'Englishes' that people speak around the world, as millions of people learn English as a second and foreign language. Currently, there is just one native speaker to every five non-native speakers of English, an incredible statistic which means that British English is a minority among the other 'Englishes'.

Why do so many people think it is better to study English than another language? Many say that English is an easy language to learn because its grammar is simple. Others say it is due to the power of the people who speak it, and Britain was a very powerful country in the 19th and 20th centuries. In addition, many British colonial countries made English their official language.

Vocabulary: Learning languages

1 🔊 56 **Match the expressions (1-5) to the pictures (A-E). Then listen and check.**

1 ☐ do a translation
2 ☐ look words up in a dictionary
3 ☐ practice the pronunciation
4 ☐ learn the meaning
5 ☐ focus on grammar

2 Underline the correct alternative.

1 Susan *said / asked* the teacher a question.
2 Martin *spoke / said* about the future of the German language.
3 Nobody *talked / answered* the question correctly.
4 The teacher *said / told* her to translate the article.
5 Melanie *told / talked* to the children about how to use a dictionary.
6 Jeremy *looked / looked up* a difficult word in the dictionary.

English is developing and changing quickly, and it is so varied that every year around 1,000 new words and expressions enter the English language from every area of life. Just take, for example, the words 'selfie', 'hater', 'follower', 'binge-watching' (watching TV series for hours) or 'mini-me' (a person similar to a younger version, for example mother and daughter). Or even 'yo' as a way of greeting people. These are all recent additions to English dictionaries and many more new words are going to appear in the near future. Mary Thorne is an English teacher in London and this is what she said on the subject: 'New English words are appearing everywhere. I think it's so important to teach my students some of them that next term I'm going to start a special course called "New Words". Students are going to study lots of new vocabulary in a fun way. The course starts on October 10th and there are already a lot of applications. It's going to be a success.'

Are we going to see an explosion of new words and expressions as the Internet and social media take control? As the world is becoming more and more global, are we going to witness the birth of a new global language where translation is probably not going to be necessary? English is definitely evolving. But one thing is sure: it is going to be important in the future and to retain its position as lingua franca.

Grammar: *be going to*

> Students **are going to study** lots of new vocabulary.
> Translation **is** probably **not going to be** necessary.
> **Are** we **going to see** an explosion of new words?
>
> ▶ Grammar reference p. 130

5 Use the prompts to write sentences with the correct form of *be going to*.

1 she / study German / next term
2 I / not spend a year / abroad
3 your parents / live in the USA / ?
4 Lola / not pass / her French exam
5 what / he / study / at college / ?
6 what / you do / on the weekend / ?
7 I / visit / Caracas / at Easter

6 Read Pablo's intentions for the summer and complete them with the correct form of *be going to* and the verbs from the box.

> visit • not sleep • travel • work • not spend • improve

Next summer:

- I ¹_____ my English
- I ²_____ across Britain by bus with my friend Freddy
- We ³_____ the Lake District
- I ⁴_____ all day
- We ⁵_____ all our money in hotels
- We ⁶_____ on a farm to pay for our vacation

3 Read the text. What does the title of the article mean? Check (✓).

☐ English is the language of the future
☐ the development of the English language
☐ learning to express the future in English

4 **CERT** Read the text again and answer the questions.

1 How many people speak English as a native language?
2 How many new 'Englishes' have appeared in recent years?
3 What did some British colonial countries do?
4 What is Mary Thorne going to do?
5 What does she think is important for her students?
6 What does she think about the course?

Watch out!

We use the Present simple to talk about schedules and timetables in the future.
*The course **starts** on October 10th.*
*Classes **finish** at 4 p.m.*

Speaking

7 **Pairwork** Take turns to ask and answer questions to talk about your future intentions. Use the verbs from the box to help you.

> be • visit • learn • travel • work • study

A What are you going to do when you finish school?
B I'm going to learn to ride a motorbike.
A Cool! I'm going to travel the world.

New Message — ⤢ ✕

Greetings from Rome

Hi Owen,

How are things? I'm in Rome, do you remember? I'm here for six months on an exchange visit with my school. It's great! I love the city. I'm staying with an Italian family and they live in the center in a really big apartment. Their son is the same age as me. His name's Luca and we do lots of things together.

We go to school together in the morning but we aren't in the same class. It's quite hard to do all my schoolwork in a different language, but I'm learning a lot of Italian now!

Last weekend, we took the train to Naples and we climbed Mount Vesuvius. It was amazing. I took loads of photos, I put them on my Instagram page. Next weekend, we're going to Venice for two days. I'm really excited! We're staying in a youth hostel and we're even hiring a gondola on Sunday! Next month, we're meeting Luca's cousins in Bologna for the weekend. I have so much to do!

I'm coming home for a week at Christmas, of course, so I'll see you then. I'm going to Jessica's Christmas party on Christmas Eve. Are you going?

Anyway, that's all for now. I'm having a pizza with my Italian schoolmates tonight. We're meeting at the metro station in 15 minutes!

Write with your news! How is everything at home?
Ciao!
Mark

Send 🗑 ▾

1 Read the email. What is Mark doing in Italy?

2 CERT Read the email again and answer the questions.

1 How long is Mark staying in Rome?
2 Who is the same age as him?
3 Where did he go last weekend?
4 Where is he staying this weekend?
5 What is he planning to do next month?
6 Where is he going tonight?

Grammar: Present continuous for future

We're going to Venice next weekend.
I'm having a pizza tonight.
We're meeting at the metro station.

We use the Present continuous for arrangements with a fixed time and place.

▶ Grammar reference p. 130

3 Do the sentences refer to a present (P) or a future (F) event? Write P or F.

1 What time are you meeting Alice on Thursday? ___
2 Where is Mark going next weekend? ___
3 Tony and Mike aren't studying. They're chatting with their friends! ___
4 Will and I are having lunch together tomorrow. ___
5 I'm not sleeping. I'm watching a movie. ___
6 Alan's taking the train to Manila at 5 p.m. ___

4 Critical thinking In pairs, discuss the following statements.

- Everyone should do an exchange visit.
- Learning another language is more important than studying math or geography these days.
- Everyone loves traveling when they're young.

be going to

1 Complete the table with the correct form of *to be*.

I	am	going to learn Chinese.
You	1 _____ (+)	going to tour France.
He / She	2 _____ (+)	going to study in the UK.
It	3 _____ (−)	going to work.
We	4 _____ (−)	going to pass the test.
5 _____?	they	going to play that song?

2 Complete the sentences with *be going to* and the verbs from the box.

> not apply • break • do • not take • start • study

1 Watch out! He's _____ that glass!
2 I _____ to Boston University this year.
3 We _____ a new course that teaches students about new words.
4 The new art teacher _____ us to the Impressionist exhibition.
5 Students _____ lots of new vocabulary this term.
6 I don't know what I _____ next year when I finish school.

3 Read the answers and write the questions.

1 _____
I'm going to study economics or law.
2 _____
My sister is going to live in France next summer.
3 _____
They're going to get married in May.
4 _____
We're going to start in five minutes.
5 _____
We're going to meet Keira Knightley!
6 _____
I'm going to read *Wonder* in the summer.

Future time expressions

4 Complete the sentences with the words from the box.

> tomorrow • in • in • next • in • after

1 We're going to start _____ 15 minutes.
2 She's going to move house _____ May.
3 I'm going to travel _____ summer.
4 I'm not going to visit you _____.
5 Sandy's going to graduate _____ a year.
6 The exam is the day _____ tomorrow.

▶ **Grammar reference & practice pp. 130-131**

Present tenses for the future

5 Underline the correct alternative to complete the rules.

*Our bus **arrives** at 5:30 in the afternoon.*
*The train **leaves** at 8:30 tomorrow morning.*
*We're **visiting** York on Sunday afternoon.*
*Mom **isn't coming**. She's **having** lunch with her friend Emma.*

We use the Present [1] *simple / continuous* to talk about timetables and future official events. We use the Present [2] *simple / continuous* to talk about fixed arrangements.

6 Write I for intention, FA for fixed arrangement and T for timetable.

1 I'm seeing Lara at 6 p.m. at the coffee shop. ____
2 Daniel's going to buy a new scooter. ____
3 The train to Tijuana leaves from platform 5 in ten minutes. ____
4 Tara's going to work in her mom's store. ____
5 We're getting the 6 o'clock train. ____
6 The French lesson is at 4 p.m. tomorrow. ____

7 Complete the sentences with the Present simple or continuous of the verbs in parentheses.

1 The train _____ (arrive) at 9 at night.
2 What time _____ you _____ (go) to the doctor's on Wednesday?
3 My judo class _____ (start) next week.
4 Our ferry _____ (depart) for Patra at 6 tomorrow morning.
5 What time _____ the movie _____ (start)?
6 We _____ (meet) this afternoon at four.

Round up

8 **CERT** Online interaction **Complete the text with the correct option (A, B or C).**

Hi Dana! Are you [1] _____ with us [2] _____?
Come on, it's going [3] _____ a wonderful day at the beach! I [4] _____ meeting Sal at the bus stop at 9 a.m. and the bus [5] _____ at 9:15 a.m. We [6] _____ to rent something, maybe a kayak or a canoe because Sal wants to see the sea caves [7] _____ the afternoon. Come on, answer the phone!

1 A going to	B coming	C come
2 A next	B the day after	C tomorrow
3 A to be	B to go	C being
4 A –	B 'm	C going
5 A leaves	B is leaving	C is going
6 A going	B 're going	C go
7 A next	B tomorrow	C in

Education

1 🔊 **57** Complete the sentences with the words from the box. Then listen and check.

> bell • lab • closes • essay • break time • degree project • school term • qualifications • roll • course

1 I love going to the science _____.
2 School _____ for the summer vacation tomorrow.
3 My grandad left school without any _____.
4 The teacher called the _____ but Peter wasn't there.
5 We are doing a school _____ about space travel.
6 When the _____ rings everybody goes home.
7 After I leave school I'm going to get a _____ in chemistry at the university.
8 I don't like speaking in public. I'm going to write an _____ for the end of _____ test.
9 I think I'll attend a language _____ to learn French in the summer.
10 My sister always has a snack at _____.

2 **CERT** Choose the correct option (A, B or C).

1 My cousin is going to _____ school next week.
   A leave   B find   C go
2 Alice wants to _____ her English, so she's going to Ireland for a month this summer.
   A understand   B improve   C look for
3 Max always _____ notes during his history lesson.
   A asks   B takes   C finds
4 Owen is very _____ at math.
   A happy   B sad   C good
5 Our teacher is going to _____ the English tests later.
   A take   B mark   C fail
6 Rachel and Sam _____ the geography test, so they're doing it again tomorrow.
   A made   B tried   C failed
7 I'm going to _____ for the science exam this weekend.
   A pass   B review   C take
8 I'm not going to _____ in college in September.
   A enroll   B write   C go

Word formation

3 🔊 **58** Complete the table with the missing nouns. Then listen and check.

verb	noun
to assign	*assignment*
to assess	1 _____
to review	2 _____
to educate	3 _____
to pronounce	4 _____
to graduate	5 _____
to behave	6 _____

4 Complete the sentences with the words from exercise 3.

1 Ms Hu gave us an _____ for next week.
2 Students must _____ correctly at all times.
3 I like French, but I think the _____ is very difficult.
4 I don't feel ready for the test. Can we _____ together one more time?
5 First, we do the exam. Then, the examiners _____ the papers and give us a mark.
6 My sister _____ last month and now she's going to take a gap year.

Listening

5 🔊 **59** Listen to the interview with Lucy and James about the summer vacation. Who's going to work?

6 🔊 **59** Listen to the interview again and write if the sentences are true (T) or false (F).

1 James isn't going to study at the university next year. ___
2 Lucy isn't thinking of doing a math degree next year. ___
3 She taught English to young children in Colombia last year. ___
4 Lucy speaks Spanish well. ___
5 School closes for the summer vacation in August. ___
6 James is going to work on a farm then go on vacation with his family. ___

Asking for and offering help

1 ▶ **Watch the video. Harry is telling Darsha about a new language he wants to learn. Why does he want to learn it?**

Darsha	What are you doing, Harry?
Harry	Nothing. Just reading.
Darsha	You're always reading. Let me see... is it a language course?
Harry	Yes. I'm studying Italian actually. But more to the point, I'm trying to...
Darsha	Why? What's the matter?
Harry	I'm going to work in Venice next summer, teaching English to kids.
Darsha	That sounds great! Italian's such a beautiful language! I'd love to learn it one day.
Harry	Yes, but it's so difficult. All those verbs!
Darsha	I speak Spanish. It helps.
Harry	Really? Could you please help me to memorise these verbs? Darsha please!
Darsha	OK, OK, I'll help you.
Harry	OK. Listen: *io ti amo, tu mi ami...*
Darsha	Not now. Let's start later Harry. I'm going to revise for German. Anyway, why did you start with the verb 'love'?
Harry	Because I'm going to meet lots of lovely Italian girls...
Darsha	Yes, of course you are. Anyway, why don't you help me with my German? You studied it last year!
Harry	German? I can't help you with that, I'm afraid. German is such a difficult language I even thought about changing to Japanese or something like that!
Darsha	I'll see you at four in the library.
Harry	Good! *Alle quattro!*
Darsha	Yeah, whatever.

Useful language

What's the matter?
Can you help me, please?
OK, I'll help you.
Why don't you help me with...?
I can't help you with that, I'm afraid.

Life Skills: School skills

• Dealing with pressure

2 ▶ **Watch the video again. Underline the mistakes in the sentences and correct them.**

1 Harry wants to learn German.
2 He thinks Italian grammar is easy.
3 Darsha can help him learn Spanish verbs.
4 Darsha speaks very good German.
5 Harry is studying German this year.
6 They are meeting at five thirty at the café.

3 **Read the situations. React in an appropriate way.**

1 Your friend is trying to learn to use her new computer. You are very good at computers.
2 Your father is picking you up at school, but he doesn't know where and when exactly.
3 Your little brother is very sweet today. You want to give him something special.

Watch out!

I'll help you.
We use *will* for spontaneous decisions and to offer help.

4 **Role play Use the prompts to make the conversation.**

Student A
• You are learning French
• French pronunciation is difficult
• Ask for help

Student B
• You speak French quite well
• Your mother is French
• Offer help
• Decide on a time and a place to meet

Evolving languages

There are at least **7,102** living languages in the world.

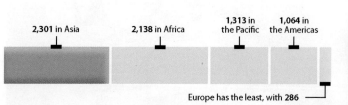

2,301 in Asia

2,138 in Africa

1,313 in the Pacific

1,064 in the Americas

Europe has the least, with **286**

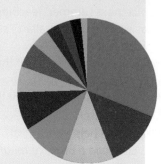

Warm up

1 Look at the charts and complete the language fact file with the numbers from the box.

1.39 billion • over 7,000 • 286 • 2,301

FACT FILE	///
World languages	
Living languages in the world	1
Languages spoken in Asia	2
Languages spoken in Europe	3
Chinese speakers	4

- Chinese 1.39 billion
- Hindi-Urdu 588 m
- English 527 m
- Arabic 467 m
- Spanish 389 m
- Russian 254 m
- Bengali 250 m
- Portuguese 193 m
- German 132 m
- Japanese 123 m
- French 118 m
- Italian 67 m

Reading

2 🔊 60 **Read and listen to the text.**

Are world languages dying?

There are over 7,000 living languages around the world, the majority of which have only a small number of speakers. More than 60% of the earth's population speaks one of only 30 of these languages as their native tongue.

English is obviously the most widely spoken language around the world ... or not? Well, no, because Chinese has, in fact, the highest number of native speakers with 1.39 billion speakers around the world. Next is Hindi-Urdu with 588 million and then English with 527 million. After that, there is Arabic and Spanish, and then languages such as Russian, Portuguese and French. The result is that two-thirds of the world's population shares just 12 languages.

So what about all the other thousands of languages? The answer is that most languages are spoken by only a small handful of people and that many of them are going to disappear – over 50% by 2100! Linguistic extinction is hitting some countries harder and faster than others – for example, in parts of the west coast of the USA and Australia there are many highly endangered languages that risk disappearing altogether. After all, do we all know Newar or Mon, or Muji and Chepang languages?

The effects of language extinction could be culturally devastating. Many of these endangered languages are such an important key to local knowledge, customs and traditions. This cultural heritage is going to inevitably disappear together with the language.

As a result of this linguistic risk, organizations are developing projects around the world that aim to prevent languages from becoming extinct. One of these is The Enduring Voices Project and another is the Endangered Languages Project which also uses modern technology to document, preserve and teach these endangered languages. One member of the project group said, 'We are going to put together a catalogue of text, audio and video files online which documents a wide range of languages that are at risk of disappearing, in order to preserve them. These languages really are so important to the world's cultural heritage that their preservation is imperative for future generations. An exhibition of our project opens in London next week. We are not going to let these cultures disappear'.

3 CERT **Read the text again and choose the correct option (A, B, C or D).**

1 Over half of the world's population...
   A speaks English.
   B speaks an endangered language.
   C speaks one of thirty languages.
   D speaks three languages.

2 Hindi-Urdu is...
   A the fifth most important world language.
   B the third most important world language.
   C the sixth most important world language.
   D the second most important world language.

3 ... are going to be extinct soon.
   A More than 50% of world languages
   B Under 50% of world languages
   C Very few world languages
   D Most Australian languages

4 Endangered languages...
   A are very difficult to learn.
   B are easy to understand.
   C are full of cultural heritage and customs.
   D are starting to decrease.

5 The Endangered Languages Project...
   A has just opened an office in London.
   B collects videos and texts about endangered languages.
   C thinks languages are not so important for future generations.
   D doesn't think the project will be a great success.

Listening

4 🔊 61 CERT **Mr Sellers is giving a geography lesson and field-trip briefing about India. Listen and complete the text with the missing information.**

INDIA

Surrounded by the Indian Ocean, the Arabian Sea and the Bay of Bengal.

Borders with Pakistan, ¹_____, Nepal, Bhutan, Myanmar and Bangladesh.

Population: ²_____ people.

Official languages of India are ³_____ and English.

⁴_____ officially recognized languages in India.

Field-trip briefing next Friday at ⁵_____.

You are going to get a list of what to ⁶_____ at the briefing.

Flight ⁷_____ at 5 a.m. on ⁸_____.

| Learn to Learn / Speaking strategies |

Oral presentations

When preparing an oral presentation, remember to choose and plan the content carefully. Here is some advice:
• collect your notes with order and clarity
• try to find the most interesting aspects of your topic
• present them in a logical order
• speak slowly and clearly
• make pauses, if necessary
• look at the audience
• always practice until you feel confident

Speaking

5 COMPETENCES **Prepare a short oral presentation about your country. Answer these questions to help you.**

• How big is the country and what is its capital city?
• What is the population?
• What is the official language of the country?
• What other languages are spoken in the country?
• Are any of them endangered languages?

Writing

6 COMPETENCES **Write a text about one of the countries from the box. Use the Internet to research some information and photos. Answer the questions in exercise 5 to help you.**

China • Indonesia • Argentina • Australia
Nepal • Korea • Ukraine • Lithuania

Choose the correct option (A, B, C or D).

1 Hurry up, the bus _____.
   A leaving   B is going to leave   C leaves   D left   ☐

2 Fred _____ French because he wants to live in Paris.
   A learning   B learn   C 's going to learn   D 'm going to learn   ☐

3 I _____ Lucia at 4 p.m. in front of the cinema.
   A 'm going to see B see   C seeing   D 'm seeing   ☐

4 You _____ lots of math if you do sciences at the university.
   A studying   B are going to study   C are studying   D going to study   ☐

5 I don't understand this text. I _____ to the teacher.
   A 'm going   B 'm talking   C 'm going to talk D talk   ☐

6 I _____ The X Factor with Mick tonight.
   A watch   B 'm watching   C going to watch   D going to watching   ☐

7 We're spending our vacation in Greece _____.
   A next summer   B last summer   C in summer   D in next summer   ☐

8 I'm going to Rome the day _____ tomorrow.
   A later   B after   C next   D in   ☐

9 When are we going to start?
   A In five minutes. B In five minutes ago.   C Next five minutes. D On five minutes.   ☐

10 Are you going to visit Sydney?
   A Yes, I'm going. B Yes.   C Yes, I am.   D Yes, I'm going to.   ☐

11 I'm going to go to Chile at the end of the _____.
   A register   B school term   C essay   D degree   ☐

12 Teachers _____ tests and homework.
   A educate   B graduate   C assess   D behave   ☐

13 My sister is going to _____ school next week. Mom's really worried.
   A find   B go   C attend   D leave   ☐

14 I'm going to write _____ about the Renaissance.
   A a project   B an essay   C a degree   D a term   ☐

15 I'm not sure about the test, I think I need to _____ more.
   A assign   B pronounce   C assess   D review   ☐

16 When I don't know the meaning of a word, I _____ in a dictionary
   A look it up   B find it   C do   D practice   ☐

17 José is panicking. He's not going to _____ the question!
   A review   B tell   C say   D answer   ☐

18 I can't stay any longer, I _____ the 5:30 p.m. train.
   A going to catch   B catching   C 'm catching   D catch   ☐

19 What are you going to do next year?
   A I'm studying art   B I going to travel   C I stay here.   D I go abroad!   ☐
     in Paris.   the world.

20 Why _____ me with my Chinese lesson?
   A don't you help   B do you help   C are you going to help D help   ☐

TOTAL _____ / 20

Ready for
PLANET ENGLISH

Grammar reference & practice

Words Plus

to be: Present simple

Affirmative	Negative
I am ('m)	I am not ('m not)
You are ('re)	You are not (aren't)
He/She/It is ('s)	He/She/It is not (isn't)
We are ('re)	We are not (aren't)
You are ('re)	You are not (aren't)
They are ('re)	They are not (aren't)

Interrogative	Short answers
Am I ... ?	Yes, you are. / No, you aren't.
Are you ... ?	Yes, I am. / No, I'm not.
Is he/she/it ... ?	Yes, he/she/it is. / No, he /she/it isn't.
Are we ... ?	Yes, we are. / No, we aren't.
Are you ... ?	Yes, you are. / No, you aren't.
Are they ... ?	Yes, they are. / No, they aren't.

We use the Present simple of the verb *be* to
* identify people and objects:
  I'm Jack and she is my sister Karen.
* talk about
  - nationalities: *'Where are you from?' 'I'm from Japan.'*
  - age: *'Is he 15 years old?' 'No, he isn't. He's 14.'*
  - jobs: *'Are you a doctor?' 'No, I'm not. I'm a dentist.'*
  - personal characteristics: *Kelly's tall and slim.*
  - feelings: *I'm hungry, but I'm not thirsty.*

Watch out!

Use *be*, not *have*, for age and feelings.
She's 8 years old.
Are you hot?

▶ **Exercises 1–3**

Plurals of nouns

To make the plural of a noun in most cases we simply add an **-s**.
apple**s**, word**s**, month**s**
For words ending with *-s, -ss, -sh, -ch, -x, -o* we add **-es**:

campu**s** → campus**es**   pea**ch** → peach**es**
bo**ss** → boss**es**   mi**x** → mix**es**
bu**sh** → bush**es**   tomat**o** → tomato**es**

For words ending with *-y*
- we add **-s** if the word ends with a vowel + *-y*:
  bo**y** → boy**s**
- we add **-ies** if the word ends with a consonant + *-y*:
  la**dy** → lad**ies**

For words ending with *-f* or *-fe*, we add **-ves**:
el**f** → el**ves**   kni**fe** → kni**ves**

▶ **Exercise 4**

Subject pronouns & Possessive adjectives

Subject pronouns							
I	you	he	she	it	we	you	they

Possessive adjectives							
my	your	his	her	its	our	your	their

Possessive adjectives go before nouns. They express 'belonging'.

I'm 15. **My** *birthday's in May.*
You're French. **Your** *family is from Paris.*
He's clever. **His** *homework is always right.*
She's tall. **Her** *friends are short.*
It's my new computer. **Its** *operating system is free.*
You're twins. **Your** *birthdays are on the same day.*
We're sporty. **Our** *favorite sport is tennis.*
They're cousins. **Their** *dads are brothers.*

Watch out!

In English, possessive adjectives do not change with plural nouns:
This is **my** *book. / These are* **my** *books.*
They relate to the possessor, not to the object:
her *book,* **her** *pens* (= belonging to a woman)
his *book,* **his** *pens* (= belonging to a man)

▶ **Exercises 5-6**

Possessive 's

Singular	Plural
Singular noun + **'s**	Plural noun + **'**
The girl's room.	*The girls' room.*

We use the possessive 's to talk about family and possessions:
He is Sarah's brother.
That's my dog's ball.
The twins' bedroom is very big.
We also use 's with irregular plural nouns:
The children's school is nice.
It's the people's decision.

▶ **Exercise 7**

Demonstrative adjectives

Singular	Plural
This	These
That	Those

We use the demonstrative adjectives to indicate how near or far someone or something is:
this *student,* **these** *books* – they are near the person who's speaking
that *car,* **those** *girls* – they aren't near the person who's speaking

▶ **Exercises 8-9**

1 Complete the conversation with the correct subject pronouns and the verb *be*.

Adriana Are these your photos, Megan?

Megan Yes, ¹ _____. In this one I'm with my mom and brother.

Adriana How old is your brother?

Megan Eighteen, like me. ² _____ twins!

Adriana Really? That's so cool! What's your mother like? ³ _____ bossy?

Megan No, ⁴ _____. She's always calm.

Adriana And do you have a sister?

Megan Yes, I do. Her name's Kate and
⁵ _____ only nine years old, but
⁶ _____ in the photo with us.

Adriana What about this photo? Are they your pets?

Megan Yes! Lola and Tiger. ⁷ _____ very big, but ⁸ _____ really clever.

2 Put the words in the correct order to make sentences.

1 Ruby / and / 16 / old / I'm / years / I'm

_____

2 Tom / cousins: / and Mark / aren't / friends / they're

_____

3 and Harry / are / parents / Suzanne / my

_____

4 aren't / children / shy / lazy / or / the

_____

5 your / Elena / sister / mom / is / your / or / ?

_____

6 from / are / Montreal / parents / your / ?

_____

3 Use the prompts to make questions, then use the words in parentheses to make answers.

1 we / late (early)

'_____?' '_____.'

2 you / thirsty (hungry)

'_____?' '_____.'

3 you / cold (hot)

'_____?' '_____.'

4 he / wrong (right)

'_____?' '_____.'

5 your clothes / dirty (clean)

'_____?' '_____.'

6 your sneakers / new (old)

'_____?' '_____.'

4 Write the plural or the singular of these nouns.

1 kiss _____   6 toy _____

2 books _____   7 beach _____

3 cities _____   8 dishes _____

4 buses _____   9 box _____

5 wife _____   10 wolves _____

5 Underline the correct alternative.

This is a photo of my grandfather. It's ¹ *his* / *her* birthday. ² *Our* / *My* brother and sister are next to him. ³ *His* / *Their* names are George and Ellie.
⁴ *Our* / *Their* parents aren't in the photo, but dad's brother is next to me. ⁵ *His* / *He's* my uncle and ⁶ *his* / *her* name's Sanjay. Of course, the lady on the right is ⁷ *his* / *my* grandmother. ⁸ *Her* / *She's* my favorite person in the whole world!

6 Complete the sentences with the correct possessive adjective.

1 _____ favorite color is orange. (Amanda)

2 _____ birthday is on Saturday. (I)

3 _____ school is near the park. (Liz and I)

4 _____ best friend is called Matt. (Jake)

5 _____ house is very big. (Rachel and David)

6 _____ playground is enormous! (my school)

7 Write the possessive form ('s) of the noun in parentheses.

1 This is my book, but that one is _____. (Tom)

2 The _____ favorite color is red. (children)

3 _____ first name is Jane. (Mrs Mason)

4 Grandad is my _____ father. (mom)

5 The _____ names are Rex and Jake. (dogs)

8 Complete the sentences with *this* or *these*.

1 _____ are my new sneakers.

2 _____ exercise is difficult.

3 Are _____ pens red?

4 _____ letters are for you.

5 Is _____ your cell phone?

6 _____ cookies are delicious.

7 _____ is a new tablet.

8 Are _____ oranges organic?

9 Is _____ my plate?

10 _____ games are boring.

9 Complete the sentences with *that* or *those*.

1 Is _____ a new video game?

2 Lucy lives in _____ house.

3 Who is _____ boy?

4 _____ pictures are really nice.

5 _____ people are from Spain.

6 Is _____ your dog?

7 _____ boys are my friends.

8 _____ is a horrible movie.

9 _____ T-shirts are wonderful.

10 Are _____ your books?

to have

Affirmative	Negative
I have ('ve)	I don't have
You have ('ve)	You don't have
He/She/It has ('s)	He/She/It doesn't have
We have ('ve)	We don't have
You have ('ve)	You don't have
They have ('ve)	They don't have

Interrogative	Short answers
Do I have ... ?	Yes, you have. / No, you haven't.
Do you have... ?	Yes, I have. / No, I haven't.
Does he/she/it has ... ?	Yes, he/she/it has. No, he/she/it hasn't.
Do we have... ?	Yes, we have. / No, we haven't.
Do you have... ?	Yes, you have. / No, you haven't.
Do they have... ?	Yes, they have. / No, they haven't.

We use the verb *have* to
- talk about possessions:
  *They **have** lots of books.*
  *I **don't have** a cell phone!*
- describe people:
  *She **has** short, blonde hair.*
  ***Does** John **have** a beard?*
- describe family relationships:
  *I **have** three cousins.*
  *How many sisters **does** she **have**?*

Watch out!

We don't use the short form in the affirmative short answers:
'Do you have short hair?' 'Yes, I have'. NOT ~~'Yes, I've.'~~

▶ Exercise 1

There is / There are

We often use *there is* and *there are* when we first refer to someone or something:
***There's** a letter on your desk.*
***There are** lots of students in my class.*

We can contract the affirmative singular form, *there is* (= *there's*), but not the plural, *there are*. Both negative forms can be contracted (*there isn't / there aren't*):
***There isn't** a window in this room.*
***There aren't** five people in that house.*

▶ Exercise 2

a/an

We use the indefinite article *a/an* to indicate an unidentified person or thing. We use **a** with singular nouns beginning with a consonant sound:
a *notebook,* **a** *child,* **a** *universe,* **a** *hotel,* **a** *yacht,* **a** *jump.*
We use **an** with singular nouns beginning with a vowel sound:
an *adult,* **an** *hour,* **an** *honour.*

the

We use *the* with specific singular and plural nouns:
***the** red carpet,* **the** *leather chairs,* **the** *lamp in* **the** *living room,* **the** *plant in* **the** *corner.*

Watch out!

We don't use *the* before nouns used in general meaning:
~~*The*~~ *kittens are cute.*
I like ~~the~~ sport clothes.
They don't eat ~~the~~ meat.

We don't use *the* with the name of countries:
Argentina is in South America.

But we use *the* with countries
- that have plural names:
  My brother is on holiday in **the Netherlands**.
  She comes from **the Philippines**.
- that have the words *Republic, Kingdom,* or *States* in their names:
  My grandparents live in **the United States**.
  ***The Islamic Republic** of Iran is in Asia.*

We use *the* with geographical names such as
- rivers and canals: *the Thames, the Panama Canal*
- oceans and seas: *the Atlantic Ocean, The Caribbean Sea*
- mountain ranges: *The Rocky Mountains, The Andes*
- groups of islands: *The Canaries, The Malvinas.*

▶ Exercise 3

Question words

We can use *Who, When, Where, Which, Why, What, How, How often* and *How long* before *do* or *does* to make *Wh-*questions. They are always at the beginning of sentences:
***Which** of these closets is yours?*
***Where** is the living room?*
***How often** do you water the garden?*

Watch out!

Note the difference between **what** and **which**:
What *is your favorite color?*
Which *is your favourite armchair: the blue one or the red one?*

▶ Exercises 4-6

1 Complete the sentences with the correct form of *have*.

1 _____ Chris _____ blond hair and blue eyes?
2 I _____ a cat or a dog, but my friends Mark and Clara _____ a big black dog.
3 Thomas _____ a toothache.
4 Daniel _____ a car. He has a bicycle.
5 Tom wants to go to the concert but he _____ a ticket. _____ you _____ a spare one?
6 I _____ a new cell phone, wow! But my sister _____ one, instead.
7 We don't like TV, so we _____ a television. _____ you _____ one?
8 I see you _____ a new games console!

2 Complete Jenny's questions about Laura's town with *Is there* or *Are there*. Then complete Laura's answers.

1 **Jenny** '_____ any stores here?
   Laura 'Yes, there _____. _____ a lot of stores.'
2 **Jenny** _____ a post office?'
   Laura 'Yes, there _____. In fact _____ two in the city center.'
3 **Jenny** _____ a zoo?'
   Laura 'No, there _____, but _____ a famous one only 30 km away.'
4 **Jenny** '_____ any shopping malls?'
   Laura 'Yes, there _____. _____ a big movie theater complex, too.'
5 **Jenny** '_____ any Chinese restaurants?'
   Laura 'No, there _____. _____ any Asian restaurants here at all.'

3 Complete the sentences with *a / an* or *the* where necessary.

1 _____ Canada is _____ very big country, and Toronto is _____ amazing city.
2 Eric lives in _____ France, but his parents are in _____ United States.
3 Paul and Janet eat _____ lunch at 1 p.m. in _____ school cafeteria.
4 'Where's _____ cat?' 'He's on _____ sofa in _____ living room.'
5 This is _____ book you wanted. I know you like reading _____ books.
6 Sophie is _____ interesting person. _____ stories she tells are always amazing.
7 _____ new teacher is really nice; he has _____ English accent.
8 Peter has _____ breakfast in bed on _____ Sundays.
9 Susan is _____ nurse: she works in _____ hospital in _____ Philippines.
10 There is _____ art exhibition in _____ town center on _____ Sunday.

4 Underline the correct alternative.

1 '*Who/Where/Why* does Marco come from?'
   'Lima in Peru.'
2 '*Which/Who/When* is Sofia's bedroom?'
   'The smallest one.'
3 '*Where/Why/How* do you make tortillas?'
   'With flour, salt, water and fat!'
4 '*Why/When/What* are the English classes?'
   'On Tuesdays and Thursdays.'
5 '*Where/How/Why* do your school friends come from different countries?'
   'Because it's an international school.'

5 Write the questions from the box next to the answers.

How is your granny? • How old is your brother?
Why is she nervous? • Who are those boys?
How high is that mountain? • What time is the football match?

1 '_____'
   'It's at 7 p.m.'
2 '_____'
   'Because there's a math test today.'
3 '_____'
   'He's twenty-five.'
4 '_____'
   'They are my new classmates.'
5 '_____'
   'She's very well, thanks.'
6 '_____'
   'It's about 1,300 meters high.'

6 Use the words in parentheses and the correct prepositions of place to answer the questions.

1 Where do you hang a picture? (wall)
   _____.
2 Where are your parents right now? (work)
   _____.
3 Where do you have P.E. lessons? (gym)
   _____.
4 Where does the train connecting France and UK travel? (water)
   _____.
5 Where are you going? (library)
   _____.
6 Where is the letter G? (letters F and H)
   _____.
7 Where does the last person in a queue stand? (everybody)
   _____.
8 Where's the title of a book? (the cover)
   _____.

can, can't

Affirmative	Negative
I can play	I can't play
You can play	You can't play
He/She/It can play	He/She/It can't play
We can play	We can't play
You can play	You can't play
They can play	They can't play

Interrogative	Short answers
Can I play?	Yes, you can. / No, you can't.
Can you play?	Yes, I can. / No, I can't.
Can he/she/it play?	Yes, he/she/it can. No, he/she/it can't.
Can we play?	Yes, we can. / No, we can't.
Can you play?	Yes, you can. / No, you can't.
Can they play?	Yes, they can. / No, they can't.

We use the modal verb *can* to express
- ability and lack of ability:
  Steve **can** *speak three languages.*
  My sister **can't** *play golf.*
  I **can** *ride a motorbike, but I* **can't** *drive a car.*
- possibility:
  The match's finished, so we **can** *leave now.*
  Can *you meet us at ten at the ice rink?*
  They **can** *come with us, or they* **can** *call a taxi.*

Can, like all modal verbs, is followed by the infinitive without *to* and has only one form for all persons.
I **can play** *basketball with you, tomorrow, and Laura* **can come**, *too.*

We use *very well, well, quite well, (not) at all* to say how good we are at something:
I can play tennis **very well**, *but Lorenzo can't play it* **at all**.
Lou is **quite good at** *horseback riding, but Jane is* **extremely good at** *it!*

▶ **Exercises 1–2**

Adverbs of manner

We form most adverbs of manner by adding *-ly* to the adjective:
slow → *slow***ly**, *bad* →*bad***ly**
*Can you speak slow***ly***, please?*

There are some spelling rules.
- If the adjective ends in *-y*, we change *-y* in *-ily*:
  angry → *angr***ily**:
  *We are going along quite happ***ily**.
- If the adjective ends in *-ic*, we simply add *-ally*:
  fantastic → *fantastic***ally**:
  *After a trick, the skater fell comic***ally** *on the ground.*
- If the adjective ends in *-ble*, we change *-ble* in *-bly*:
  *possib***le** →*possib***ly**:
  *Today the weather is terrib***ly** *hot.*

Watch out!

Some adjectives have irregular adverb forms:
good → *well, fast* → *fast, hard* → *hard, late* → *late*
I don't feel very **well** *today.*
He's speaking too **fast**.
Adverbs of manner usually go after the object or before the verb, not between the verb and object:
He examined the picture **carefully**. / *He* **carefully** *examined the picture.*
(NOT *He examined* **carefully** *the picture.*)

▶ **Exercises 3–5**

Object pronouns

Subject pronouns	Object pronouns
I	me
you	you
he	him
she	her
it	it
we	us
you	you
they	them

Object pronouns are used to replace nouns:
'I don't like **chocolate**.' *'Really? I love* **it**!'
'Is that Millie's **dad**?' *'Yes, that's* **him**.'
Object pronouns go after, not before, the verb:
I know **him**.
We can't see **them**.
They are often used after prepositions:
Hey, I'm talking **to you**. *Look* **at me**.
Hurry! They're waiting **for us**.

▶ **Exercises 6-7**

1 **Write *A* (ability) or *P* (possibility) next to the sentences.**

1 Sorry I can't come with you. _____
2 Can you play basketball? _____
3 You can take your friend Marina with you at the party. _____
4 My baby sister can't walk, she's too young! _____
5 You can go to London by plane or by train. _____
6 She got very good grades, so she can go to a better university now. _____

2 **Look at the table, and write what people can or can't do.**

	Andy	Maria and Jon
bake a cake	✓	✗
speak French	✗	✓
swim	✗	✗
ski	✓	✓
do karate	✓	✓
ride a horse	✗	✗

1 Can Andy bake a cake or swim?
   He _____ but he
   _____.

2 Can Maria and Jon swim or speak French?
   They _____ but they
   _____.

3 Can Maria and Jon ski or ride a horse?
   They _____ but they
   _____.

4 Can Andy do karate or speak French?
   He _____ but he
   _____.

5 Can Maria and Jon bake a cake or do karate?
   They _____ but they
   _____.

6 Can Andy ride a horse or ski?
   He _____ but he
   _____.

3 **Write the adverb next to the adjective.**

1 interesting _____
2 nice _____
3 complete _____
4 loud _____
5 quiet _____
6 angry _____
7 kind _____
8 tragic _____
9 funny _____
10 soft _____

4 **Correct the mistake in each sentence.**

1 He feels stressed because he works very hardly.
2 Read carefully the details before doing the test.
3 Don't eat too quick, take your time!
4 I can't hear the music good. Could you turn it up?
5 He did bad in the exam and didn't pass it.

5 **Complete the sentences with an appropriate adverb of manner.**

1 Careful! You'll fall if you run so _____.
2 Come over here very _____, or you'll wake the baby.
3 The instructions are quite complicated so read them _____.
4 I don't speak French very _____ at all. I find it really hard.
5 Explain that to me again, please – and can you speak more _____?
6 Dad's talking really _____ at Peter. What did he do?

6 **Complete the mini conversations with the correct subject or object pronouns.**

1 A Do _____ like my new bike?
   B Yes, I like _____ a lot.
2 A Are these our new books?
   B Yes, put _____ in your bags, please.
3 A We're so thirsty. Can you bring _____ some water, please?
   B Of course.
4 A Personally, _____ don't like Miss Jones.
   B Really? I quite like _____.
5 A Stop fighting and listen to _____!
   B OK, Mom. Sorry.
6 A Does your mom know your new teachers?
   B No, _____ doesn't know _____ at all.

7 **Complete the text with the object pronouns from the box.**

> her • him (x 2) • it • me • them • us (x 2)

Hi! I'm Pedro. I'm 16 and I'm from San Antonio. Music is my life – I'm crazy about [1] _____! My favorite bands are Greta Van Fleet and The Vamps. I love listening to [2] _____. I'm in a band, The Raiders. This is a picture of [3] _____ all at Felipe's house. He's only 14, but he can play the guitar really well. His mom's a musician and he learned from [4] _____. Felipe's on the right of the photo and I'm sitting next to [5] _____. I'm the lead singer. The other boy, next to [6] _____ with the guitar, is my cousin Carlos. The boy on the left of the picture is older than the rest of [7] _____: he's 18. His name's Javi and he plays the drums. I don't know [8] _____ very well yet, but he's good friends with Carlos.

Present simple

We use the Present simple to talk about permanent states and regular habits in the present, and things that are always true:

*I **live** in Istanbul.*
*He **plays** football at weekends.*

*We **don't work** on Saturdays.*
***Does** water **boil** at 100°?*

Affirmative	Negative
I work	I don't work.
You work	You don't work.
He/She/It works	He/She/It doesn't work.
We work	We don't work.
You work	You don't work.
They work	They don't work.

Interrogative	Short answers
Do I work?	Yes, you do. / No, you don't.
Do you work?	Yes, I do. / No, I don't.
Does he/she/it work?	Yes, he/she/it does. No, he/she/it doesn't.
Do we work?	Yes, we do. / No, we don't.
Do you work?	Yes, you do. / No, you don't.
Do they work?	Yes, they do. / No, they don't.

Watch out!

Note the spelling of the third person singular affirmative verb form:

- most verbs add *-s*: *drinks, speaks, works*
- verbs ending in *-ch, -o, -sh, -ss, -x, -z* add *-es*: *watches, washes, goes*
- verbs ending in consonant + *-y* change *y* in *-ies*: *studies, cries, flies*

*He **lives** in Manila. She **studies** a lot.*

We form negatives with *don't / doesn't* and the main verb:

*Jim **doesn't speak** French very well.*
*I **don't know** the meaning of this word.*

We form interrogatives with *do / does* and the main verb:

*(Wh-*word) + *do / does* + subject + main verb.

***Does** she **like** pizza?*
*What **do** you **want** for lunch today?*
*What **does** he **watch** on TV?*

▶ Exercises 1-3

Prepositions of time

We use **at**
- with clock times:
  *Classes start **at** 8:30 a.m.*

- with specific times of day, or mealtimes:
  *My mom goes running **at** lunchtime.*

- with festivals:
  *We visit grandparents **at** Christmas.*

We use **in**
- with months, years, seasons, and longer periods of time:
  *They won the Superbowl **in** 1995.*
  *We go on vacation **in** June.*

- with periods of time during the day:
  *I usually read a book **in** the evenings.*

We use **on**
- with days of the week, and parts of days of the week:
  *I go swimming **on** Mondays.*
  *They play with their game console **on** the weekend.*

- with dates:
  *My sister was born **on** April 1st.*

- with special days:
  *My grandparents often have a party **on** their anniversary.*
  *My mom always prepares my favorite cake **on** my birthday.*

▶ Exercises 4-5

Adverbs and expressions of frequency

0% never > hardly ever > rarely > sometimes > often > very often > usually > always **100%**

We often use adverbs of frequency with the Present simple. They go before the main verb, but follow the verb *be*.

*Do you **often** cry?*
*He's **always** hungry!*

We also use other expressions of frequency with the Present simple (for example, *every day/week/month, once/twice a day/week, on Mondays/Tuesdays*). They usually go at the end of the sentence.

*We have a French lesson **twice a week**.*
*Does he work **every day**?*

We use *How often...?* to ask about frequency.

*'**How often** do you take a shower?' 'I **usually** take a shower **once a day**.'*

▶ Exercises 6-8

1 Complete the sentences with the correct form of the Present simple of the verbs in parentheses.

1 Fred and Lou _____ (go) to school by bus.
2 Mom _____ (not have) time for breakfast!
3 We _____ (wake up) early on weekdays.
4 Sam's brothers _____ (not like) pasta.
5 Mike _____ (study) hard before exams.
6 Frank _____ (not speak) any languages.

2 Complete the text using an appropriate verb or auxiliary.

My aunt has an interesting job. On Mondays, she
[1] _____ really early, at 5:45 in the morning.
She [2] _____ a shower, [3] _____ dressed and
[4] _____ breakfast, then she [5] _____ home
at 7:00 a.m. She [6] _____ work at 8 o'clock and
finishes 22 hours later!
What job [7] _____ she do? Well, she [8] _____
work in an office: she's an airplane pilot! She
[9] _____ on the London–Sydney route and the
flight is always about 22 hours. It's tiring, but there
are secret bedrooms on the plane where pilots can
sleep!
When my aunt [10] _____ to London, it's usually
the middle of the night, but luckily she [11] _____
live far from the airport. She sometimes [12] _____
me with her on flights – she's great!

3 Use the prompts to write questions in the Present simple. Then write short answers that are true for you.

1 you / often / see your friends / after school / ?
_____? _____
2 you / always / do your homework / in the evenings / ?
_____? _____
3 your parents / drive you / to school / ?
_____? _____
4 your best friend / have lunch / at school / ?
_____? _____
5 your English teacher / often / give tests / ?
_____? _____
6 you and your friends / do projects / together / ?
_____? _____

4 Write the correct preposition: on, in or at.

1 ____ Clara's birthday   7 ____ Sunday
2 ____ winter   8 ____ 2014
3 ____ the morning   9 ____ the 19th century
4 ____ August 10th   10 ____ Halloween
5 ____ breakfast time   11 ____ Tuesday morning
6 ____ the end of the   12 ____ Easter
  movie

5 Complete the sentences with at, in, on.

1 The kids are always hungry ____ dinner time.
2 What do you usually do ____ the weekend?
3 Gardens are lovely ____ spring.
4 We get up late ____ Sunday mornings.
5 School starts ____ September.
6 My birthday is ____ October 30th.
7 I like to look at the stars ____ night.
8 The train leaves ____ 11:45 a.m.

6 Rewrite the sentences using the adverbs in parentheses.

1 He's in the kitchen after he gets up. (always)
2 When they are sick, they watch TV. (never)
3 We don't have a big lunch on Saturdays. (usually)
4 They wake up early if there's no school. (never)
5 Before you have dinner, do you help your mom in the kitchen? (sometimes)
6 Dad works in the garage after he gets home. (often)
7 When the children finish school, Mom's at home. (hardly ever)
8 Does Peter eat before he goes to school? (always)

7 Reorder the words to make sentences.

1 late / My / friend / sometimes / for / is / school
_____
2 plays / Marta / rarely / computer games
_____
3 grandparents / visit / you / at Christmas / often / Your
_____
4 eggs / Simon / eats / never
_____
5 Sarah / on Sundays / early / rarely / gets up
_____
6 finish / classes / We / at 1.00 p.m. / our / on Fridays / always
_____

8 Complete the sentences so they are true for you.

1 I _____ watch television in the evenings.
2 I _____ do my homework at school.
3 On weekends I _____ get up early.
4 My family _____ goes to Europe on vacation.
5 My father _____ cooks dinner for us.
6 I _____ play sports after school.

Present continuous

Affirmative	Negative
I am ('m) studying.	I'm not studying.
You are ('re) studying.	You are not (aren't) studying.
He/She/It is ('s) studying.	He/She/It is not (isn't) studying.
We are ('re) studying.	We are not (aren't) studying.
You are ('re) studying.	You are not (aren't) studying.
They are ('re) studying.	They are not (aren't) studying.

Interrogative	Short answers
Am I studying?	Yes, you are. / No, you aren't.
Are you studying?	Yes, I am. / No, I'm not.
Is he/she/it studying?	Yes, he/she/it is. No, he/she/it isn't.
Are we studying?	Yes, we are. / No, we aren't.
Are you studying?	Yes, you are. / No, you aren't.
Are they studying?	Yes, they are. / No, they aren't.

We use the Present continuous
- to talk about things that are happening at the moment of speaking:
  I**'m not playing** football today because it**'s raining**.
- to talk about things that are happening around the time of speaking or in this period:
  I**'m reading** a good book **this week.**

Spelling rules

There are some spelling rules about how to make the continuous form of verbs.
We simply add -ing to most verbs:
work → work**ing**; eat → eat**ing**; play → play**ing**.
The verbs ending in consonant + -e drop the e before adding -ing:
have → hav**ing**; write → writ**ing**; make → mak**ing**.
The verbs ending in consonant + vowel + consonant double the consonant before adding -**ing**:
step → stepp**ing**; cut → cutt**ing**; tap → tapp**ing.**

State verbs

Verbs which describe a state (for example, like, hear, know, want, understand) are NOT normally used with continuous tenses:
~~Are you wanting some money?~~ **Do** you **want** some money?
~~We aren't liking this film.~~ We **don't like** this film.

Some verbs, such as think, can be used in both simple and continuous forms, but the meaning changes slightly:
I **think** Rome is more attractive than Paris. (= my opinion is that ...)
Keep quiet! I**'m thinking**. (= I'm reflecting)

▶ Exercises 1-2

Present simple vs Present continuous

Present simple	Present continuous
• things that are always true: Water **boils** at 100°. • things that happens regularly: We **go** to the theater every Friday. • with adverbs of frequency: I **always have** breakfast. She **never arrives** late. They **often go** to the movies. • with timetables: The train to Buenos Aires **leaves** at 8:15 a.m.	• a temporary activity: I**'m boiling** some water to make tea. • things that are happening now, at the time when we are talking: I**'m going** to the store **now**. • for future arrangements: We **are going** to the beach **tomorrow**.

▶ Exercises 3- 4

Whose

We usually use whose to indicate possession, especially in questions to ask about which person owns something. We use it before nouns instead of a possessive; it can be used as an adjective, or as a pronoun:
Whose cell phone is it? / Whose is the cell phone?

▶ Exercise 5

Possessive pronouns

Possessive adjectives	Possessive pronouns
my	mine
your	yours
his	his
her	hers
its	--
our	ours
your	your
their	theirs

We use a possessive pronoun instead of a full noun to avoid repeating words:

My sneakers and **yours** are identical. (yours = your sneakers)
Her sister and **his** are in the same class. (his = his sister)
Your bike is blue, **mine** is red. (mine = my bike)
Our house and **theirs** are new. (theirs = their house)

Watch out!

We don't use possessive pronouns before nouns, or after another determiner:
I like **your** T-shirt. (possessive adjective)
Sam has a new backpack: it's red, like **yours**. (possessive pronoun)

▶ Exercise 6

1 Complete the text with the Present continuous of the verb in parentheses.

Hi! I ¹_____ (shop) in the city center with Megan today. At the moment I'm trying on some clothes. Right now I ²_____ (wear) a yellow top, jeans and trainers, but I'm not buying them. Megan ³_____ (choose) some jewelry in a shop opposite this one. She ⁴_____ (look for) her mom's birthday presents this week! Are you doing anything at the moment? Do you want to meet us? We ⁵_____ (not stay) here for much longer. I'm hungry and I ⁶_____ (think) about lunch! We're near Café Ten. Text me if you can come!

+   Send

2 Use the prompts to make questions and short answers using the Present continuous.

1 your dad / work / today / ?
A _____?
B Yes, _____.

2 your mom / cook dinner / now / ?
A _____?
B No, _____.

3 you and your friends / play football / ?
A _____?
B No, _____.

4 I / eat too many sweets / ?
A _____?
B No, _____.

5 the students / eat at the cafeteria / today / ?
A _____?
B Yes, _____.

6 Samuel / chat to his friends online / ?
A _____?
B Yes, _____.

3 Underline the correct alternative.

1 Please be quiet. We *watch / are watching* a documentary.
2 Phillip *plays / is playing* baseball every week for the school team.
3 I can't come out this evening. I *study / am studying* for the geography test.
4 What *do you do / are you doing* in the kitchen? You *make / are making* a real mess!
5 They *enjoy / are enjoying* pop music but they *don't listen / aren't listening* to it all the time.
6 It *takes / is taking* twenty minutes to get to the town center from the school.
7 *Do you buy / Are you buying* the same fashion magazine every week?
8 We *just sit / are just sitting* at home right now because it *rains / is raining* really heavily.

4 Complete the text with the Present simple or the Present continuous of the verbs in parentheses.

Omar   Where ¹_____ (you, work) at the moment?
Tim   On a farm in Argentina! My best friend ²_____ (stay) with me at the moment, too.
Omar   Do ³_____ (you, like) it there?
Tim   Oh yes, it's good fun. I ⁴_____ (prefer) the lifestyle in the countryside. It's calm and relaxing.
Omar   What things ⁵_____ (learn)?
Tim   We ⁶_____ (have) horseback riding lessons next week.
Omar   Wow, that sounds great! ⁷_____ (you, plan) to visit Patagonia?
Tim   Oh yes. I ⁸_____ (go) next month.

5 Use the prompts to make questions. Then write the answers using the word in parentheses.

1 Whose / those bikes / be? (they)
A _____?
B _____.

2 Whose / this book / be? (you)
A _____?
B _____.

3 Whose / this car / be? (we)
A _____?
B _____.

4 Whose / that digital camera / be? (I)
A _____?
B _____.

5 Whose / these jeans / be? (he)
A _____?
B _____.

6 Whose / this video game / be? (she)
A _____?
B _____.

6 Make questions using the first part of the prompts and *whose*. Then write the answers using the second part.

1 red scarf / Janine
_____? _____.

2 that backpack / Tom
_____? _____.

3 new car / my dad
_____? _____.

4 pencils / Mary
_____? _____.

5 purple socks / Martin
_____? _____.

6 black jacket / my sister
_____? _____.

Countable and uncountable nouns

Countable nouns have a singular and a plural form:
*I have a math **book** and two English **books** in my backpack.*
Uncountable nouns only have the singular form, but they never take the indefinite article (*a / an*):
*Is there **butter** and **sugar** in this recipe?*
*We need **time** to finish the job.*
To express a quantity with uncountable nouns, we can use phrases like *a piece of, a slice of, a bottle of*:
*That's **an interesting piece of news**.*
*I bought **a packet of spaghetti**.*

> ### Watch out!
>
> In English, these common nouns are uncountable: *furniture, homework, hair, money, news, spaghetti, advice, baggage, information.*
> *Our **homework** is really hard.*
> *Her **hair** is blonde.*

Some, any

We use *some* and *any* with plural countable nouns and uncountable nouns.
We use *some* in affirmative sentences:
*You need **some eggs** (countable) and **some flour** (uncountable) to make pasta.*

We use *any* in questions and negative sentences:
***Do** you have **any** bananas? (countable) I **don't** have **any snacks** for school. (countable)*
***Is there any** cheese? (uncountable) I **don't** eat **any** meat. (uncountable)*

We can use *some* in questions, especially when we expect the answer *yes*:
*Did your grandma give you **some** money for your birthday?*
*Would you like **some** coffee?*

Much, many, a lot of

With plural countable nouns we can use *many* or *a lot of* to express an undefined large quantity:
***Many / A lot of** doctors say daily physical activity is good for your health.*
*I don't eat **many / a lot of** sugary foods.*
*Did you buy **many / a lot of** burgers?*

With uncountable nouns we use *much* or *a lot of* to express an undefined large quantity. Note that we never use *much* in affirmative sentences:
*I have **a lot of information** about healthy diet.*
*There isn't **much / a lot of** time – we have to hurry!*
*Do you have **much / a lot of** work to do?*

A few, a little

To talk about small quantities, we use *a few* with plural countable nouns and *a little* with uncountable nouns:
*There are **a few types** of rice that cook in a couple of minutes!*
*Mom, can you give me **a little money** for a snack, please?*

How much / How many

We use *How much* with uncountable nouns and *How many* with countable nouns to ask about quantity:
***How much water** do you drink?*
***How many pizzas** are here?*

▶ Exercises 1-4

Imperatives

We use the base form of the verb for affirmative imperatives and *don't* + base form for negative imperatives.

We use imperatives to give instructions, orders and advice:
***Put** the shopping bag here.*
***Go away** and **don't come** back!*
***Don't drink** so much cola.*

We also use imperatives to make suggestions and requests:
***Try** this recipe: it's great!*
***Close** the door, please.*

Be / Don't be + adjective is a common imperative form:
***Be** careful or you'll fall over!*
***Don't be** late for the party.*

▶ Exercise 5

Verbs of preference

Verbs like *love, like, can't stand, hate* are called verbs of preference; they can be followed by
- a noun: *I **love pizza**!*
- an object pronoun: *Lara is my new classmate. I **like her**.*
- a verb in the *-ing* form: *Joe **hates doing** his homework.*

For the spelling rules of the *-ing* form, see Grammar reference 5.

▶ Exercises 6-7

1 Underline the correct alternative.

1 Can I have *any/some/an* hot chocolate, please?
2 We don't have *any/some/a* tomatoes. Can you buy *some/any/an* for me?
3 There isn't *any/some/a* sugar in the cupboard.
4 You need to do *any/some/a* physical activities.
5 When I cook a new dish, I don't ask for *any/some/an* advice: I want to do it alone.
6 Do you want *any/some/a* cup of tea without milk? There isn't *any/some/an* in the fridge.
7 Dad doesn't want *any/some/a* juice, but can you give him *any/some/a* bottle of water, please?
8 We really need *any/some/a* new furniture for the kitchen. There's nowhere to put all the food!

2 Complete each sentence with *some* or *any*.

1 There isn't _____ water in this bottle.
2 Bring _____ cheese to the picnic if you want.
3 We can't do without _____ rice or pasta!
4 Could you put _____ herbs into the soup?
5 Is there _____ juice in the fridge?
6 How about _____ sweets for the trip?

3 Complete the telephone conversation using ONE appropriate word in each space.

Dad Hi, Jamie. I'm in the supermarket, but I can't remember what Mom said we need. Can you check in the kitchen, please?
Jamie Ha ha... yes, no problem, Dad. What do you want to know?
Dad Do we have ¹ _____ eggs?
Jamie Hmm... there's only one. And there isn't ² _____ milk. I think we need ³ _____ orange juice, too, Dad.
Dad Right, OK. And what about vegetables?
Jamie Well, we have ⁴ _____ broccoli and ⁵ _____ carrots. But there aren't ⁶ _____ onions.
Dad Is there ⁷ _____ pasta?
Jamie We have ⁸ _____ brown pasta, but I don't really like that.
Dad Anything else?
Jamie Yes, can you get ⁹ _____ yogurt and ¹⁰ _____ packet of chocolate cookies, please? Oh, and there isn't ¹¹ _____ bread or cheese in the house and I'm really hungry!
Dad Eat ¹² _____ apple then, Jamie!
Jamie Hmmm. Remember the shopping list next time, Dad!!

4 Complete the sentences with *much* or *many*.

1 I don't know if I have _____ money left after my vacation.
2 There aren't _____ sports that you can do here.
3 Don't be sad: I don't think _____ people pass their driving test the first time!
4 There aren't _____ teachers in our school.
5 There wasn't _____ useful information online.
6 How _____ carrots and potatoes do you want?
7 There wasn't _____ news about the election.
8 How _____ physical exercise do you do?
9 How_____ students went on the school trip?
10 Did you invite _____ friends to the party?
11 How _____ rice do we need?
12 There isn't _____ tuna in my salad. It's boring!

5 Match the beginnings (1-6) to the endings (a-f) of the imperative sentences.

1 Don't cook   a ☐ any alcohol: it's bad for your health!
2 Eat   b ☐ some exercise everyday.
3 Don't drink   c ☐ up late at night.
4 Do   d ☐ your food in much oil.
5 Don't stay   e ☐ things that cause stress.
6 Avoid   f ☐ a balanced, healthy diet.

6 Write sentences with a verb of preference and the correct form of the words given.

1 Jason / ☺ / do / martial arts / after school
   _____

2 We / ☺☺ / go climbing / on weekends
   _____

3 Mom and I / ☹ / play / chess
   _____

4 William / ☹☹ / dance / at parties
   _____

5 I / ☺ / use / social media / to relax
   _____

7 Complete the conversation using the correct form of the verb in parentheses and the *-ing* form of the verbs from the box.

| be • dance • do • listen • play (x 3) • sing |

My sister and I are very different. I ¹ _____ (love) soccer. It's my favorite sport, but my sister Irene ² _____ (not like) it at all. Why ³ _____ (I / like) soccer? Because I ⁴ _____ (love) outside and competing in games. Instead, Irene ⁵ _____ (hate) any kind of physical activity! She's very musical though: she can play the violin, sing and dance. I'm so different! Of course I ⁶ _____ (like) to music, but I ⁷ _____ (not like) and I ⁸ _____ (can't stand) songs.

to be: Past simple

Affirmative	Negative
I was	I wasn't
You were	You weren't
He/She/It was	He/She/It wasn't
We were	We weren't
You were	You weren't
They were	They weren't

Interrogative	Short answers
Was I … ?	Yes, you were. / No, you weren't.
Were you … ?	Yes, I was. / No, I wasn't.
Was he/she/it … ?	Yes, he/she/it was. No, he/she/it wasn't.
Were we … ?	Yes, we were. / No, we weren't.
Were you … ?	Yes, you were. / No, you weren't.
Were they … ?	Yes, they were. No, they weren't.

We use the Past simple of *be* to talk about past states:
*I **was** sick last week.*
*He **wasn't** happy with the result.*
***Were** they at home yesterday?*

We often use past time expressions with the Past simple, like *last night, yesterday afternoon, in 2019, in June, on Monday, at 8 o'clock, three weeks ago, at midnight, two days ago*:
*We **went** to a new restaurant **last night**.*
*He **starred** in his first movie **in 2001**.*
*They **left** for Japan **yesterday morning**.*
*She **won** her first video game tournament **three days ago**.*

> **Watch out!**
>
> We use the Past simple of *be* with *born* to say when or where someone or something was born:
> *When **were** you **born**? I **was born** in 2007.*
> *K-pop **was born** in South Korea.*

▶ **Exercises 1-5**

Past simple

Affirmative
I worked
You worked
He/She/It worked
We worked
You worked
They worked

We use the Past simple to talk about finished actions in the past:
*I **walked** to school **yesterday**.*
*We **watched** this movie **last month**.*
*She **played** Snow White when she was at **primary school**.*

Regular verbs

We form the Past simple affirmative of regular verbs by adding *-ed* to the base form of the verb:
*call → call**ed**, work → work**ed**, play → play**ed***
*We **played** tennis this morning.*
*They **worked** hard yesterday.*

Note the spelling rules.
- If a verb ends in *-e*, we add *-d*:
  *live → live**d**, hate → hate**d***
  *My father **lived** in Argentina as a child.*
- If a verb ends in a consonant + *-y*, the *-y* changes to *-ied*:
  *try → tr**ied**, worry → worr**ied***
  *They **tried** to call you yesterday.*
- If a one-syllable verb ends in one vowel + one consonant, we double the consonant before adding *-ed*:
  *stop → stop**ped**; tap → tap**ped***
  *The teacher **tapped** on the screen and the app **stopped**.*

Irregular verbs

Unlike regular verbs, irregular verbs don't add *-ed* to the base form but have their own past form.

*He **went** to school by bus today.*
*Last week she **won** a prize.*
*Last term we **made** a movie for the final exam.*

See pages 142-143 for the Past simple affirmative form of irregular verbs.

▶ **Exercises 6-7**

1 Complete the sentences with the affirmative form of be in the Past simple.

1 We _____ in this classroom last year.
2 The weather _____ bad yesterday.
3 Last term my exams _____ difficult.
4 Jo and I _____ tired after school.
5 Megan _____ very happy last week.
6 I _____ nervous on the first day of school.

2 Rewrite the sentences from exercise 1 using the negative form.

1 _____ .
2 _____ .
3 _____ .
4 _____ .
5 _____ .
6 _____ .

3 Complete the sentences with the correct Past simple form of be.

1 My grandmother _____ a dentist for forty years, but now she's retired.
2 _____ your brother an assistant in a sports shop last summer?
3 The receptionist _____ in the hotel yesterday: it was closed.
4 Where _____ you and Liam last night?
5 _____ Carl and Sam at the doctor's yesterday?
6 Her grandparents _____ from the UK. They were from Canada.

4 Write questions for the answers given. Use Who, Why, When, Where, How many or What time and the Past simple form of be.

1 _____ ?
   I was at school at 7:45 a.m. this morning.
2 _____ ?
   She was at the police station last night.
3 _____ ?
   There were twenty students in the library.
4 _____ ?
   The receptionist was in the office.
5 _____ ?
   Last Wednesday we were in Europe.
6 _____ ?
   They were late because there was no bus.
7 _____ ?
   They were our new neighbors.
8 _____ ?
   My last vacation was last summer.

5 Use the prompts to make questions with be born. Then write answers that are true for you.

1 when / your mother / born
   _____ ?
   _____ .
2 where / you / born
   _____ ?
   _____ .
3 when / your best friend / born
   _____ ?
   _____ .
4 where / your / English teacher / born
   _____ ?
   _____ .
5 where / your / grandparents / born
   _____ ?
   _____ .

6 Write the Past simple of the irregular verbs.

1 buy _____
2 do _____
3 take _____
4 have _____
5 bring _____
6 come _____
7 go _____
8 get up _____
9 tell _____
10 put _____
11 eat _____
12 drink _____
13 write _____
14 make _____
15 read _____
16 give _____

7 Complete the sentences with the Past simple of the verbs from the box. Which verbs are irregular?

> arrive • change • go • help • learn • listen • miss
> paint • post • speak • teach • visit • wait

1 I _____ my sister in the hospital last night. She has a broken leg.
2 The students _____ to Miami on a school trip.
3 David _____ his mom to cook dinner.
4 We _____ our bedroom a green color.
5 Eliza _____ to her friend in New York on Skype last night.
6 We _____ planes on the way from Los Angeles to Chicago.
7 I _____ a comment about the game on Facebook this morning.
8 She _____ for the bus for 40 minutes, but it didn't come.
9 We _____ to ride our bikes years ago.
10 Miss Smith _____ math to me at primary school. She was a good teacher.
11 The students _____ late for the exam because they _____ their train.
12 We _____ to the band playing until midnight. The gig was fantastic.

Grammar reference

Past simple

Negative
I didn't work
You didn't work
He/She/It didn't work
We didn't work
You didn't work
They didn't work

Interrogative	Short answers
Did I work?	Yes, I did. / No, I didn't.
Did you work?	Yes, you did. / No, you didn't.
Did he/she/it work?	Yes, he/she/it did. No, he/she/it didn't.
Did we work?	Yes, we did. / No, we didn't.
Did you work?	Yes, you did. / No, you didn't.
Did they work?	Yes, they did. / No, they didn't.

For both regular and irregular verbs, we use the auxiliary *did + not* for the negative form followed by the base form of the verb:
We **didn't like** the concert.
I went to the reception desk but I **didn't see** anyone.
They **didn't watch** The X Factor final last night: the TV **didn't air** it.
Last summer, she **didn't go** on vacation to Acapulco with her family.

For both regular and irregular verbs, we use the auxiliary *did* for the interrogative form followed by the base form of the verb:
Did they **ask** a question about the exam?
What time **did** you **get up** today?
What team **did** he **play for** last year?
Did he **buy** a railcard for his last vacation?

▶ Exercises 1-5

could

Affirmative	Negative
I could	I couldn't
You could	You couldn't
He/She/It could	He/She/It couldn't
We could	We couldn't
You could	You couldn't
They could	They couldn't

Interrogative	Short answers
Could I?	Yes, I could. / No, I couldn't.
Could you?	Yes, you could. / No, you couldn't.
Could he/she/it?	Yes, he/she/it could. No, he/she/it couldn't.
Could we?	Yes, we could. / No, we couldn't.
Could you?	Yes, you could. / No, you couldn't.
Could they?	Yes, they could. / No, they couldn't.

We use *could*, the Past simple of *can*, to express ability and possibility or permission in the past.
It is followed by the base form of the verb and has the same form for all the persons:
I **could skate** when I was 5 years old!
When she was a child, my mom **could go** to school on foot alone.
Could you **stay up** late at weekends when you were a child?

We use *could + not* (*couldn't*) for the negative form:
Last year I **couldn't** buy the plane tickets for our vacation.
I invited them to join us at the campsite but they **couldn't** come.
We **couldn't use** our cell phones during the test.

▶ Exercise 6

1 Underline the correct alternative.

1 Did you *see / saw* Mel's new house yesterday?
2 We *didn't left / didn't leave* the beach resort for the whole vacation.
3 *Did Maria book / Does Maria booked* the tickets online?
4 Where *did you buy / did you bought* your new backpack?
5 Why did your family *move / moved* to Brazil last year?
6 Last summer my brother *find / found* a really nice apartment by the sea.

2 Complete the sentences with the Past simple of the verbs from the box.

live • eat • become • bring • forget • cost • ride • go

1 Rob _____ a doctor when he was 25.
2 Our vacation in the Caribbean _____ a fortune.
3 They _____ some drinks to the party.
4 We _____ through the woods to get to the lake.
5 I'm sorry, I _____ to tell you about it.
6 My grandparents _____ near the river.
7 Luis never _____ a motorbike when he was young.
8 We _____ a delicious lasagna at the new Italian restaurant.

3 Complete each sentence with the negative or affirmative form of the Past simple of the verb in parentheses.

1 Bill usually eats cereal for breakfast. (eat)
He _____ cereal yesterday.
He _____ toast.
2 Elijah usually wakes up at 7:00 a.m. (wake up)
He _____ at 7:00 a.m. yesterday.
He _____ at 8:00 a.m.
3 Annie usually takes a shower in the mornings. (take)
She _____ a shower yesterday morning.
She _____ a bath.
4 Jim and Claire usually read the Sunday newspaper. (read)
They _____ it last Sunday.
They _____ the news online.
5 Oscar usually leaves the house at 7:45 a.m. (leave)
He _____ at 7:45 a.m. today.
He _____ at 8:30 a.m.
6 Mom always buys presents for our birthday. (buy)
She _____ any presents this year.
Our dad _____ them all!

4 Put the words in the correct order to write questions and short answers.

1 you / Did / the computer / by yourself / repair / ? (✓)
_____
2 safely / Did / ship / they / your suitcase / ? (✓)
_____
3 the camping site / easy / Was it / to find / ? (✗)
_____
4 to the beach / Was / near / the youth hostel / ? (✗)
_____
5 speak English / on holiday / you met / Did / the people / ? (✓)
_____
6 arrive / on time / the train / Did / at the station / ? (✗)
_____

5 Use the prompts to write questions in the Past simple. Then write answers that are true for you.

1 What / you / do / yesterday evening / ?
_____
_____
2 Where / you / go / last summer / ?
_____
_____
3 When / your family / get up / today / ?
_____
_____
4 How / you / come / to school / today / ?
_____
_____
5 When / you / learn / to swim / ?
_____
_____
6 How / your birthday party / be / last year / ?
_____
_____

6 Complete the sentences with the correct form of *could*.

1 When I was young, I _____ play the violin: it was too difficult for me!
2 My grandfather _____ play chess and he was the best!
3 _____ they go abroad with their old passports?
4 We _____ board the train: the door was blocked.
5 It was very late when you got to the restaurant: _____ you eat?
6 Tom _____ run very fast when he was fifteen. Now he's improved.
7 When I called Emma, she arrived as fast as she _____.
8 Sorry, I _____ make it on time yesterday: the streets were jammed.

9 | Grammar reference

Comparative adjectives

We use comparative adjectives + *than* to compare two people, animals, places or things:
*Giraffes are **taller than** elephants.*
*Danny is **younger than** me.*
*The USA is **bigger than** the UK.*

We form the comparative of short adjectives like this.
- We add *-er* to the end of most one-syllable adjectives:
  *Winter is **colder than** fall.*
- If the adjective ends in *-e*, we add *-r*:
  *A ship is **larger than** a boat.*
- If the adjective ends in a single vowel + consonant, we double the consonant and add *-er*:
  *My friend Tony is **taller than** me.*

We add *-ier* to the end of two-syllable adjectives that end in consonant + *-y*:
*I think this blue dress is **prettier than** the floral one.*
*This suitcase is **heavier than** I expected.*

To form the comparative of most long adjectives (adjectives that have two or more syllables) we add *more* before them:
*The math test was **more difficult** than the art one.*
*Dr Smith's lectures are **more interesting** than Dr Jones'.*

> **Watch out!**
>
> Some adjectives have an irregular comparative form.
> *good* → *better*
> *bad* → *worse*
> *far* → *farther/further*

▶ Exercises 1-2

Superlative adjectives

We use superlative adjectives to say that something has more of a particular quality than others in the same group.
*Whales are **the heaviest** mammals on Earth.*
*This is **the coldest** period of the year.*

We normally use the definite article *the* before superlative adjectives.

We form the comparative of short adjectives like this.
- We add *-est* to the end of most one-syllable adjectives:
  *Lucy is **the fastest** runner of the team.*
- If the adjective ends in *-e*, we add *-st*:
  *A bank is **the safest** place to save your money.*
- If the adjective ends in a single vowel + consonant, we double the consonant and add *-est*:
  *Antarctica is **the biggest** desert in the world.*

We add *-iest* to the end of two-syllable adjectives that end in consonant + *-y*:
*Yesterday we watched **the scariest** movie ever!*

To form the superlatives of most long adjectives (adjectives that have two or more syllables) we add *most* before them.
*My mom's cakes are **the most delicious** thing on Earth!*

> **Watch out!**
>
> Some adjectives have an irregular superlative form.
> *good* → *the best*
> *bad* → *the worst*
> *far* → *the farthest/ the furthest*

▶ Exercises 3-4

(not) as ... as

We use *as* + adjective + *as* to say that two things are similar or equal:
*Math is **as difficult as** science.*
*My sister is **as tall as** me.*
We use *not as* + adjective + *as* to say that one thing has less of a quality than another:
*This orange cake is **not as sweet as** the chocolate one.*
*Your flowery dress is **not as beautiful as** your black one.*

▶ Exercise 5

too, (not) enough

We use *too* + adjective to say that the quality described is more than we want or need:
*I didn't like that coat. The fabric was **too heavy**.*
*Don't miss tomorrow's meeting: it's **too important**!*

> **Watch out!**
>
> Never use *much* before an adjective:
> *These shoes are too tight for me.* (NOT *too ~~much~~ tight*)

We use adjective + *enough* to say that the quality described is the right amount, and adjective + *not enough* to say that it isn't sufficient. Note that *enough* always follows the adjective:
*The teacher's instructions were **clear enough**.*
*We left before the fashion show ended: it was**n't interesting enough**.*

Expressions with *too* and *enough* are often followed by *to* + infinitive:
*The weather wasn't **warm enough to wear** a T-shirt.*

▶ Exercise 6

very, extremely

We use *very* and *extremely* to make adjectives stronger:
*Stella McCartney's new collection is **extremely expensive**.*

1 Complete the sentences with the correct comparative form of the adjectives from the box.

bad • busy • cold • comfortable • dangerous • difficult good • happy • quick • tall

1 In Italy, January is _____ than April.
2 My English is _____ now than it was last term. I've studied a lot!
3 I couldn't get a table in the restaurant. It was _____ than usual.
4 Skyscrapers are _____ than apartment blocks.
5 Tom passed his driving test this morning. He's _____ than he was yesterday!
6 I'm going to the doctor. My headache is _____ than before.
7 Cities are usually _____ than small towns: there is a lot of crime.
8 I don't understand this lesson. It is _____ than the last one we did.
9 I hate this school computer: it's really slow! My laptop is _____ than this.
10 My dad's office chair hurts his back. He wants to buy a _____ one.

2 Use the prompts to write comparative sentences.

1 biology / interesting / history
   _____
2 oranges / sweet / lemons
   _____
3 the afternoon / warm / the morning
   _____
4 my dog / friendly / your cat
   _____
5 the Andes / snow / the Rocky Mountains
   _____
6 my dad / old / my mom
   _____
7 my sneakers / fashionable / my other shoes
   _____
8 fruit juice / healthy / cola
   _____

3 Complete the sentences with the correct superlative form of the adjectives in parentheses.

1 I told you: John is _____ (smart) of us all.
2 This is _____ (good) cheesecake in the store.
3 Molly has a new pet: it's _____ (cute) kitten in the world!
4 Toby is _____ (intelligent) boy in our class.
5 Pedro knows _____ (funny) jokes!
6 Which is _____ (busy) city in the world?
7 I got _____ (bad) grades in the class.
8 Scott is _____ (tall) of the four friends.

4 Complete the sentences with the correct comparative or superlative form of the adjectives in parentheses.

1 His last movie is _____ (spectacular) of all!
2 Let's meet in the school library. It's _____ (quiet) than the other rooms.
3 My bedroom is _____ (warm) room in the house.
4 I think soccer is _____ (popular) sport in the world.
5 City life is _____ (exciting) than life in the countryside.
6 Martin is _____ (good) player of our baseball team.

5 Use the prompts to write sentences with (*not*) *as … as* that are true for you.

1 playing sports / watching TV (relaxing)
   _____
2 taking a test / writing an essay (stressful)
   _____
3 school lunch / lunch at home (tasty)
   _____
4 the weekend / weekdays (busy)
   _____
5 walking / taking the bus (enjoyable)
   _____
6 speaking English / reading English (easy)
   _____

6 Complete the second sentence with the words in parentheses so that it has the same meaning as the first sentence. Use *too* or *enough* each time.

1 The red car is too slow to win the race. (fast)
   The red car _____ to win the race.
2 The weather wasn't dry enough to play outside. (wet)
   The weather _____ to play outside.
3 There's the right amount of space in the classroom for two more desks. (big)
   The classroom _____ for two more desks.
4 The exam didn't seem easy enough to complete in an hour. (difficult)
   The exam _____ to complete in an hour.
5 Was the boy the right age to drive a moped? (old)
   Was the boy _____ to drive a moped?
6 We aren't tall enough to join the basketball team. (short)
   We're _____ to join the basketball team.

be going to

Affirmative	Negative
I am ('m) going to play.	I am not ('m not) going to play.
You are ('re) going to play.	You are not (aren't) going to play.
He/She/It is ('s) going to play.	He/She/It is not (isn't) going to play.
We are ('re) going to play.	We are not (aren't) going to play.
You are ('re) going to play.	You are not (aren't) going to play.
They are ('re) going to play.	They are not (aren't) going to play.

Interrogative	Short answers
Am I going to play?	Yes, you are. / No, you aren't.
Are you going to play?	Yes, I am. / No, I'm not.
Is he/she/it going to play?	Yes, he/she/it is. No, he/she/it isn't.
Are we going to play?	Yes, we are. / No, we aren't.
Are you going to play?	Yes, you are. / No, you aren't.
Are they going to play?	Yes, they are. / No, they aren't.

We use *be going to* + the base form of the main verb to talk about plans and future intentions:
*What **are you going to study** next year?*
*I'**m going to have** a party for my birthday this Friday.*
*Dad **isn't going to make** dinner tonight.*
***Are** we **going to eat** at that new sushi restaurant this weekend?*

The future form *be going to* is often used when there is evidence for a prediction, especially when it is expected to happen soon:
*We'**re going to buy** more food: Joe and Annie are coming to dinner.*
*Look out! You'**re going to drop** that bottle!*
*Why are you wearing your bikini? **Are** you **going to sunbathe** in the garden?*
*Look at those black clouds. I'**m not going to paint** the fence.*

▶ Exercises 1-3

Present simple and Present continuous for the future

We can also use the Present continuous to express future arrangements with a fixed time and place by adding a future time expression (*this evening, tomorrow, next week, ...*).
*I'**m meeting** Ann for dinner **on Friday evening**.*
*Mom'**s picking us up this afternoon** after the match.*

We generally prefer to use the Present continuous for fixed future plans and *be going to* for future intentions. Compare:
*I'**m studying** French.*
(Present continuous meaning 'now')
*I'**m studying** French with Lisa **next Monday**.*
(Present continuous + time expression = future plan)
*I'**m going to study** French more carefully.*
(*be going to* = future intention)

Future time expressions

When we use the Present continuous to talk about plans and arrangements for the future, we usually add some future time expressions to show that the action is not happening now:
*I'**m working** on my project. (= now)*
*I'**m working** on my project **next week**. (= future)*

Common future time expressions are *this afternoon, tonight, tomorrow, next week, in a month, next year* etc:
*I'**m studying** abroad **this summer**.*
*Mom **is making** her famous pizza **on Saturday evening**.*
*We **are moving** to the new house **in June**.*
*School **is ending in a month**!*

▶ Exercises 4-6

1 Complete each sentence with the correct form of *be going to* and a verb from the box.

| not eat • book • not buy • learn • not go • study |

1 Kate _____ to play the violin.
2 Michael _____ tonight. He had a big lunch.
3 Dad _____ me a new cell phone. I'm so upset!
4 _____ Meg and Al _____ the tickets online?
5 _____ your sister _____ travel and tourism at the university?
6 I'm _____ sightseeing tomorrow. I'm tired.

2 Mel and her mom are going on vacation. Put the words in the correct order and make questions.

1 are / going to / Mel and her mom / when / the airport / leave / for / ?
_____

2 time / are / what / arrive / going to / they / hotel / at / their / ?
_____

3 Mel / who / Paris / is / see / in / going to / ?
_____

4 going to / are / they / eat / what / ?
_____

5 visit / monuments / are / they / which / going to / ?
_____

6 return / when / going to / are / home / they / ?
_____

3 Now read Mel's diary and answer the questions from exercise 2.

> **Friday**
> • leave for the airport: 4:30 p.m.
> • arrive at the hotel: 9 p.m.
>
> **Saturday**
> • see my French cousins
> • try local food
> • visit the Eiffel tower
>
> **Sunday**
> • return home: 3 p.m.

1 _____
2 _____
3 _____
4 _____
5 _____
6 _____

4 Present continuous or *be going to*? Underline the correct alternative.

1 I've already decided. I *won't / am not going to* talk to him ever again!
2 You *are opening / are going to open* a new shop, so do you need an architect?
3 Hurry up. We *are leaving / are going to leave* on the 10:15 a.m. train.
4 I've bought this old bookshelf, because I *am going to repaint / am repainting* it.
5 Mom can't take you to football training. She *is having / is going to have* a job interview at 4:30 p.m.
6 'Where are you going?' 'To the backyard. I'*m cutting / am going to cut* the grass.'

5 Match the beginnings (1-6) of the sentences with their endings (a-f).

1 Don't forget!
2 'Can you lend me *The Hobbit* book?'
3 'Why are you buying so many cakes?'
4 'Please, can you give this DVD to Jaime?'
5 Let's meet at the station.
6 I'm so excited!

a ☐ 'We are going to have a party.'
b ☐ I am going on vacation to Europe tomorrow!
c ☐ 'Sorry, I can't. I am going to read it soon.'
d ☐ The boys are playing in Los Angeles next week.
e ☐ 'Yes, of course. I am seeing him this evening.'
f ☐ The train arrives at 7:25 p.m.

6 Complete the sentences with the correct form of Present simple, Present continuous or *be going to* and the verbs in parentheses.

1 Take an umbrella. It _____. (rain)
2 Don't hurry. The movie _____ at 7:30 p.m. (start)
3 I _____ to the concert tonight. I already have a ticket. (go)
4 'Why are you leaving? Are you finished?' 'No, I am not. But I _____ a break.' (take).
5 Louis can give Mom the box. He _____ her in the afternoon. (see)
6 The flight number AA 3018 _____ at 11:15 a.m. (leave)
7 Betty is going to driving lessons. And then she _____ a motorbike. (buy)
8 I can't eat anything today. I _____ an appointment at the hospital tomorrow. (have)
9 Fasten your seatbelts, please. The plane _____ in five minutes. (land)
10 They _____ another museum in our town on September 1st. (open)
11 I'm sorry. We can't come at 10 o'clock. We _____ a real estate agent. (meet)
12 I can't wait till tomorrow. We _____ to Acapulco. (fly)

beard (n.)

moustache (n.)

long (adj.) hair

short (adj.) hair

straight (adj.) hair

wavy (adj.) hair

curly (adj.) hair

bald (adj.)

braces (n.)

freckles (n.)

glasses (n.)

piercings (n.)

slim (adj.)

well-built (adj.)

Appearance

1 Match the words (1–8) to the definitions (a–h).

1	bald	a ☐	Someone who is not fat.
2	freckles	b ☐	Holes for jewelry on the face or body.
3	slim	c ☐	Someone with little or no hair.
4	glasses	d ☐	Hair that grows above a man's mouth.
5	beard	e ☐	Someone with a large, strong body.
6	piercings	f ☐	Small brown marks on the face and body.
7	well-built	g ☐	Something you wear to help you see.
8	moustache	h ☐	Hair that grows under a man's mouth.

2 Can you remember the meanings of these words related to appearance? Which are positive (+) and negative (-)? Which are neutral (N)?

good-looking ☐   handsome ☐   overweight ☐   plain ☐
pretty ☐   short ☐   tall ☐   thin ☐   ugly ☐

3 Read the description of Ed Sheeran and answer the questions.

Ed Sheeran is a British musician. He was born in February 1991 in England. He isn't very tall and he's a bit overweight, but I think he's quite good-looking.

He has short, red hair, a beard and a moustache. His eyes are blue and he has glasses. He sings and he plays the guitar. In my opinion, 'Perfect' is his best song.

1 Where is Ed Sheeran from?

_____

2 How old is he?

_____

3 Is he very slim?

_____

4 What kind of hair does he have?

_____

5 What color are his eyes?

_____

4 Write a paragraph (about 80 words) describing yourself. Use the text about Ed Sheeran to help you. Include:

- where you are from and your age
- your build (tall, short, slim...)
- your hair (color, type...), eyes and other features
- an interesting fact about yourself

Rooms & furniture

1 Write the name of a room where people normally do each of these activities.

1 cook a meal _____
2 watch TV _____
3 sleep _____
4 have a wash _____
5 prepare food _____
6 keep documents _____
7 put umbrellas _____
8 have dinner _____
9 keep clothes _____
10 clean teeth _____
11 write an email _____
12 relax and chat _____
13 enter the house _____
14 eat meals _____

2 Delete one item that you would never find in each room.

3 Write a paragraph (80–100 words) describing your home. Include:

- what rooms there are
- a description of your bedroom
- what you like/don't like about your home

bedroom

bathroom

dining room

kitchen

living room

hallway

study

architect

artist

builder

cleaner

dentist

farmer

fire fighter

hairdresser

journalist

lawyer

mechanic

nurse

office worker

photographer

police officer

politician

receptionist

sales assistant

Jobs

1 Complete with the names of the jobs in the pictures. Some can go in more than one category.

Jobs ...
1 where you often work outside: _____
_____
2 where you often work alone: _____
_____
3 that can be dangerous: _____
_____
4 that are creative: _____
_____
5 where you meet a lot of people: _____
_____
6 where you help people: _____
_____

2 Look at the pictures. Which person...

1 works in agriculture? _____
2 works in politics? _____
3 greets people in a hotel? _____
4 examines and repairs teeth? _____
5 interviews people? _____
6 helps people accused of crimes? _____
7 draws and paints pictures? _____
8 takes photos? _____
9 cleans offices and houses? _____
10 works in a hospital? _____
11 sells things in a shop? _____
12 arrests criminals? _____

3 Write a paragraph (80–100 words) describing the jobs that some of your relatives (parents, uncles, aunts...) do. Include:

- the name of the job and where they work
- what activities they do for this job
- whether you would like to do the job

Remember!

unemployed = without a job
retired = without a job because of old age

With the economic crisis, many young people are unemployed.
My grandfather was a doctor, but now he's retired.

Daily routine

catch the bus

do homework

finish classes

get dressed

get up

go to bed

go to school

have a break

take a shower

have breakfast

have lunch

have dinner

leave home

meet friends

relax

start classes

wake up

watch TV

1 **Number the activities in the order in which you normally do them on a school day.**

a ☐ catch the bus
b ☐ do my homework
c ☐ finish classes
d ☐ get dressed
e ☐ get up
f ☐ go to bed
g ☐ leave home
h ☐ take a shower
i ☐ have breakfast
j ☐ start classes
k ☐ wake up
l ☐ watch TV

2 **Complete each sentence with the correct form of a suitable daily routine verb.**

1 I always _____ at 6 a.m. when my alarm clock rings.
2 Tom usually _____ in the school cafeteria at 1 p.m.
3 In the mornings Mom and I _____ together, but my dad usually eats before we wake up.
4 Every Saturday afternoon, I _____ and together we go to the town center.
5 On Sundays, ____ you _____ later than on school days?
6 Joe's dad wakes him up at 8 a.m, but he never _____ before 8:30.
7 I always choose my clothes and then _____ before I have breakfast.
8 After school, Sarah _____ (usually math!) on her laptop for an hour.

3 **Complete Max's email to a foreign exchange student with suitable expressions.**

> ● ○ ○ ✉ ↩ reply
>
> Hi,
> I can't wait to meet you when you come for the school exchange trip next month! Here's the information you wanted about my typical school day here in Lima. Mom ¹ _____ me _____ early, at 6:30 every morning. 😣 First, I take a shower and I ² _____ in my (horrible!) school uniform. Then I ³ _____ with my sister: usually cereal with milk. We ⁴ _____ at 9 a.m. and we have eight lessons every day.
> At 10:15 we ⁵ _____ for fifteen minutes so I usually go outside with my friends. Then, at 12:45 we ⁶ _____ : I sometimes eat in the school cafeteria, but usually my mom gives me sandwiches. My favorite day is Thursday because we do sport in the afternoon. We ⁷ _____ at 3:15 p.m., but I don't always go straight home. I usually go to my friend Jorge's house and we ⁸ _____ together. When you and the other foreign students come here, I hope the teachers will give us less homework!!
> See you next month,
> Max

4 **Write a paragraph (80–100 words) describing your school day. Include:**

- when you get up, have breakfast, etc
- how you get to school
- your lessons and your favorite day

art

cafeteria

classroom

computer room

drama

English

geography

gym

principal's office

history

information technology (IT)

laboratory

library

math

music

physical education (PE)

science

student lounge

School

1 Write the words from the pictures in the correct category.

Subjects	Places

2 Complete this virtual guide to Springfield High School with the correct words from exercise 1.

| ALUMNI | SCHOOL APP SUPPORT | LEARNING PLATFORM | WORK FOR US | ADMISSIONS | CONTACT US |

| About Us | Academic Results | School Life | Learning | Extra Curricular | Houses |

Welcome to Springfield School! Here is a quick virtual guide to help you find your way around!

As you enter the school you pass the ¹ _____ - so don't run or shout!

On the ground floor there are two ² _____ for ³ _____, with male and female changing rooms and easy access to the playing fields outside. At the back of the school is the ⁴_____ for lunch and a ⁵ _____ for relaxing with your classmates.

On the first floor there are ⁶ _____ for ⁷ _____ experiments and three ⁸ _____ you can use in the breaks for any ⁹ _____ work or online research. There is also a ¹⁰ _____ for reading or quiet study on this floor.

On each floor there is a map showing you the location of all the other ¹¹ _____ including the ¹² _____ room for acting classes.

3 Write an online virtual guide to your school or college (80 -100 words). Include information about:

- where all the important rooms and areas are
- how many specialist rooms there are and where you can find them
- what you can do and where

Food & drink

1 Complete the mind maps with the names of the food and drink in the photos. *Milk* can go in two categories.

onions

Vegetables

Fruit

Dairy

Cereals

Sweet things

Meat

Fish

Drinks

apples

cookies

bread

butter

cheese

chicken

chocolate

coffee

eggs

hamburger

honey

juice

milk

onions

oranges

pasta

potatoes

rice

salad

salmon

spinach

strawberries

sugar

tea

tomatoes

tuna

yogurt

2 Write a paragraph (about 80 words) describing your eating habits. Include:

- what you usually have for breakfast, lunch and dinner
- what other things you eat or drink during the day
- your favorite things to eat and drink

audience

award

comedian

costumes

documentary

dressing room

filmmaker

performance

playwright

presenter

talent show

reporter

script

set

sitcom

soundtrack

stage

studio producer

theater

TV series

Entertainment

1 Complete the mind maps with the words in the pictures.

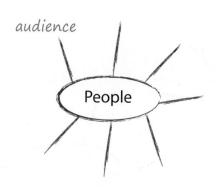

audience

People

Places

Things

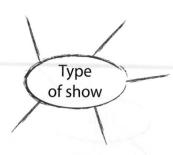

Type of show

2 Write a review (80-100 words) for a TV or theater show you saw. Include:

- what you saw when and where
- who wrote it or was in it
- what you particularly liked about it

Vacations

1 Write a type of vacation or accommodation for each definition.

1 A place where you can stay in a tent, a campervan or a chalet. _____

2 A cheap hotel with very simple facilities, popular with young backpackers. _____

3 A vacation where you travel from place to place by car. _____

4 A small traditional house or villa. _____

5 A vacation near the sea. _____

6 A place to stay that is on water. _____

7 A winter vacation in the snow. _____

8 A small hotel, often owned by a family. _____

9 A small house, often made of wood, for a vacation at the sea or in the mountains. _____

10 A vacation where you can practice speaking to people of a different nationality. _____

2 Last month Andy spent a week with a family in Berlin, Germany. Complete the website reviews with the words in the box.

apartment • city • exchange • vacation • hotel • sightseeing • walking

Review your guest

Andy was a great guest. He was on a language ¹ _____ and his German is not bad. Most days he explored the ² _____ on his own. We gave him a map and he went ³ _____ in Berlin. At the weekend, I offered to be his guide. He enjoyed staying in my home with my family for his ⁴ _____. He said it was better than staying in a ⁵ _____.

Review your host

I stayed in Ingrid's vacation ⁶ _____ with her and her family. It's in the city center: perfect! Ingrid was a great host and I think my German improved a lot. On the weekend, I really wanted to go ⁷ _____ in the park, but she took me to some museums instead. Not really my thing, so the other days I borrowed a map and explored on my own. Berlin is a great city!

3 Write a paragraph (80-100 words) describing your last, or best, vacation. Include:

• what type of vacation it was and who you went with
• where you went and the type of accommodation you stayed in
• what you did while you were on vacation

activity vacation

beach vacation

camping vacation

driving vacation

language exchange

sightseeing vacation

skiing vacation

walking vacation

B&B (bed and breakfast)

campsite

campervan

chalet

cottage

vacation apartment

hotel

houseboat

tent

youth hostel

Clothes

1 Write the name of an article of clothing or an accessory from this page next to each sentence.

1 It can be very heavy when it's full of books!

_____

2 It stops your pants from falling down! _____

3 Girls (and some Scottish men!) wear this. _____

4 They protect your eyes ... and they look cool!

_____

5 Use it to tell the time (when your cell phone is broken!) _____

6 Cover your head with one in winter for the cold ... and in summer for the sun! _____

7 Decorate your hands with these ... and wear a gold one when you get married! _____

8 Casual pants invented in 1873 by Levi Strauss!

_____

Accessories

bracelet   necklace   earrings

sunglasses   watch   ring

2 Complete the email with the words from the box.

coat • hat • jeans • sandals • shorts • socks
sneakers • T-shirts

○○○   ✉   ↩ reply

Hi Molly,
Well, here I am in Detroit visiting my Dad. It's a great city, but there's one bad thing: the weather.
Today I'm wearing a warm [1] _____ on my head, a jumper, and my Dad's winter [2] _____ ... and I'm inside the house! The heating is broken and it's really cold!
And, believe it or not, I forgot to bring my favorite Nike [3] _____, so I'm wearing my summer [4] _____ on my feet – without [5] _____, of course!
I was expecting the sun, so I have three pairs of [6] _____ and lots of [7] _____ in my bag.
No pants, not even my [8] _____!
Before coming here, Mom offered to pack my bag for me but I refused. Never again!
Harry

3 Write a paragraph (about 80 words) describing your clothes. Include:

* what your favorite clothes are
* what you are wearing today
* what you usually wear to school

backpack   dress   coat   T-shirt   shirt

pants

sock   sneaker   shoe

jacket   hat   scarf

hoodie   pullover

shorts   glove   skirt

belt

sandal   boot   jeans   pumps

Education

grammar

qualifications

a degree

a dictionary

a language course

a school project

a translation

an essay

the bell

the pronunciation

the meaning

the roll

1 Write the correct words to complete the expressions.

1 attend _____
2 call _____
3 do _____, _____
4 focus on _____
5 get _____, _____

6 learn _____
7 look words up in _____
8 practice _____
9 ring _____
10 write _____

2 Complete Bethany's blog post with the missing words.

Here's how I'm going to live and work in Japan one day:
I'm going to ¹ _____ a language course this year and
² _____ the basics of Japanese.
Then I'm going to find an app to ³ _____ the pronunciation
(because I know it's hard!).
I'm going to ⁴ _____ a daily translation of all my favorite
manga cartoons by looking up ⁵ _____ I don't know in a
dictionary so I can ⁶ _____ the meaning.
Then I'm going to ⁷ _____ on grammar and ⁸ _____
some qualifications in spoken Japanese first before going on to get
a ⁹ _____ in Japanese and write – ¹⁰ _____ and stuff.
Simple, no? 😊

3 Write a blog about your future learning plan (80-100 words).
Include:

- what you are going to learn
- how you are going to learn it
- what you are going to do with your new skills

Irregular Verbs

Base form	Past simple	Past participle	Translation
be /biː/	was /wɒz/ were /wə/	been /biːn/	
become /bɪˈkʌm/	became /bɪˈkeɪm/	become /bɪˈkʌm/	
begin /bɪˈgɪn/	began /bɪˈgan/	begun /bɪˈgʌn/	
break /breɪk/	broke /brəʊk/	broken /ˈbrəʊk(ə)n/	
bring /brɪŋ/	brought /brɔːt/	brought /brɔːt/	
build /bɪld/	built /bɪlt/	built /bɪlt/	
buy /bʌɪ/	bought /bɔːt/	bought /bɔːt/	
catch /katʃ/	caught /kɔːt/	caught /kɔːt/	
choose /tʃuːz/	chose /ˈtʃəʊz/	chosen /ˈtʃəʊzn/	
come /kʌm/	came /keɪm/	come /kʌm/	
cost /kɒst/	cost /kɒst/	cost /kɒst/	
cut /kʌt/	cut /kʌt/	cut /kʌt/	
do /duː/	did /dɪd/	done /dʌn/	
draw /drɔː/	drew /druː/	drawn /drɔːn/	
dream /driːm/	dreamed /driːmd/ dreamt /dremt/	dreamed /driːmd/ dreamt /dremt/	
drink /drɪŋk/	drank /draŋk/	drunk /drʌŋk/	
drive /drʌɪv/	drove /drəʊv/	driven /ˈdrɪvn/	
eat /iːt/	ate /eɪt/	eaten /ˈiːt(ə)n/	
fall /fɔːl/	fell /fɛl/	fallen /ˈfɔːlən/	
feel /fiːl/	felt /fɛlt/	felt /fɛlt/	
fight /fʌɪt/	fought /fɔːt/	fought /fɔːt/	
find /fʌɪnd/	found /faʊnd/	found /faʊnd/	
fly /flʌɪ/	flew /fluː/	flown /fləʊn/	
forget /fəˈgɛt/	forgot /fəˈgɒt/	forgotten /fəˈgɒtn/	
forgive /fəˈgɪv/	forgave /fəˈgeɪv/	forgiven /fə(r)ˈgɪv(ə)n/	
get /gɛt/	got /gɒt/	got /gɒt/ gotten /ˈgɒt(ə)n/	
give /gɪv/	gave /geɪv/	given /ˈgɪv(ə)n/	
go /gəʊ/	went /wɛnt/	gone /gɒn/	
grow /grəʊ/	grew /gruː/	grown /grəʊn/	
have /hav/	had /həd/	had /həd/	
hear /hɪə/	heard /hɜːˈ(r)d/	heard /hɜːˈ(r)d/	
hit /hɪt/	hit /hɪt/	hit /hɪt/	
keep /kiːp/	kept /kɛpt/	kept /kɛpt/	
know /nəʊ/	knew /njuː/	known /nəʊn/	
learn /ləːn/	learned /ˈləːnɪd/ learnt /lɜːˈ(r)nt/	learned /ˈləːnɪd/ learnt /lɜːˈ(r)nt/	
leave /liːv/	left /lɛft/	left /lɛft/	

Base form	Past simple	Past participle	Translation
lend /lɛnd/	lent /lɛnt/	lent /lɛnt/	
let /lɛt/	let /lɛt/	let /lɛt/	
lose /luːz/	lost /lɒst/	lost /lɒst/	
make /meɪk/	made /meɪd/	made /meɪd/	
mean /miːn/	meant /mɛnt/	meant /mɛnt/	
meet /miːt/	met /mɛt/	met /mɛt/	
pay /peɪ/	paid /peɪd/	paid /peɪd/	
put /pʊt/	put /pʊt/	put /pʊt/	
read /riːd/	read /rɛd/	read /rɛd/	
ride /raɪd/	rode /rəʊd/	ridden /ˈrɪdn/	
ring /rɪŋ/	rang /raŋ/	rung /rʌŋ/	
run /rʌn/	ran /ræn/	run /rʌn/	
say /seɪ/	said /sɛd/	said /sɛd/	
see /siː/	saw /sɔː/	seen /siːn/	
sell /sɛl/	sold /səʊld/	sold /səʊld/	
send /sɛnd/	sent /sɛnt/	sent /sɛnt/	
show /ʃəʊ/	showed /ʃəʊd/	showed /ʃəʊd/ shown /ʃəʊn/	
shut /ʃʌt/	shut /ʃʌt/	shut /ʃʌt/	
sing /sɪŋ/	sang /sæŋ/	sung /sʌŋ/	
sit /sɪt/	sat /sat/	sat /sat/	
sleep /sliːp/	slept /slɛpt/	slept /slɛpt/	
speak /spiːk/	spoke /spəʊk/	spoken /ˈspəʊk(ə)n/	
spend /spɛnd/	spent /spɛnt/	spent /spɛnt/	
stand /stand/	stood /stʊd/	stood /stʊd/	
swim /swɪm/	swam /swam/	swum /swʌm/	
take /teɪk/	took /tʊk/	taken /ˈteɪkən/	
teach /tiːtʃ/	taught /tɔːt/	taught /tɔːt/	
tell /tɛl/	told /təʊld/	told /təʊld/	
think /θɪŋk/	thought /θɔːt/	thought /θɔːt/	
throw /θrəʊ/	threw /θrəʊn/	thrown /θrəʊn/	
understand /ʌndəˈstand/	understood /ʌndəˈstʊd/	understood /ʌndəˈstʊd/	
wake /weɪk/	woke /wəʊk/	woken /ˈwəʊkən/	
wear /wɛː/	wore /wɔː/	worn /wɔːn/	
win /wɪn/	won /wʌn/	won /wʌn/	
write /rʌɪt/	wrote /rəʊt/	written /ˈrɪtn/	

Punctuation & Phonetics

Punctuation Guide

A	capital letter
a	lower case
.	period (British English: full stop)
,	comma
:	colon
;	semicolon
'	apostrophe
?	question mark
!	exclamation point (British English: exclamation mark)
-	hyphen
-	dash
...	dots / ellipsis
/	slash
" "	quotation / speech marks
( )	parentheses (British English: brackets)
[ ]	brackets (British English: square brackets)
aaa	italics
aaa	bold
&	ampersand (= and)
*	asterisk
#	hash sign
@	at

Alphabet and phonetics

A	/eɪ/	**B**	/biː/	**C**	/siː/	**D**	/diː/	**E**	/iː/	**F**	/ef/	**G**	/dʒiː/	**H**	/eɪtʃ/	**I**	/aɪ/
J	/dʒeɪ/	**K**	/keɪ/	**L**	/l/	**M**	/m/	**N**	/n/	**O**	/əʊ/	**P**	/piː/	**Q**	/kjuː/	**R**	/ɑː/
S	/es/	**T**	/tiː/	**U**	/juː/	**V**	/viː/	**W**	/ˈdʌbljuː/	**X**	/eks/	**Y**	/waɪ/	**Z**	/zed/		

Vowels

/iː/	s**ee**	/i/	happ**y**	/æ/	c**a**t	/ʌ/	j**u**mp	/ɔː/	f**our**	/ɒ/	g**o**t	/ə/	th**e**
/ɪ/	**i**t	/e/	b**e**d	/ɑː/	f**a**ther	/ʊ/	l**oo**k	/u/	us**u**ally	/uː/	tw**o**	/ɜː/	p**ur**ple

Diphthongs

/eɪ/	d**ay**	/aʊ/	n**ow**
/aɪ/	n**i**ne	/ɪə/	h**ear**
/ɔɪ/	b**oy**	/eə/	h**air**
/əʊ/	g**o**	/ʊə/	t**our**

Consonants

/p/	**p**en	/k/	**c**ar	/θ/	**th**ink	/ʃ/	**sh**e	/tʃ/	**ch**air	/ŋ/	si**ng**
/b/	**b**ook	/ɡ/	**g**ive	/ð/	**th**is	/ʒ/	vi**si**on	/dʒ/	**j**uice	/r/	**r**un
/t/	**t**able	/f/	**f**ive	/s/	**s**it	/h/	**h**e	/m/	**m**e	/l/	**l**ook
/d/	**d**esk	/v/	**v**ery	/z/	**z**oo	/w/	**w**e	/n/	**n**o	/j/	**y**ou

be – Present simple

Affirmative Form		Negative Form	
Full	**Short**	**Full**	**Short**
I am	I'm	I am not	I'm not
you are	you're	you are not	you aren't
he / she / it is	he's / she's / it's	he / she / it is not	he / she / it isn't
we are	we're	we are not	we aren't
you are	you're	you are not	you aren't
they are	they're	they are not	they aren't

Interrogative Form	Short Answers	
	Affirmative	**Negative**
Am I... ?	Yes, you are.	No, you aren't.
Are you... ?	Yes, I am.	No, I am not.
Is he / she / it... ?	Yes, he / she / it is.	No, he / she / it isn't.
Are we... ?	Yes, we are.	No, we aren't.
Are you... ?	Yes, you are.	No, you aren't.
Are they... ?	Yes, they are.	No, they aren't.

be – Past simple

Affirmative Form	Negative Form	
	Full	**Short**
I was	I was not	I wasn't
you were	you were not	you weren't
he / she / it was	he / she / it was not	he / she / it wasn't
we were	we were not	we weren't
you were	you were not	you weren't
they were	they were not	they weren't

Interrogative Form	Affirmative Short Answers	Negative Short Answers
Was I... ?	Yes, you were.	No, you weren't.
Were you... ?	Yes, I was.	No, I wasn't.
Was he... / she... ? / it... ?	Yes, he / she / it was.	No, he / she / it wasn't.
Were we... ?	Yes, we were.	No, we weren't.
Were you... ?	Yes, you were.	No, you weren't.
Were they... ?	Yes, they were.	No, they weren't.

can, can't

Affirmative Form	Negative Form	Interrogative Form	Short answers	
			Affirmative	**Negative**
I can play	I can't play	Can I play?	Yes, you can.	No, you can't.
You can play	You can't play	Can you play?	Yes, I can.	No, I can't.
He/She/It can play	He/She/It can't play	Can he/she/it play?	Yes, he/she/it can.	No, he/she/it can't.
We can play	We can't play	Can we play?	Yes, we can.	No, we can't.
You can play	You can't play	Can you play?	Yes, you can.	No, you can't.
They can play	They can't play	Can they play?	Yes, they can.	No, they can't.

Could, couldn't

Affirmative Form	Negative Form	Interrogative Form	Short answers	
			Affirmative	**Negative**
I could	I couldn't	Could I?	Yes, you could.	No, you couldn't.
You could	You couldn't	Could you?	Yes, I could.	No, I couldn't.
He/She/It could	He/She/It couldn't	Could he/she/it?	Yes, he/she/it could.	No, he/she/it couldn't.
We could	We couldn't	Could we?	Yes, we could.	No, we couldn't.
You could	You couldn't	Could you?	Yes, you could.	No, you couldn't.
They could	They couldn't	Could they?	Yes, they could.	No, they couldn't.

Verb Tables

Present simple – Regular Verbs

Affirmative Form	Negative Form	
	Full	**Short**
I live.	I do not live.	I don't live.
You live.	You do not live.	You don't live.
He / She / It lives.	He / She / It does not live.	He / She / It doesn't live.
We live.	We do not live.	We don't live.
You live.	You do not live.	You don't live.
They live.	They do not live.	They don't live.

Interrogative Form	Short Answers	
	Affirmative	**Negative**
Do I live...?	Yes, you do.	No, you don't.
Do you live...?	Yes, I do.	No, I don't.
Does he / she / it live...?	Yes, he / she / it does.	No, he / she / it doesn't.
Do we live...?	Yes, we do.	No, we don't.
Do you live...?	Yes, you do.	No, you don't.
Do they live...?	Yes, they do.	No, they don't.

Present continuous

Affirmative Form	Negative Form	
	Full	**Short**
I am walking.	I am not walking.	I'm not walking.
You are walking.	You are not walking.	You aren't walking.
He / She / It is walking.	He / She / It is not walking.	He / She / It isn't walking.
We are walking.	We are not walking.	We aren't walking.
You are walking.	You are not walking.	You aren't walking.
They are walking.	They are not walking.	They aren't walking.

Interrogative Form	Short Answers	
	Affirmative	**Negative**
Am I walking?	Yes, you are.	No, you aren't.
Are you walking?	Yes, I am.	No, I'm not.
Is he / she / it walking?	Yes, he / she / it is.	No, he / she / it isn't.
Are we walking?	Yes, we are.	No, we aren't.
Are you walking?	Yes, you are.	No, you aren't.
Are they walking?	Yes, they are.	No, they aren't.

Spelling variations

Spelling rules for the Present simple third person

-ch, -sh, -ss, -x, -zz, -o	watch	wash	kiss	relax	buzz	do
-es	watch**es**	wash**es**	kiss**es**	relax**es**	buzz**es**	do**es**

consonant + -y	study	vowel + -y	play
-ies	stud**ies**	**-s**	play**s**

Present continuous spelling rules

Base form	eat	play	study	have	stop	lie
-ing form	eat**ing**	play**ing**	study**ing**	hav**ing**	stop**ping**	ly**ing**

Past simple – Regular verbs

Affirmative Form	Negative Form	
	Full	Short
I walked.	I did not walk.	I didn't walk.
You walked.	You did not walk.	You didn't walk.
He / She / It walked.	He / She / It did not walk.	He / She / It didn't walk.
We walked.	We did not walk.	We didn't walk.
You walked.	You did not walk.	You didn't walk.
They walked.	They did not walk.	They didn't walk.

Interrogative Form	Short Answers	
	Affirmative	Negative
Did I walk?	Yes, you did.	No, you didn't.
Did you walk?	Yes, I did.	No, I didn't.
Did he / she / it walk?	Yes, he / she / it did.	No, he / she / it didn't.
Did we walk?	Yes, we did.	No, we didn't.
Did you walk?	Yes, you did.	No, you didn't.
Did they walk?	Yes, they did.	No, they didn't.

Past simple – Irregular verbs: *to go*

Affirmative Form	Negative Form	
	Full	Short
I went.	I did not go.	I didn't go.
You went.	You did not go.	You didn't go.
He/She/It went.	He/She/It did not go.	He/She/It didn't go.
We went.	We did not go.	We didn't go.
You went.	You did not go.	You didn't go.
They went.	They did not go.	They didn't go.

Interrogative Form	Short answers	
	Affirmative	Negative
Did I go?	Yes, you did.	No, you didn't.
Did you go?	Yes, I did.	No, I didn't.
Did he/she/it go?	Yes, he/she/it did.	No, he/she/it didn't.
Did we go?	Yes, we did.	No, we didn't.
Did you go?	Yes, you did.	No, you didn't.
Did they go?	Yes, they did.	No, they didn't.

be going to

Affirmative Form		Negative Form	
Full	Short	Full	Short
I am going to walk.	I'm going to walk.	I am not going to walk.	I'm not going to walk.
You are going to walk.	You're going to walk.	You are not going to walk.	You aren't going to walk.
He / She / It is going to walk.	He / She / It's going to walk.	He / She / It is not going to walk.	He / She / It isn't going to walk.
We are going to walk.	We're going to walk.	We are not going to walk.	We aren't going to walk.
You are going to walk.	You're going to walk.	You are not going to walk.	You aren't going to walk.
They are going to walk.	They're going to walk.	They are not going to walk.	They aren't going to walk.

Interrogative Form	Short Answers	
	Affirmative	Negative
Am I going to walk...?	Yes, you are.	No, you aren't.
Are you going to walk...?	Yes, I am.	No, I'm not.
Is he / she / it going to walk...?	Yes, he / she / it is.	No, he / she / it isn't.
Are we going to walk... ?	Yes, we are.	No, we aren't.
Are you going to walk... ?	Yes, you are.	No, you aren't.
Are they going to walk... ?	Yes, they are.	No, they aren't.

Map of the United Kingdom of Great Britain and Northern Ireland

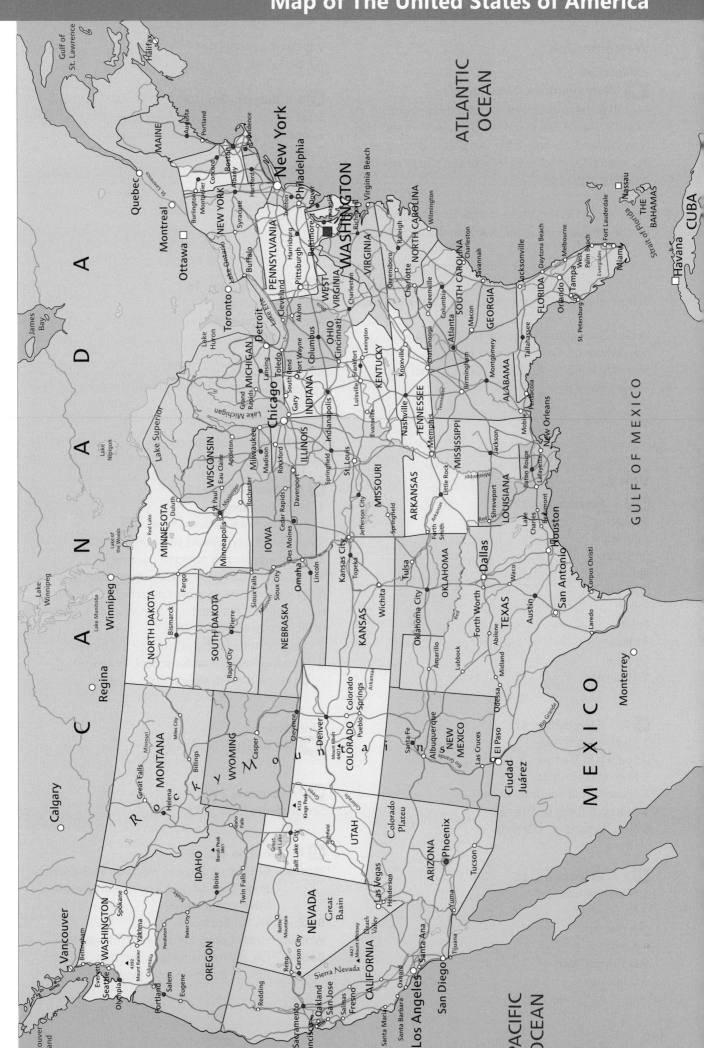

Audioscripts and videoscripts

Welcome Unit

Videoscript
 **Many countries, one language**

English is the language of the 'English speaking World' – the United Kingdom, the USA, Australia and New Zealand. It's one of the two official languages in Canada, together with French, and also in Ireland, together with Irish.

What about the rest of the world? English is the official language in Liberia, Kenya and South Africa.

In South America, it's the official language in Guyana.

People speak English also in Nigeria, Ghana and India.

English is an official language or lingua franca somewhere on every continent in the world! And there are millions of students, like you, that study English every day.

Unit 1

🔊 1 Exercise 1 p. 12
Mexican
American
Brazilian
Italian
Spanish
British
Polish
Turkish
Chinese
Vietnamese

🔊 2 Exercise 3 p. 12
1 Thailand is in Asia.
2 Spain is in Europe.
3 Nigeria is in Africa.
4 Ecuador is in South America.
5 Alaska is in North America.
6 New Zealand is in Oceania.

🔊 3 Exercise 2 p. 16
1 H blonde hair
2 G curly hair
3 A glasses
4 F a beard
5 D straight hair
6 C freckles

7 B long hair
8 E blue eyes

🔊 4 Exercise 3 p. 16
1 tall
2 short
3 slim
4 round
5 pretty
6 good-looking
7 young
8 old

🔊 5 Exercise 4 p. 16
Jim – grandfather
Margaret – grandmother
Lisa – mother
Colin – father
Richard – uncle
Louise – aunt
Rachel – sister
Josh – brother
Gemma, Joe and Mark – cousin

🔊 6 Exercise 5 p. 16
1 'Mom, I'm hungry.'
  'Your sandwich is on the table.'
2 Are you thirsty? Would you like a drink?
3 My little brother is afraid of the dark.
4 I'm so cold. Can you close the door, please?
5 Please open the window. I'm so hot!
6 'So, Zurich is the capital of Switzerland. Am I right?'
  'No, you're wrong. It's Bern.'
7 I have no time for breakfast, I'm in a hurry!
8 'Morning Paulie, time for school, wake up!'
  'Oh no please! I'm sleepy!'

Videoscript
 See Student's Book p. 17

🔊 7 Exercise 2 p. 18
See Student's Book p. 18

🔊 8 Exercise 4 p. 19
Woman Good morning and welcome to the School Book Club. So, just a couple of questions. What's your name?
Bobbie Hi. I'm Bobby.
Woman Hello, Bobby. What's your full name?
Bobby Oh, my full name is Robert Luis Gordon, but I'm Bobby to my friends.

Woman	How old are you, Bobby?
Bobby	I'm 15.
Woman	And you are American, is that right?
Bobby	Yes, I am. But my mom's from Colombia.
Woman	Really? Nice. Now, what's your favorite school subject?
Bobby	History. I'm a huge fan! I'm in the School History Society too.
Woman	That's very good, Bobby. And who's your favorite author?
Bobby	Dan Brown is one of my favorites, and Toni Morrison. I love all her books, especially Beloved. And I also like Ken Follett. He's British.
Woman	That's great, Bobby, she's one of my favorite too. Last question: what are the important things in your life?
Bobby	The important things in my life? Well, books of course. Then all my friends and my cat Dino, who's 12 years old, and my dog Flaca. They're fantastic!
Woman	Well Bobby, welcome to the School Book Club. Have fun!
Bobby	Thank you, this is awesome, I'm so excited!

Unit 2

🔊 9 **Exercise 2 p. 22**
1 D living room
2 C bedroom
3 F bathroom
4 A kitchen
5 B hall
6 E yard

🔊 10 **Exercise 6 p. 23**
1 G bookcase
2 B lamp
3 D table
4 C closet
5 E bed
6 F chair
7 A window
8 H door

🔊 11 **Exercise 8 p. 23**
1 D in
2 C on
3 F under
4 H behind
5 B next to
6 G between

7 E opposite
8 A near

🔊 12 **Exercise 4 p. 25**
B&B	Hi Henry, this is your room. There is a double bed, a closet and a desk. There are also two lamps on the desk.
Henry	Is there an internet connection?
B&B	Yes, there is.
Henry	Is there a password?
B&B	No, there isn't. It's free Wi-Fi.
Henry	Excellent. Is that my bathroom?
B&B	Yes, it is. There is a shower but there isn't a bath...
Henry	No problem, I like showers! Are there other people in the house?
B&B	No, there aren't.

🔊 13 **Exercise 5 p. 26**
Hi Fran, I have a great new apartment in the center of town! There's a new kitchen with a table, a stove and a fridge, but no dishwasher. There is a very large window in the living room and there's a sofa and two big armchairs too. There's a double bed in the bedroom and a big closet. And in the bathroom there's a bath and a shower. Come and visit soon! But where are you?

Videoscript
▶ See Student's Book p. 27

🔊 14 **Exercise 2 p. 28**
See Student's Book p. 28

🔊 15 **Exercise 4 p. 29**
Interviewer	Good morning! Today we're here to talk about houses with our listener Julie. Can you tell me about your house Julie?
Julie	Of course: I really love my house! It is in the center of the town and it's very modern and quite big. The walls are white and there are lots of big silver windows and gray doors in it. There are two floors in the house with a balcony upstairs outside one of the three bedrooms. The roof is flat, so there isn't a chimney. Downstairs there is a small terrace with tables and chairs, and a tiny utility room, too. There isn't a garage, but there is a small garden near the house.
Interviewer	Oh, your house seems really lovely, Julie.
Julie	Yes, it really is.

Audioscripts and videoscripts

Unit 3

🔊 **16** **Exercise 2 p. 32**
1 E nurse
2 A doctor
3 G driver
4 L teacher
5 J architect
6 I receptionist
7 B journalist
8 C waiter/waitress
9 F businessman/businesswoman
10 H sales assistant
11 D athlete
12 K tennis instructor

🔊 **17** **Exercise 1 p. 36**
1 A **virtual assistant** works from home and assists customers online.
2 A **stylist** knows about fashion.
3 A **sports manager** is good at organising teams and competitions.
4 An **influencer** shows and suggests products online.
5 A **organic food producer** produces natural foods with no chemicals.
6 An **app developer** is good at creating apps for smartphones.
7 A **social media manager** makes your posts catchy and visible to a lot of people.
8 A **psychologist** helps you with your mental health.
9 A **personal assistant (PA)** is good at organising other people's work.
10 An **accountant** manages your finances.

🔊 **18** **Exercise 4 p. 36**
1 basketball
2 athletics
3 baseball
4 tennis
5 ice skating
6 horseback riding
7 yoga
8 jogging
9 martial arts
10 gymnastics
11 volleyball
12 soccer

🔊 **19** **Exercise 5 p. 36**
1 I go ice skating in winter.
2 He does martial arts every Thursday.
3 We do yoga at the weekends.
4 They play football for the school team.
5 She goes horseback riding on Saturday mornings.
6 We play volleyball at the beach.
7 He does athletics in the summer.
8 Do you do gymnastics at school?

🔊 **20** **Exercise 6 p. 36**

Manager	So Josh, tell me about yourself. Can you speak any foreign languages?
Josh	Yes, I can speak Russian and a bit of Spanish. My mother's Russian, and my girlfriend is from Mexico.
Manager	Great. Are you good at smartphones and computers?
Josh	I'm absolutely excellent at computers, I want to be an app developer one day.
Manager	That's good. How about numbers? Are you good at them? There's a lot of math to do here.
Josh	Well, I can do math pretty well, but it's not my favorite thing, really.
Manager	Now, you have a bicycle, right? Can you ride fast?
Josh	Oh yes, I can ride very fast.
Manager	That's perfect. Can you work in the evenings and at weekends?
Josh	Evenings and Saturdays are OK, but on Sunday morning I usually have a soccer match.
Manager	Fine. You can start on Monday as a food delivery cyclist. Orders arrive on your smartphone, you go to the restaurant and then to people's houses. Remember to check that payment is correct. Be kind and ride fast. Maybe next month we can move you to the office. You can speak three languages, a lot of tourists call us for food delivery.
Josh	Thank you, I'm very happy to hear that.

Videoscript
 See Student's Book p. 37

🔊 **21** **Exercise 2 p. 39**
See Student's Book p. 38

🔊 **22** **Exercise 4 p. 39**
We're all really excited because breaking or breakdancing is in the Olympic Games for the first time from 2024! People think you can just do it without any training - but you really can't! Here's a typical training day for me. So I go to the gym at 6 a.m. and workout really hard. Then at 7 I can either have a massage or spend time in the pool.

At 8 a.m. I have breakfast. It can't be sugary but can be anything which releases energy slowly (like porridge, eggs and toast, fruit).
Then at 10 a.m. we have classes where we can work on our dance moves. It's pretty physical: you can burn 400 calories in an hour, so you can't do it without energy drinks.
Lunch is at 12:30 p.m. It can't be too heavy because we do some weight training at 2 p.m. to become fit and strong, too.
If I can, I usually have a quick siesta at 3 p.m., before practicing dance routines in the afternoon 4-6.
If you don't have competitions you can eat a normal dinner at 7 in the evening and then just work on the music and creative moves after that.

Unit 4

🔊 23 **Exercise 1 p. 42**
1 catch the bus
2 have lunch
3 go to bed
4 get dressed
5 take a shower
6 do my homework
7 wake up
8 get to school

🔊 24 **Exercise 4 p. 46**
1 It's half past twelve.
2 It's ten o'clock.
3 It's twenty to seven.
4 It's ten past eight.
5 It's quarter past five.
6 It's quarter to ten.

🔊 25 **Exercise 6 p. 46**
Hi! I'm Rashid, I'm 16 and I live in Bristol, England. My week is a bit boring. Mondays to Fridays I usually wake up at 7 and have breakfast with my family. I leave home at 8 and catch the bus to school. It only takes 15 minutes, I don't live too far from school. I always have lunch in the school canteen at 1:30, the food is not so bad, although I prefer my mum's food! My favourite lesson is P.E. and it's on Friday morning. We've got a huge rugby pitch, I love rugby. What do I do after school? Well, I go to music class, I play the ukulele, or maybe I try to... Then I go home and I do my homework in my bedroom. At weekends, life gets much more interesting! Especially when I go surfing with my brother in Cornwall. It doesn't happen very often, but it's just fantastic.

Videoscript
▶ See Student's Book p. 47

🔊 26 **Exercise 2 p. 49**
See Student's Book p. 48

🔊 27 **Exercise 4 p. 49**

Interviewer	So, Stella. You've got an unusual job. What do you do?
Stella	I'm a zoo keeper.
Interviewer	A zoo keeper?
Stella	Yes, that's right. I work in a zoo. I work with gorillas.
Interviewer	That's interesting.
Stella	Yes, it is, but it's difficult. I get up very early in the morning. I start work at 6 and I finish work very late, at about 9.
Interviewer	Really? What's a typical day for you?
Stella	Well, in the morning I make breakfast for the gorillas. Then I clean their homes and I give them medicines.
Interviewer	Do you play with the animals?
Stella	Yes, I do. It's important for the gorillas to be healthy, so I exercise with them for an hour every day.
Interviewer	What do you do in the afternoon?
Stella	I look at the data about the gorillas. I write about them on my computer.
Interviewer	Do you like your job, Stella?
Stella	Yes, I do. I love it and I love the gorillas.

Unit 5

🔊 28 **Exercise 1 p. 52**
1 music
2 geography
3 history
4 art
5 science
6 drama
7 information technology
8 math
9 physical education
10 English

🔊 29 **Exercise 6 p. 56**

Mandy	What subjects do you have today, Helen?
Helen	I have English at 9 o'clock and then I have history.
Mandy	What do you have after break?
Helen	I think it's math. Yes, math for an hour, and then I have science.

Audioscripts and videoscripts

Mandy	When do you have P.E.?
Helen	P.E.? You mean physical education? It's after lunch. I have P.E. at 2 o'clock.
Mandy	So what's your last lesson today?
Helen	It's geography. Then I go home – hurrah!

Videoscript
▶ See Student's Book p. 57

🔊 30 **Exercise 2 p. 58**
see Student's Book p. 58

🔊 31 **Exercise 4 p. 58**

Interviewer	Hi Clint. Tell us where you're studying this year. Where is your school?
Clint	I'm not going to school this year, I'm learning at home with my brother and sister.
Interviewer	You're learning at home?! Who are your teachers?
Clint	My parents are teaching us. My dad is teaching us science, geography and Spanish. My mum is teaching us maths, English and history.
Interviewer	This method is called 'homeschooling', right?
Clint	Yes, that's right. In homeschooling you follow the school programme but you learn at home. We study the same subjects our friends study at school, and Mum and Dad use the same books as the teachers use at school, but we study at our own speed at home.
Interviewer	Do you like learning with this method?
Clint	Yes, I do.
Interviewer	Why do you like it?
Clint	Well, it's more interesting. We don't spend all day in a classroom, sitting at a desk. We study in the mornings, then in the afternoons we go out. We visit a museum, or we go to a beach, or we visit a castle. Mum and Dad show us things we're learning about in our lessons.
Interviewer	Can you give me an example?
Clint	Yes, I can. In history we're learning about the Normans and Norman castles. So my mum wants to take us to see Warkworth Castle.
Interviewer	Warkworth Castle? Is it in the north of England?
Clint	Yes, that's right. It's a real Norman castle. It's awesome!

Unit 6

🔊 32 **Exercise 1 p. 62**
1 D water
2 J strawberries
3 A sandwich
4 B salad
5 K cheese
6 F fish
7 I peppers
8 G rice
9 L cake
10 H cola
11 C pasta
12 E chicken
13 O bread
14 P lentils
15 N soup
16 Q eggs
17 R butter
18 M grapefruit

🔊 33 **Exercise 2 p. 66**
1 c a carton of milk
2 d a slice of cake
3 h a bag of chips
4 g a can of cola
5 b a bar of chocolate
6 a a loaf of bread
7 e a bowl of cereal
8 f a packet of flour

🔊 34 **Exercise 3 p. 66**
1 f mix: to put two or more food together so they become one
2 d add: to put something with something else to make it bigger
3 h bake: to cook in the oven
4 g fry: to cook food in hot oil or fat
5 c stir: to mix an ingredient into a liquid by moving a spoon
6 a boil: to cook food in very hot water
7 b roast: to cook in an oven or over a fire
8 e steam: to cook food by heating it in steam from boiling water

🔊 35 **Exercise 5 p. 66**

Waitress	Hi. What would you like?
Luke	A cheese sandwich, please and a black coffee.
Waitress	Any dessert?
Luke	Yes, please. I'd like ice cream with fruit.
Waitress	OK thanks. And you, madam?
Judy	I'd like fish and chips.

Waitress	OK and to drink?
Judy	A bottle of mineral water please.
Waitress	Any dessert for you?
Judy	I don't like ice cream...
Waitress	We have chocolate cake. It's very good.
Judy	Oh, I like that! OK, chocolate cake for me.
Waitress	Perfect!

Videoscript
▶ See Student's Book p. 67

🔊 36 **Exercise 2 p. 68**
See Student's Book pp. 68-69

🔊 37 **Exercise 4 p. 69**

Interviewer	Hi David. You're also a big fan of the Slow Movement, right?
David	Yes, I am. I'm part of a group called Slow Cities.
Interviewer	Slow Cities?
David	Yes. I'm from London but I'm living in a place called Ludlow now. Ludlow is a 'slow city'.
Interviewer	What is a 'slow city'?
David	It's a city where people choose a slow, relaxed lifestyle.
Interviewer	Why do they want a slow lifestyle?
David	Well, cities like London, New York and Tokyo are too fast and too noisy. People get really stressed living there. They're always running. So they come to Ludlow. In Ludlow it's very quiet.
Interviewer	Why is it so quiet?
David	There aren't a lot of cars. People don't drive, they cycle. And they work in the town, they don't drive long distances to get to work.
Interviewer	Do they work long hours?
David	No, they don't. Most offices close at half past 4, then people have time to relax after work.
Interviewer	What do they do after work?
David	They play sports, visit friends, cook dinner, spend time with their families. I'm having tennis lessons this month and I'm studying Spanish at an evening class too.
Interviewer	It sounds lovely.
David	It is!

Unit 7

🔊 38 **Exercise 1 p. 72**
1 C play video games

2 G watch YouTube or Netflix
3 B hang out with friends
4 F go out on my hoverboard
5 H go to a music festival
6 A listen to music
7 E watch a theater show
8 D go to the movies

🔊 39 **Exercise 1 p. 76**
Job: reporter, comedian, presenter, producer, filmmaker, playwright
Place: stage, theater, studio, set
Other: performance, sitcom, audience, documentary, award, reality show, episode, costumes, soundtrack, script

🔊 40 **Exercise 3 p. 76**
1 punk
2 hip hop
3 new age
4 country
5 blues
6 grunge
7 gospel
8 jazz
9 rock
10 heavy metal
11 rap
12 classical

🔊 41 **Exercise 4 p. 76**

David	What are you listening to, Julie?
Julie	My iPod.
David	I can see that! I mean, what music are you listening to?
Julie	Oh right, sorry. It's a new gospel choir called Hallelujah.
David	Really? Do you like that kind of music?
Julie	Yes, actually. You should listen to them. I saw them in concert last month. Their music was just beautiful.
David	Mmm, well, it isn't my kind of thing. I prefer hip hop and grunge. I went to a grunge music festival last month with Jacob and we had the most amazing time!
Julie	Mmm, well, each to their own, I suppose. My brother likes that kind of music but I prefer more peaceful stuff like new age or soul music.
David	No, that's all just too relaxing for me. Now, you know what I really love...punk music!
Julie	Oh no, really?!
David	Yeah, it's great! I love listening to it when I'm studying.

Audioscripts and videoscripts

Julie	Ah well, that explains why you didn't pass the math exam then!
David	Ha ha, very funny! No, I'm serious. You should try listening to it. You know, there's a new punk band called Craze playing at the Exhibition Centre next weekend. Do you want to come with me? I could get tickets...
Julie	No thanks, David. I'm going to a nice jazz concert with Melanie on Saturday, but maybe next time...

Videoscript
▶ See Student's Book p. 77

🔊 42 **Exercise 2 p. 78**
See Student's Book pp. 78-79

🔊 43 **Exercise 4 p. 79**
What do I do in my free time? What's my favorite type of entertainment? Well, I like watching TV, like everyone, I love Netflix and going to the movies. I watch my favorite soaps in the evening and I do sports too – I do Zumba and I play hockey at school. But my favorite thing of all is probably reading. Yes, I know, reading is boring, but not for me. I love reading! People think I'm a bit old-fashioned because I always have my nose in a book but I don't care! I started reading as a hobby when I was about eight and I always had a book in my bag. Then when I was 11, my aunt bought me a Kindle for my birthday and that was like a reading revolution for me! Now I can download ebooks and read wherever I am. Ebooks are quite cheap so my hobby isn't expensive either. I read all sorts of books – horror, fantasy, adventure stories, everything really, but my favorites are science fiction books. I downloaded a great book last night. It's the first Hunger Games book. I can't wait to start reading it!

Unit 8
🔊 44 **Exercise 1 p. 82**
By air: airplane, helicopter, glider
By rail: train, tram, subway
By road: bus, scooter, taxi, truck, motorbike, bicycle, car
By sea: ferry, ship

🔊 45 **Exercise 1 p. 86**
1 We only had three days and we decided on a city vacation to Paris. It was short, but we had a great time!

2 The best sightseeing tour of London is on board the hop-on-hop-off bus.
3 We went to Dublin – Joseph, Mike and me. There wasn't much money, so we stayed in a youth hostel.
4 When I travel, I prefer B&B accommodations because I love meeting the local people.
5 The return trip was a nightmare because our flight was delayed.
6 The best part of the vacation was a one-day excursion to the small islands by boat.
7 The guided tour of the Transport Museum wasn't that interesting.
8 As soon as we put up the tent in the campsite it started to rain!

🔊 46 **Exercise 4 p. 86**
1 A go straight on
2 D turn left
3 B go past
4 E cross the road
5 F take the second road on the right
6 C turn right

🔊 47 **Exercise 5 p. 86**

Phil	Excuse me, can you tell me the way to the police station?
Woman	Oh dear, what happened?
Phil	I lost my passport, I think I forgot it on the train. When I got off at the train station it wasn't in my knapsack.
Woman	Right. Now, for the police station go straight on until King's Square, then take the first road on the right.
Phil	So, straight on, then the first road on the right.
Woman	Correct. Walk for about four hundred meters, go past the cathedral until you get to a Chinese restaurant.
Phil	Cathedral, then Chinese restaurant...
Woman	Yes. At the Chinese restaurant, cross the road, take York Street, then turn right and the police station is at the end of Queen's Road.
Phil	Oh. It sounds very far from here...
Woman	Oh, it's not that far. When you get to Queen's Road, go past the football stadium...
Phil	Go past the stadium? It is too far, and I'm carrying a very heavy knapsack. Is there a bus stop near here?
Woman	Sure. Just cross the road, it's over there, opposite the bank. Take bus number 54. It's just four stops from here.
Phil	Thank you so much, it was very kind of you.
Woman	You're welcome. And good luck with your passport!

Videoscript

▶ See Student's Book p. 87

🔊 48 **Exercise 2 p. 88**

See Student's Book p. 88

🔊 49 **Exercise 4 p. 89**

1

This is an important announcement about the bus service to Camden this evening. The 19:45 service was cancelled due to a street accident on the High Street. As a result, the next service at 20:15 was also delayed by 15 minutes. The 20:45 bus service to Camden leaves from bay 22. Thank you for your patience.

2

Katy	What time does Alex's party start tonight?
Jack	Erm, it says half past eight on the invitation.
Katy	OK, and where is it?
Jack	At Zio Peppe's, the new Italian restaurant in Chelsea.
Katy	Great! Can you drive there?
Jack	No way! Parking is terrible in that area. Let's take the bus.
Katy	... or the Tube... I hate buses.
Jack	Oh, you're so difficult. Let's just take a cab... it can drop us off outside the restaurant, then we can get a Tube home maybe... if it isn't too late.
Katy	OK, good idea!

3

Journalist	So Ella, we understand you saw the accident in Westminster Street yesterday afternoon.
Ella	Yes, I did. I had a violin lesson yesterday so I was on my way there when it happened. There were lots of buses and cars around so it was very busy as usual. I didn't take the bus yesterday because there were some delays to the service so I decided to take the Tube from Victoria to Westminster. I sometimes walk but it was raining yesterday and I didn't want to get wet. Anyway, when I came out of the Tube station, I heard a loud bang and then there was chaos...

4

Tom	Grandad, I'm doing a school project on how people got to work in the past. Can you help me?
Grandad	Of course, I can. What do you want to know?
Tom	How did you get to work?
Grandad	Well, when I started working, we didn't all have cars, you know. Not like today... we walked or took the bus.
Tom	So, you took the bus or walked to work...?
Grandad	Neither!
Tom	Ah, so did you take the Tube then?
Grandad	No, I didn't. I took the river bus very morning. At that time, the boat traveled up the Thames every morning and dropped off at Westminster Pier and Greenwich Pier.
Tom	Wow, that sounds like fun!
Grandad	Yes, I suppose so, but it was very cold some mornings too!

Unit 9

🔊 50 **Exercise 1 p. 92**

1 designer label: a famous company that makes expensive clothes, bags or other accessories
2 popular retail stores: clothes shops you find in every town or city
3 must-have: something highly fashionable and in demand
4 catwalk: the place where models walk during a fashion show
5 vintage: clothes in a style from the past
6 timeless: clothing that never goes out of fashion
7 fashion victim: somebody who wears fashionable clothes that sometimes make him/her look silly
8 old-fashioned: clothes that are no longer in style

🔊 51 **Exercise 1 p. 96**

Clothes: pants, cardigan, dress, pullover, boots, sneakers, skirt, jacket, top
Accessories: flip flops, beanie, gloves, earrings, necklace, belt, watch, scarf, shoulder bag

🔊 52 **Exercise 3 p. 96**

1 savings
2 credit card
3 cash machine / ATM
4 coins
5 bills
6 cash register
7 tip
8 wallet

🔊 53 **Exercise 4 p. 96**

Emma	That was a great meal!
Hannah	It was... it was really tasty! Much better than the Mexican last week. I didn't like that at all. Anyway, I suppose we should go.

Liam Yeah. Let's ask for the bill.

Hannah Do you pay at the till?

Liam No, you just leave the money on the table.

Emma Should we leave a tip?

Liam Let me see how much money I have in my wallet... I'm a bit broke at the moment.

Emma Oh come on Liam... you have loads of coins and notes in your wallet!

Hannah And you have a credit card... if you want to pay for us, too!

Liam Ha ha! You're the one with the savings, Hannah!

Hannah I wish! I had to ask my dad for a loan the other day because I went to the ATM and my bank balance was in the red!

Emma That's because you buy too many clothes! How many new dresses did you buy last year? And you bought a new watch and some cargo pants the other day...

Hannah Yeah, I know, you're right. I just love shopping!

Liam Sounds like you need to save a bit more money, Hannah, so I say 'no tip'!

Hannah Liam! The waitress was really good. Let's leave her a few coins.

Liam OK OK...

Videoscript
▶ See Student's Book p. 97

🔊 54 **Exercise 2 p. 98**
See Student's Book pp. 98-99

🔊 55 **Exercise 3 p. 99**

Grant What are you doing, Megan?

Megan I'm doing some online shopping.

Grant Again?!! You bought some clothes last week online...

Megan Yes, I know. But I'm looking for some shoes now.

Grant More shoes?

Megan Yes, vegan ones...

Grant What? You're a vegan now... when did you stop eating meat?

Megan I didn't. I'm just a very environmentally conscious shopper.

Grant Really? So tell me about these vegan shoes.

Megan Well, think about it. Those leather shoes you're wearing aren't sustainable or very animal friendly... so, it's simple, vegan shoes are kinder to the world... and they're nicer than you think. Look, there are loads of colors and they're actually extremely stylish.

Grant Yeah, I suppose so. They're not as bad as I thought.

Megan So, what do you think? Shall I buy the blue ones or the green ones?

Grant Well, I don't like the green ones at all, so buy the blue ones, they're nicer.

Megan Do you want anything?

Grant I like the hiking boots, but they're more expensive than normal ones. Look, they cost 169 dollars.

Megan Yeah, but they're better quality than non-vegan ones.

Grant The sneakers are cool though. Are there any of the blue ones in a size 11?

Megan Let's see... erm, no, just 12 or 13.

Grant Oh well, no good then. Never mind!

Unit 10

🔊 56 **Exercise 1 p. 102**
1 B do a translation
2 A look words up in a dictionary
3 C practice the pronunciation
4 D learn the meaning
5 E focus on grammar

🔊 57 **Exercise 1 p. 106**
1 I love going to the science lab.
2 School closes for summer vacation tomorrow.
3 My grandad left school without any qualifications.
4 The teacher called the roll but Peter wasn't there.
5 We are doing a school project about space travel.
6 When the bell rings everybody goes home.
7 After school I'm going to get a degree in chemistry at the university.
8 I don't like speaking in public. I'm going to write an essay for the end of school term test.
9 I think I'll attend a language course to learn French in the summer.
10 My sister always has a snack at break time.

🔊 58 **Exercise 3 p. 106**

assign	assignment
1 assess	assessment
2 review	review
3 educate	education
4 pronounce	pronunciation
5 graduate	graduation
6 behave	behaviour

🔊 59 **Exercise 5 p. 106**

Martin Thanks guys, for agreeing to talk to me today during your precious break time! So, first question... what are you going to do next

	year when you leave school?
James	I'm going to apply to Bristol University to study math. I'm going to an Open Day next Thursday. The course looks really interesting and I think a degree in math is a better qualification than a degree in French or something like that.
Lucy	I don't agree! I think languages are so important that everybody should study one. I'm going to study a language. But first I'm going to take a gap year.
Martin	That's very interesting!
Lucy	Yes, I'm meeting some people on the weekend who taught English to primary school children in Colombia last year. They're going to tell me about their experience.
Martin	Many young people take a gap year after school now. Where are you going to travel to?
Lucy	I'm not sure yet. I speak Spanish… I'm an intermediate level, so I'm thinking of going somewhere in South America too. I'm going to do an advanced Spanish course during the summer vacation to improve my language. The course starts in August and lasts for four weeks.
Martin	Does school close soon?
James	Yes, we're finishing school on 20th July…
Martin	And what are you going to do, James?
James	Vacation first! I'm going to visit Barbados with my family, then I'm going to work on my uncle's farm for the rest of the vacation. It's going to be very hard.
Martin	Well, good luck guys! Thanks for your time. Your interview will be online tomorrow!

Videoscript
See Student's Book p. 107

60 Exercise 2 p. 108
See Student's Book p. 108

61 Exercise 4 p. 109
OK, everybody, so today we're going to talk a little bit about India. Are you all ready for your trip next week? Nervous, excited…? Well, geographically, India is surrounded by the Indian Ocean in the south, the Arabian Sea in the southwest and the Bay of Bengal in the southeast, and it shares a border with Pakistan, China, Nepal, Bhutan, Myanmar and Bangladesh. It is also the second most populous country in the world with over 1.2 billion people. So what about its language? Does anybody know which language people speak in India? Indian?! Well, the official language of the Government of India is Hindi, that's H-I-N-D-I, but English is very important too, so people use both Hindi and English for official purposes. Indian states have the power to specify their own official language, so as a result there are 22 officially recognized languages in India. Can you imagine learning 22 languages?! So, this is India! An amazing country, and I'm sure we're going to have a wonderful trip. Remember, there will be a field trip briefing next Friday evening at 7:30 p.m. in the sports hall. We will give you a list of everything you need to pack and details about the flight to the capital, New Delhi, which, remember, leaves Manchester Airport at 5 a.m. on May 20th. So, see you all on Friday!

**Ready for Planet English - Elementary
Student's Book**

Editorial project and coordination: Simona Franzoni
Editors: Francesca Seracini, Simona Bagalà
Language revision: Kathy Metzger, Rebecca Raynes
Art director: Marco Mercatali
Page design: Sergio Elisei
Illustrated by: Laura Désirée Pozzi
Picture editor: Giorgia D'Angelo
Production manager: Francesco Capitano
Page layout: Quarta di Copertina

Cover
Cover design: Paola Lorenzetti
Photos: Shutterstock

© 2024 ELI S.r.l.
P.O. Box 6
62019 Recanati
Italy
Tel. +39 071 750701
Fax +39 071 977851
support@elipublishing.com
www.elipublishing.com

No unauthorised photocopying

All rights reserved. No part of this publication may be
reproduced, stored in a retrieval system, or transmitted,
in any form or by any means, electronic, mechanical,
photocopying, recording or otherwise, without the prior
written permission of ELI.

This book is sold subject to the condition that it shall
not, by way of trade or otherwise, be lent, resold, hired
out, or otherwise circulated without the publisher's
prior consent in any form of binding or cover than that
in which it is published and without a similar condition
being imposed on the subsequent purchaser.

While every effort has been made to trace all the
copyright holders, if any have been inadvertently
overlooked the publisher will be pleased to make the
necessary arrangements at the first opportunity.

The Publisher would like to give a special thanks to
Emma Hill and Niccolò Caderni for their kindness and
support during the video production in London.

Printed by Tecnostampa – Pigini Group Printing Division
– Loreto, Trevi – Italy 22.83.148.1

Photo Acknowledgements

All photos by Shutterstock, except:
Alamy: p. 44; Eli Archives: p. 48 (top), p. 57 (book cover),
p. 102 (B, D); Gettyimages: p. 14 (Joe and Lucy), p. 19 (C),
p. 38 (B), p. 39 (C), p. 48 (bottom), p. 74, p. 92 (bottom),
p. 98 (top right), p. 99; Istock: p. 61.
Sitography: youtube.com/khanacademy;
khanacademy.org (p. 59).

Video Acknowledgements

Commissioned video production in London: Mainline
Design Ltd (David Turner & Nilesh Mistry), London.

Culture videos: ELI Archives

DLA Digital Learning Associates